A WRITING
APPRENTICESHIP

A WRITING APPRENTICESHIP

FIFTH EDITION

Norman A. Brittin
Auburn University

Ruth L. Brittin
Auburn University

Holt, Rinehart and Winston
New York   Chicago   San Francisco   Dallas
Montreal   Toronto   London   Sydney

Library of Congress Cataloging in Publication Data

Brittin, Norman A comp.
  A writing apprenticeship.

  Includes index.
  1. College readers. 2. English language—Rhetoric.
I. Brittin, Ruth L., joint author. II. Title.
PE1417.B714   1981   808'.0427   80-23807

ISBN 0-03-55421-7

NOTE TO THE FIFTH EDITION

In revising *A Writing Apprenticeship* for the fifth edition, we have held firmly to the principles on which the earlier editions were based. Therefore the book is arranged according to the same patterns as before. We have, however, somewhat decreased the number of selections in Description and Narration and increased those in Exposition. The chief new addition is a glossary of terms, which we hope will enhance the practicability of the text. Some of the material in the introduction to the Argument section is also new and stems from a contemporary example.

One-third of the selections are fresh ones. We chose them in part to achieve interesting variety, and we hope that the bearing of many of them on current issues will prove to be thought-provoking.

For criticisms and suggestions we are grateful to Orvis C. Burmaster, Boise State University; Michael L. Dickmeyer, Metropolitan Technical Community College; Dr. Wilfred O. Dietrich, Blinn College; Drewey Wayne Gunn, Texas A&I University; Mary Eugenia Kilgallen, Ferris State College; Barry Logan, California State University; Anne S. Peets, Albany Junior College; Nancy Powers, University of North Alabama; Sylvia Bowen Price, Blinn College; Donna Cobb Vogt, Texas A&I University. We deeply appreciate the wise counsel, constant good humor, and friendship of Richard S. Beal over many years.

N. A. B.
R. L. B.
Auburn, Alabama
October 1980

Foreword to
the Instructor

This text is designed as an unpretentious, practical instrument for the teaching of composition. Many students coming to college have not read much, nor have they written much in any of their high school classes. Consequently they have very little idea of how to write English sentences according to standard patterns or how to compose solid and effective paragraphs. They are frequently set to studying material that is over their heads—material far too long and complex to serve as a model for writing. So the students often flounder around, trying to put together five hundred words on topics that are vaguely associated with the material read and that freshmen frequently are as yet too ignorant to write about. The material in this text was carefully chosen so that students would not be thrust into writing situations that are bound to be unprofitable.

As a matter of common sense, it is well to start students off by presenting paragraphs that they can use as models. There is a long and approved tradition of learning to write by imitation. But if students are really to learn by imitation, they must have models brief enough to imitate. Thus many of the selections in this book contain only one paragraph; more than half of the selections contain no more than four paragraphs.

Along with the imitable model goes the practicable writing assignment. The assignments should permit the student to follow the pattern established by the paragraph. The assignments here call upon students to imitate the models on topics that are within their experience or require only direct observation of life about them.

It is hoped, too, that the very concept of apprenticeship in writing, as explained in the first pages, will produce in students a healthy, commonsense attitude toward composition. The selections in the text are examples of serious, craftsmanlike writing that in a great many respects is easily imitable by beginners. Though the names of many famous authors appear in the table of contents, the selections, which have considerable variety, do not represent the undesirable extremes of either the belletristic or the utilitarian.

The material is arranged so that it gradually becomes more complex, and the suggested assignments naturally sometimes become longer. The selections are varied enough that the text will suit freshmen of different levels of proficiency. After a while the students should feel that they are making definite progress. By the time they have had the experience of writing single paragraphs and linked paragraphs of the types assigned, they should have laid a really effective foundation for writing practically anything they will be called upon to write later.

The work sections accompanying the selections apply, of course, to the methods by which the authors composed their work and are designed both to make students understand some of the standard practices in writing and to inculcate in them the habit of critical reading. As students direct their attention closely to sentence patterns, paragraph patterns, and diction, in the way that the study questions ask them to do and that the requirement of imitation imposes upon them, they will learn a good deal about efficient reading as well as about writing. In the work sections, necessary terms like *topic sentence* and *transition* are introduced along the way in such a manner that students should become accustomed to employing them practically and naturally. The attention to diction varies with the vocabulary difficulty of the different selections; but the word-study included should help students overcome scantiness of vocabulary and set them off on the right foot, by making them more aware of word-roots.

The text was devised with both the experienced and inexperienced instructor in mind. It is believed that the experienced instructor will feel that the strategy of this text is a sound one; it is hoped that the inexperienced instructor will find the text informative and effective.

N. A. B.
R. L. B.
Auburn, Alabama
October 1980

CONTENTS

SECTION ONE   Description and Narration   1

SECTION TWO   Exposition   61

Foreword to the Student

Writers and people who teach writing often call it a craft. A craft is an art or occupation that requires a special skill. If you wish to learn a craft, whether it is pottery making, carpentry, weaving, or silversmithing, you must have instruction and practice. Suppose you were an apprentice to a potter or a carpenter. Before the potter gave you a ball of clay to turn on the wheel or before the carpenter put a saw into your hands, you would have to watch the master's skilled hands handle the clay, handle the saw and the board. Then, as the apprentice, you would try to do exactly what the master craftsman did, with the same smoothness and precision. At first, you would be awkward, but as you became more familiar with the material used, with the tools, and with the problems that the craft had been created to solve, you would gradually improve.

If you wish to learn the craft of writing, you must go about it in the same way. You learn by imitating the work of those who are master craftsmen. . . .

Remember that as an apprentice, you would first be put to making small pots, not great vessels; you would first be shown how to saw boards accurately, not given a house to build. In the early stages of your apprenticeship, the projects would be small; only gradually would they become larger and more complicated. But after you had learned to do the little things well—after you had mastered the basic operations—you would be able to create larger things, too, with success.

Similarly, in developing special skill in writing, you cannot start by composing an epic or a novel. First you must learn how to compose sentences and paragraphs. You must learn how to value words in terms of their special meanings, and you must learn how to place them in the right spots (paying attention also to the rules of grammar and syntax) so that they will form effective statements. And you must combine the sentences into paragraphs that are effective for various purposes. Anyone who can write a good paragraph can write a book. In other words, if you had enough writing skill to compose a good paragraph, you would be able, if you acquired enough knowledge, to create paragraph after paragraph until you had written a book.

Thus, if you were a carpenter's apprentice, you would know very little, at first, about saws, hammers, planes, boards, planks, and nails; but after you had worked steadily with them for a few years and had learned the principles of using them, you would have the ability to build a house. Though few college freshmen will ever actually write books, they will all certainly write many other things: papers, reports, letters, speeches, articles. And, if they have learned through direction and practice how to write sentences and paragraphs, they have learned the essential skills of the writing craft.

This book provides masters and models; it provides direction and practical patterns as guides. Do the writing assignments, always imitating the work of some master (and learning through answering questions the principles that have guided master writers), and you will eventually be able to produce writing that can pass inspection. You will have served your apprenticeship; you will be able to call yourself at least a journeyman writer.

A WRITING
APPRENTICESHIP

SECTION ONE

Description and Narration

Human beings are always interested in other human beings. Perhaps the majority of people are interested in people more than in anything else. Often, in conversation, one hears: "What did she look like?" "What was she wearing?" "What does he look like?" To answer such questions, we describe.

In describing, we note the details we have observed, or, more precisely, details that we have been made aware of by the use of our senses—sight, hearing, taste, smell, touch. All of the environment—the world of people, the world of nature, and the man-created world—comes to us first through the senses; and if we are to communicate to others what our experiences in the environment are like, we must report through words what our senses have told us. Even so common an experience as washing one's face in the morning provides numerous sense impressions—the flashing on of the light in the bathroom; the gleam of chromium and porcelain; gray steam rising and clouding the mirror; the scalding feel of overhot water; the response of the nerves to contrasting cold or lukewarm water; the smells of soap, shaving cream, and toothpaste; and the feel of the soft tubes or of the bar of soap: cold hardness if new, wet slippery smoothness if used. Nor is the ear dull to varied sounds: the splash, hiss, trickle, or gurgle of water, the rubbing of palms, popping and roaring in the ears. Maybe, because of familiarity, we pay little attention to these sense impressions—but they exist, they *are* in their totality the experience that we have had, and if we were to become blind, deaf, or nerve-dead, the experience would undergo radical change.

If anyone tries to answer questions about people or about environment— "What does that place look like?" "What kind of house does so-and-so live in?" "So you have been to———! What is it like? How did you feel when you saw it? Is it pleasant? Is it scary? Is it fantastic? Is it picturesque? Is it beautiful?" the person asked is often likely, in conversation, to give answers that are not adequate, being too hurried, too broad, too lacking in details. In writing description, however, it is possible to take time to set down details that will show with exactness just how someone looks: the person's height, shape of head, color of hair, way of gesturing or walking, shade of complexion, look of eye, twist of mouth—all these pieces of evidence can be recorded if the writer looks closely enough and if he or she can think of effective terms to express them. In order to be accurate and to be interesting, we must notice details and be able to report them in abundance. But writers must also notice telling details—that is, the particular details that give them their impressions of people and of places. A place may be awesome or dreary or uncomfortable or colorful (and a colorful place may be unpleasantly gaudy or delightfully harmonious) or spacious or crowded, and so forth. To convey the impressions that the senses have given mankind, it is essential to find words that are just right.

Description/Characterization/Exposition

In the most exact meaning of the term, *description* is writing that conveys these sense impressions; but writing about people and places may also have informational purposes which are combined with description; description may lead to or be blended with character study; and description is often a necessary element in storytelling.

A large part of our lifetime is taken up by our associations with other people. We are constantly trying to become acquainted with them, trying to get to *know* them. Description is important in this effort, for it lets us know what sense impressions people arouse. What different pictures are conveyed by the words "tall, dignified gentleman" and "little roly-poly fellow"! Yet, one would be more fascinated by a further report: "tall, dignified—but stupid"; "little roly-poly fellow—but sharp, even waspish"!

People are interested in surface appearances, but they are even more interested in what lies behind them. "What *kind* of person is this? What are his qualities? What are the elements of his character?" Thus people are frequently led, as they talk or write about human beings, to go from description to characterization—after surveying the outward appearance, to penetrate to the inner being, the character. Of course, this calls for more knowledge, more thought, more analysis. But people are always doing it, informally as they make mental notes or chat with friends, formally as they write letters of recommendation and make other appraisals.

Though, as has been said, writing about the environment is often descriptive (it aims to make us *see* a place and sometimes to experience it with our other senses), such writing may also, at times, be as much informational as descriptive. To know that the Washington Monument is 555 feet high does not make a person see the exact look of it, but this information might be a necessary part of an article about Washington, D.C. In practice, description and informational writing, which is called *exposition,* often go together.

Description/Narration

Likewise, in a story an author often tells how both places and people look; the reader generally wishes to know something about the background of the place where the story happens. Often, too, the author relates in stories how places, people, and actions affect the feelings of other people. That is, description and storytelling (or narration) usually go together. The following episode from a narrative of travel in nineteenth-century Palestine shows how closely description and narration can be combined. It is an account of building a fire in the desert. Notice how the narrator concentrates on the action involved in starting the fire and how he includes numerous and precise details.

A spot for the fire was found with some difficulty, for the earth was moist, and the grass high and rank. At last there was a clicking of flint and steel, and presently there stood out from the darkness one of the tawny faces of my muleteers, bent down to near the ground, and suddenly lit up by the glowing of the spark, which he courted with careful breath. Before long, there was a particle of dry fibre or leaf that kindled to a tiny flame; then another was lit from that, and then another. Then small, crisp twigs, little bigger than bodkins, were laid athwart the glowing fire. The swelling cheeks of the muleteer, laid level with the earth, blew tenderly at first, then more boldly, and the young flame was daintily nursed and fed, and fed more plentifully till it gained full strength. At last a whole armful of dry bushes was piled up over the fire, and presently, with a loud, cheery cracking and crackling, a royal tall blaze shot up from the earth, and showed me once more the shapes and faces of my men, and the dim outlines of the horses and mules. . . .[1]

Kinglake makes us see the muleteer's "tawny" face and his "swelling cheeks." He makes us hear the fire "cracking and crackling." He makes us visualize the entire action through the images he creates; for example, "the young flame was daintily nursed and fed." Moreover, the feelings of the narrator are conveyed in words such as "loud, cheery" and "royal tall blaze."

While describing the fire itself, Kinglake tells us the story of building the fire, relating the series of actions that make up the whole episode. The episode has a beginning, a middle, and an ending. The author tells us how at first the fire was just a spark, how it gradually grew larger, and how at last it shot up from the earth, thus bringing the incident and our suspense to an end.

Narration

The episode that follows contains a larger proportion of pure narration.

A sergeant in the first platoon senses the predicament. If his men are isolated, they will likely be destroyed. He makes his decision quickly. Motioning his men to follow, he rises and with a submachine gun charges head-on toward one of the enemy positions two hundred yards away.

On the flat, coverless terrain, his body is a perfect target. A blast

[1] A. W. Kinglake, *Eothen* (1844).

of automatic fire knocks him down. He springs to his feet with a bleeding shoulder and continues his charge. The guns rattle. Again he goes down.

Fascinated, we watch as he gets up for the third time and dashes straight into the enemy fire. The Germans throw everything they have at him. He falls to the earth; and when he again pulls himself to his feet, we see that his right arm is shattered. But wedging his gun in his left armpit, he continues firing and staggers forward. Ten horrified Germans throw down their guns and yell, *"Kamerad"* ["Comrade": signal of surrender].[2]

This episode from a famous World War II story shows us several things about narration. (1) A story has a setting; that is, the time and place in which the action occurs. (2) A story involves a protagonist, or chief actor, and other characters, one or more of whom will be antagonists of the chief actor. Here the sergeant is the protagonist; his men are characters favorable to him; and the enemy consists of antagonistic characters. (3) A story involves conflict, or a struggle between one character and another or with one character against a force. The sergeant fights the Germans. (4) In a story we feel suspense because we are uncertain of the outcome of the struggle. The sergeant is charging head-on against an enemy position. We wonder if he can succeed. When he is knocked down and wounded, we wonder if he can go on. (5) The material in a story is organized to form a plot. The separate events in this selection are related in the order in which they occur. The sergeant decides to charge; he is knocked down; he goes on; he is hit; he still goes on; he charges the enemy; finally they surrender. Our suspense is over. While reading, we were aware of certain points that make up the whole action, and these points, taken together, make up the plot.

This episode is almost entirely narration; it contains a few descriptive details such as "flat, coverless terrain" or "a bleeding shoulder." However, in the context of intense action, these details provide just enough information to make us aware of the setting and the sense impressions of the characters.

In the section that follows, the apprentice writer is given models for several kinds of descriptive writing and for relatively simple narration. Since everyone is in continual communication with people, it is easy to observe them. To describe people is one of the simplest writing exercises with which to start, and writing description is an excellent discipline for the writing apprentice because it begins to train the powers of observation and shows the value of sharp, clear details. Some of the selections provide examples of characterization; others provide models for the description of varied places. Many of the models come from stories. The section ends with readings that contain more narration than description.

[2] From *To Hell and Back* by Audie Murphy. Copyright 1949 by Audie Murphy. Reprinted by permission of Holt, Rinehart and Winston.

Martin Luther King, Jr.

ROBERT PENN WARREN

He looks like his pictures. He is a shade less than medium height, a tidily made, compact man, the head rather large but rounded and compact too, the lips rather full but drawn back at the corners under a narrow close-trimmed mustache to emphasize this impression of compactness, the nose broad rather than projecting, the ears close-set, the hairline already receding, the hair growing close and cut short to define the shape of the skull. Compactness and control—that is the first impression, even in the natural outgoing cordiality at the moment of greeting, when the eyes brighten. At the handshake you notice that the hand is unusually large for a man of his stature, a strong hand. He has the tight-packed skin of a man who will be fat some day if he doesn't watch it, a skin with a slight sheen to its brownness. His dark clothing sits rather close on him, too, emphasizing again that compactness and completeness, nothing loose or shaggy or tweedy—a sheen to things. The shoes are of highly-polished, hard-glazed black leather, with elastic inserts that make them fit as tight and flexible as skin. He has a natural grace of movement as he turns to sit down at his desk. He could, you think, move fast and effectively.

STUDY QUESTIONS

Organization and Content

1 Which words are the key terms of Warren's paragraph?
2 Which parts of the word-portrait of King are brought out first?
3 Which elements come later? How is the first impression reinforced in sentences 4–7?
4 Do you think that Warren used any principle of arrangement when he wrote the paragraph? Could the nine sentences just as well appear in reverse order, or even be mixed up, without losing any of the effect?
5 Which of Warren's terms suggest something of King's character?

Sentence Structure

1 Which are the shortest sentences? How many words does the longest sentence have? Does Warren use a variety of sentence length?

From *Who Speaks for the Negro?* by Robert Penn Warren. Copyright © 1965 by Robert Penn Warren. Reprinted by permission of Random House, Inc.

2 Show how Warren packs many descriptive details into his longest sentence by using the same grammatical pattern many times.
3 Warren holds the paragraph together (that is, he has good *transition*) by often using *he* and *his*. At what place in the sentences do these words appear?
4 Explain how the final sentence element is added in the same way at the end of sentences 4, 5, and 6.

Diction

1 Which words indicate the main impression of the subject that Warren wishes to convey? Which words then best make us see precise details that support the main impression?
2 Are nouns, verbs, or adjectives most effective in this description?
3 Warren says that there was nothing "loose or shaggy or tweedy" about King's clothing. What terms contrast positively with these three adjectives?

Assignment

Present in one paragraph a word-portrait of someone that you know well—a friend, a member of your family, or some citizen of your town. Stress one main impression that this person gives.

Kittredge of Harvard

ROLLO WALTER BROWN

1   The sight of him as he came to the ten-o'clock class was in itself something that had to be recognized as dramatic. In the pleasant autumn or spring, men stood high on the steps or out on the turf in front and watched in the direction of Christ Church to see who could catch the first glimpse of him.

2   "There he comes!" somebody called, and then everybody who was in a position to see watched him as he hurried breezily along—a graceful, tallish man in very light gray suit and gray fedora hat, with a full square beard at least as white as his suit, who moved with energy, and smoked passionately at a big cigar. Students used to say that he smoked an entire cigar while he walked the short distance along the iron fence of the old burying ground and across the street to Johnston Gate. But as he came through the gate he

From *Harvard Yard in the Golden Age*, by Rollo Walter Brown. Copyright 1948 by Current Books, Inc., by permission of Current Books, Inc., A. A. Wyn Publisher, New York.

tossed the remnant of his cigar into the shrubbery with a bit of a flourish, and the students still outside hurried in and scrambled up the long stairway in order to be in their places—as he liked—before he himself entered. If any of them were still on the stairway when he came in at the outer door like a gust, they gave way and he pushed up past them, and into the good-sized room and down the aisle to the front, threw his hat on the table in the corner, mounted the two steps to the platform, looked about with a commanding eye, and there was sudden silence and unrestrained expectancy.

STUDY QUESTIONS

Organization and Content

1 Why is paragraph 1 so short?
2 Why did Brown decide to start paragraph 2 where he did and as he did?
3 Paragraph 2 has four sentences. What determines the order in which they are arranged? Does the paragraph have a beginning, a middle, and an end?

Sentence Structure

1 Sentence 1, paragraph 1, is almost exactly balanced before and after *was*. Describe the pattern of balance in terms of subject, predicate nominative, and modifying clauses and prepositional phrases.
2 Does the author have any purpose in placing the word *dramatic* at the end of sentence 1?
3 How does Brown proceed in sentence 1, paragraph 2, from the observers to the subject of his description (Kittredge), and then to the physical details that begin the description of the subject?
4 What purpose is served by placing *But* (an important word in our language) at the beginning of sentence 3, paragraph 2?
5 What is the relation of the second half of sentence 3 to the first half? Could the second half just as well come first?
6 Sentence 4, paragraph 2, is the longest sentence in the description (seventy-one words). Why should it be so long? If it were divided into two or three shorter sentences, how would the effect be changed?
7 How does Brown manage the attention given to the students and to Professor Kittredge in sentence 4, paragraph 2?

Diction

(The vocabulary given in this section throughout the book is taken from the text in the exact form in which it appears and in the order of appearance within the article.)

1   What is the key word of paragraph 1 (and of the whole description)?
2   Would there be any difference if *grass* or *ground* were used instead of *turf*? *Look, observation, sight,* or *view* instead of *glimpse*?
3   What is the meaning of *breezily*? of *passionately*?
4   Which adjectives help you most to visualize Kittredge?
5   What effect do these phrases have: "with a bit of a flourish," "like a gust"?
6   There are more than a dozen verbs in sentences 3 and 4, paragraph 2. What is the effect of having so many, and which are the most specific?
7   What effect do the last two adjectives have?

Assignment

Brown used his observations of Professor Kittredge to produce in a few words a brilliant description of a forceful personality. Observe the approach of one of your teachers to his classroom or office, or of a businessman to his place of work, and in the same way as Brown, show your reader (a friend in another town, perhaps) the special and specific look, walk, and manner of your subject. Other possibilities are: a preacher coming to the pulpit to preach a sermon or a politician arriving to make a speech before a specific audience.

Juan Chicoy

JOHN STEINBECK

1   The electric lantern, with a flat downward reflector, lighted sharply only legs and feet and tires and tree trunks near to the ground. It bobbed and swung, and the little incandescent bulb was blindingly blue-white. Juan Chicoy carried his lantern to the garage, took a bunch of keys from his overalls pocket, found the one that unlocked the padlock, and opened the wide doors. He switched on the overhead light and turned off his lantern.

2   Juan picked a striped mechanic's cap from his workbench. He wore Headlight overalls with big brass buttons on bib and side latches, and over this he wore a black horsehide jacket with black knitted wristlets and neck. His shoes were round-toed and hard, with soles so thick that they seemed swollen. An old scar on his cheek beside his large nose showed as a shadow in the overhead light. He ran fingers through his thick, black hair to get it all in the mechanic's cap. His hands were short and wide and strong, with square fingers and nails flattened by work and grooved and twisted from

having been hammered and hurt. The third finger of his left hand had lost the first joint, and the flesh was slightly mushroomed where the finger had been amputated. This little overhanging ball was shiny and of a different texture from the rest of the finger, as though the joint were trying to become a fingertip, and on this finger he wore a wide gold wedding ring, as though this finger was no good for work any more and might as well be used for ornament.

A pencil and a ruler and a tire pressure gauge protruded from a slot in his 3 overalls bib. Juan was clean-shaven, but not since yesterday, and along the corners of his chin and on his neck the coming whiskers were grizzled and white like those of an old Airedale. This was the more apparent because the rest of his beard was so intensely black. His black eyes were squinting and humorous, the way a man's eyes squint when he is smoking and cannot take the cigarette from his mouth. And Juan's mouth was full and good, a relaxed mouth, the underlip slightly protruding—not in petulance but in humor and self-confidence—the upper lip well formed except left of center where a deep scar was almost white against the pink tissue. The lip must have been cut clear through at one time, and now this thin taut band of white was a strain on the fullness of the lip and made it bunch in tiny tucks on either side. His ears were not very large, but they stood out sharply from his head like seashells, or in the position a man would hold them with his hands if he wanted to hear more clearly. Juan seemed to be listening intently all the time, while his squinting eyes seemed to laugh at what he heard, and half of his mouth disapproved. His movements were sure even when he was not doing anything that required sureness. He walked as though he were going to some exact spot. His hands moved with speed and precision and never fiddled with matches or with nails. His teeth were long and the edges were framed with gold, which gave his smile a little fierceness.

STUDY QUESTIONS
Organization and Content

1 What preparatory function does paragraph 1 serve? What things are stressed in sentences 1 and 2? in 3 and 4?
2 This description is more detailed than the preceding one. More attention is given to the dress, physical appearance, and expression of the subject. Which details are most vividly presented in paragraph 2?
3 Which material in paragraph 3 resembles, and which differs from, the material in paragraph 2?
4 In what places does Steinbeck go beyond the description of observed details to give some hints of Juan Chicoy's character? What general impression of the man is left with you?

Sentence Structure

1   A succession of details is presented in paragraph 1. They are connected in each sentence by the coordinating conjunction *and*. Which things are thus connected in sentence 1?

2   Which verbs in sentences 2, 3, and 4 of paragraph 1 are connected by *and*? How do these sentences differ in grammatical type from sentence 1?

3   Point out how sentence 4 is almost exactly balanced. How is the balanced arrangement of sentence 4 different from that of sentence 3?

4   Show how by using *he* and *his* (referring to Juan) Steinbeck has linked together all the sentences of paragraph 2. (Thus the paragraph has effective transition.) Does he do the same in paragraph 3?

5   Sentence 6, paragraph 2, is elegantly designed to express parallel ideas. Show what pairs and trios of words are joined in parallel structure.

6   Paragraph 3 is substantial; it has twelve sentences varying in length from eleven to forty-two words. Writers often try to achieve variety of sentence structure as well as of length. How much variety of structure does Steinbeck use? Do the sentences all begin with subjects, or do some begin with dependent grammatical elements?

Diction

1   Most of the words in this selection are simple and easy to understand. A few have Latin origins: for example, *reflector, incandescent,* and *protruded*. What are the exact meanings of these three words? List other words formed from the same roots as these.

2   Paragraph 1 has ten verbs. Which ones are the most vividly specific?

3   Which of the many adjectives in paragraph 2 have the greatest descriptive value?

4   What does the unusual term *mushroomed* mean in sentence 7, paragraph 2? What picture does it make you see?

5   Are *mushroomed* and *tucks* (sentence 6, paragraph 3) metaphors?

6   Point out similes in sentences 2, 4, and 7 of paragraph 3. Which one is the simplest? Do they all make you visualize some detail?

7   Are *petulance* and *taut* well-chosen words? Can you find any synonyms that might be better?

Assignment

In order to introduce a character at the beginning of a story, write one or two paragraphs in which you describe a person getting ready to do his or her regular work. Write in Steinbeck's manner, and make the reader aware of many specific details that reveal the subject as an unmistakable individual.

Khan, Indian Police Official

JOHN FREDERICK MUEHL

Khan indeed looked official. I had expected far less, even from a deputy 1
superintendent of police. He wore brown shorts and a topee and a Sam
Browne belt with a bandoleer of bullets slung across his chest, crossing his
body from upper right to lower left and terminating in a distinctly lethal-
looking pistol. He was incredibly fat, and these leather accoutrements did
nothing to diminish the size of his waistline; rather they made him look
like a dray horse in harness, some great Belgian stallion trapped out for the
fair.

Yet I took an instinctive liking to Khan. There was about him an air of 2
tremendous vitality, and as he walked out on the porch to greet me that
first day, his short arms beat the air in his very enthusiasm. The thing that
amazed me most, though, was his voice. It was the deepest and most reso-
nant that I ever have heard, and as he laughed and called out his welcome
from the veranda, it was like something from the score of a Wagnerian
opera.

"Come in!" he commanded. He could do nothing but command, en- 3
dowed by nature with a voice box like his. "Come in! What on earth are
you doing in this place? You must stay with me here! Come in! Come in!"

I must confess that I stood for a moment and stared, so different was this 4
man from the one I had pictured.

"Well, don't stand there!" he roared to a servant. "Get his luggage!" 5

And it was thus that I first was introduced to Khan. . . . 6

I had ample time to watch Khan at work. He was conducting routine in- 7
terviews, or so I thought at the time, and yet his approach to the villagers
even then was unique. There was, about Khan, none of that brusque and
officious quality I had noticed in so many of the petty bureaucrats, particularly in Kathiawar and in Bursad. He was kindly and sympathetic in his
talks with the cultivators; it seemed that he spent half his time in trying to
allay the fears and quiet the suspicions which they all had formed of the
government generally. Even in the face of the most obvious and stubborn
resistance to his simplest questions he maintained his calm. It was interesting to watch the reaction of the villagers. They seemed as surprised by all
this as I was myself.

Khan was a shrewd man. His very genius perhaps lay in his harmless ap- 8
pearance, for he resembled nothing so much as the stereotype village police

officer, lazy, corrupt, anxious only for order, and that on whatever terms it could be had. He now seemed to be proceeding on a routine tour of inspection. His interviews were desultory and his manner was casual; such an appearance of indolence and disinterest did he give that the people he talked to were invariably overconfident. But he was like a sleeping watchdog. Just one stray word, just a sentence out of place would jar him awake. He would swing his feet down off of the table, shift his enormous bulk in his chair, point a finger and ask a question, and a whole week's work would have been thus accomplished. He was not nearly so much a detective as a psychiatrist, but then his job was to pick the brains of the villagers, to extract just a tenth of the invaluable information that to them was simple common knowledge. I noticed that he never asked a direct question. He seemed to sense that there was enough animosity so that to identify the very information he wanted would be the surest way of closing it to discussion. Rather he would talk around the question in his mind, probing and prodding, testing for reactions, piecing together every raise of an eyebrow, every halt or stammer or hesitation in speech.

STUDY QUESTIONS

Organization and Content

1   What kinds of descriptive details does Muehl present in paragraph 1? What different kinds of details appear in paragraph 2? What is the key word in paragraph 2?
2   What further impressions of Khan does Muehl convey in paragraphs 3–5?
3   What qualities of Khan's character are brought out in paragraph 7?
4   Does the picture of Khan at work in paragraph 8 reinforce the description of him in paragraph 2, or does it seem inconsistent?
5   To what extent has Muehl ventured into characterization?
6   What sentences are most effective for physical description, and which for interpretation of character?

Sentence Structure

1   Point out the variety of sentence length in paragraph 1.
2   Which is the most picturesque part of paragraph 1, sentence 4? How does Muehl arrange the sentence so as to emphasize that part?
3   The beginnings and endings of sentences, paragraphs, and themes are positions that deserve emphasis. How does Muehl throw emphasis on the final word of paragraph 2, sentence 3?
4   How is the idea of paragraph 2, sentence 3, developed in a cumulative way in sentence 4?

5   In paragraph 7, sentence 4, what is the relation of the two parts?
6   Point out how the adjectives are placed in paragraph 8, sentence 2.
7   Identify the series of parallel sentence elements in paragraph 8, sentences 8 and 10.

Diction

1   If you are unsure about the meanings of these words, look them up: *topee* (paragraph 1), *unique, brusque, officious* (7), *desultory, indolence, animosity* (8).
2   Which words in paragraph 1, sentence 3, have the most power to make you visualize Khan?
3   What do the similes contribute to paragraphs 1 and 2? Muehl must have assumed that his readers would be familiar with Belgian stallions and Wagnerian opera. If a reader should not know them, would Muehl lose much descriptive effect?
4   How is the ''sleeping watchdog'' simile in paragraph 8, sentence 5, different from the other two similes?
5   Which verbs convey vivid impressions in paragraphs 2–5?
6   Compare paragraph 8, sentences 5 and 12, with paragraph 8, sentences 9–11, in terms of their concrete and specific words.

Assignment

1   Describe how someone (however unlikely looking) looks while doing his or her work. Like Muehl, stress the person's appearance, manner, and technique of operation. You may go into character, too, but it would be good if actions implied character. Some suggestions: a doctor, minister, counsellor, coach, or policeman.
2   In a similar type of paper, tell about the habits of a person; then relate the appearance of the person to his or her character. It might be well if, before writing, you made a list of details that give life to the subject. Write about someone you know well—a roommate, laboratory partner, teammate or relative.

Mrs. Jack Gardner

CLEVELAND AMORY

1   For a Boston Society which has never lacked for grandes dames to have to admit that its greatest was not a Bostonian at all but a New York import is a stern story indeed. Furthermore this greatest of grandes dames was a lady who persisted in regarding herself as a sort of dedicated spirit to wake up Boston. The daughter of a New York dry-goods merchant named David Stewart, she was christened Isabella. In the year 1860 she married John Lowell Gardner, son of the last of Boston's East India merchants, and moved to Boston. From then until her death in 1924 at the age of eighty-five Isabella Stewart Gardner proceeded to do everything that Proper Boston women do not do, and then some. "In a Society," wrote Lucius Beebe, "where entertaining Major Higginson at tea and sleigh-riding on the Brighton Road on Sunday afternoon were the ultimate public activities endorsed by decorum, she soon became far from anonymous."

2   Mrs. Gardner didn't drink tea; she drank beer. She adored it, she said. She didn't go sleigh-riding; instead, she went walking down Tremont Street with a lion named Rex on a leash. She gave at-homes at her Beacon Street house and received her guests from a perch in the lower branches of a mimosa tree. Told that "everybody in Boston" was either a Unitarian or an Episcopalian, she became a Buddhist; then when the pleasure of that shock had worn off she became such a High-Church Episcopalian that her religion differed from Catholicism only in respect to allegiance to the Pope. Advised that the best people in Boston belonged to clubs she formed one of her own named the "It" Club. In Boston one coachman was enough for anybody. But Mrs. Gardner soon showed she wasn't anybody. She kept two footmen as well as a coachman and rarely drove out in her carriage without all three of them in full livery. Warned that a woman's social position in Boston might be judged in inverse ratio to her appearance, she spent thousands of dollars a year on the latest Paris fashions. She saw Cabots and Lowells leave their jewels in their safe-deposit boxes; she picked out her two largest diamonds, had them set on gold wire springs and wore them waving six inches above her hair like the antennae of a butterfly. Mrs. Gardner even told risqué stories and told them in mixed company—at the same time, her bout with Buddhism behind her, each Lent with much fanfare she piously atoned for her misdeeds by scrubbing the steps of the Church of the Advent and sending out black-bordered invitations to Holy Communion.

3   Hypnotic was the word for this woman. She had a way with her. Plain of face to the point of homeliness and short of stature, she had a strikingly

From *The Proper Bostonians* by Cleveland Amory. Copyright 1947, 1975 by Cleveland Amory. Reprinted by permission of E. P. Dutton.

curvaceous figure and attracted artists by the score, most of whom offered to paint her merely for the pleasure of doing so. When she finally chose John Singer Sargent to do her portrait, she once more showed her scorn for Bostonian propriety by having him paint her in a black low-necked dress with a rope of pearls around her waist and a black shawl drawn tightly around her hips. Exhibited at the gentlemanly St. Botolph Club in the winter of 1888–1889, the picture caused so much comment that her husband had it removed and declared it would never be exhibited again as long as he lived. So far as it is known this is the only occasion he or anyone else ever told Mrs. Gardner what to do. "To dominate others," writes her biographer and present-day executor, Morris Carter, "gave Mrs. Gardner such pleasure that she must have regretted the passing of slavery."

STUDY QUESTIONS
Organization and Content

1 What is the main theme that continues throughout this account of the famous Mrs. Gardner?
2 Paragraph 2 does not have any general statement to serve as a topic sentence. What idea would cover the many details mentioned in paragraph 2?
3 What relation does paragraph 2 have to paragraph 1?
4 How does the principal thought of paragraph 3 contrast with that of paragraph 2?

Sentence Structure

1 Note that the author begins many of his sentences with dependent phrases or clauses. He uses the participial modifier as in: "Told that 'everybody in Boston' . . ." in paragraph 2, the appositive as in: "The daughter of a New York dry-goods merchant . . ." in paragraph 1, the adjective plus modifiers in the "Plain of face to the point of homeliness . . ." in paragraph 3, and a series of prepositional phrases as in: "From then until her death . . ." in paragraph 1. Does he overdo the opening with dependent elements?
2 However, the first several sentences of paragraph 2 are of a different type. Explain what their difference is.
3 What is the effect of this "change of pace" in the early part of paragraph 2?
4 To what extent would you say that Amory has achieved variety in his sentence style in these paragraphs?

Diction

1 Look up *grandes dames, ultimate, decorum, livery, risqué, fanfare, atoned, propriety.*

2   What are the chief differences among the beliefs of Unitarians, Episcopalians, and Buddhists?

3   Comment on the effect of these terms: *and then some, bout, curvaceous.* Are all three of them colloquial terms? Be sure that you know what *colloquial* means (it has nothing to do with locality).

Assignment

Write two or three paragraphs about an unconventional person. To do justice to your model, Mrs. Jack Gardner, choose the most unconventional person you have ever known, one who has seemed "wild" and who has delighted in challenging social conventions wherever he or she has lived.

Note that though there is some description here, the author places most stress upon Mrs. Gardner's activities and personality. He does not say much about her character or temperament. Sentence 2 of paragraph 1 gives necessary information in this respect and so does the last sentence of paragraph 3. Paragraph 2 is devoted entirely to the actions of Mrs. Gardner. Do the same in your paragraphs; an honest report of facts is generally very effective.

Another promising subject would be some distinctive well-publicized person such as Elvis Presley, George Wallace, Howard Hughes, or Jerry Brown.

Roxanne of Watts, California

CAROLYN SEE

1   When domestic misery hits in Watts, it immediately and inextricably combines with social disaster. Consider Roxanne, who had lived in Watts for about seven years. Her man left her on the day of Kennedy's assassination in 1963, and she remembers not knowing which she was crying for— her President's death, or her man's absence. She wasn't in enough control to delegate this tear for this, this for that. Roxanne and her sister were raised in Arkansas by strict, prosperous parents. The girls "went bad"—became pregnant—as teenagers, their parents departing from the Negro stereotype by disowning them. Their parents don't write now, or send money, or ask for pictures of their numerous grandchildren.

2   Like thousands of whites and blacks before them, Roxanne and her sister

From "Three Family Dropouts in Watts." Reprinted from the January 29, 1967, issue of *West* by permission of the author.

came to Los Angeles and began to live the strange, isolated present-tense life of people new to Southern California. Roxanne brought two children with her, both illegitimate, from two different casual encounters. It's not that she wanted them to be casual. Roxanne describes herself as the kind of woman no man would stay with. She hasn't a dazzling personality or ready wit. She isn't cut out to be someone's mistress, but someone's wife. She wants to take care of her children and keep a house and wait all day for her husband to come home and tell her his ideas, his experiences. Waiting is Roxanne's most distinctive trait, but she isn't waiting for anyone. She has never lived with a man for over a week, and those weeks are months apart. Roxanne refutes the theory that Negro women are always strong, competent and tough. She is gentle and shy, and these typically "feminine" attributes have almost ruined her life.

Hearing about Roxanne, you expect to see someone sadly plain. In fact, she is stunning and doesn't know it, with a perfect young body and hair worn casually in loose curls, reminiscent of Nancy Wilson as much as anyone else. But she's Nancy Wilson in a shiny blue gabardine skirt, a cheap, see-through nylon blouse, scuffed slippers, and one 79-cent touch of bravado—a red lace bra. Roxanne is all alone. She sits alone in her house in back of another house, denied even the company of the street. She has her children for company—four of them now—but no friends. **3**

Roxanne's house is built in the Spanish style of the 1920s. The living room has a beamed ceiling stenciled with antiqued cabbage roses. The art work is 40 years old and faded into delightful shades of green and rose and brown. The front door is fake hand-hewn wood with giant hinges. The walls have ornate wrought-iron electric fixtures. It's the kind of house you walk into and think, "Oh for a couple of gallons of white paint!" Then, sitting a while, you see the holes in the plaster, holes in the linoleum, the torn front screen where flies come in. And the darkness of the kitchen—dark because some previous tenant painted the windows to save the expense of buying curtains. A naked wire dangles from one of the fixtures. The television set is broken. The plumbing smells bad. You see two or three roaches, and Roxanne says she's afraid at night for the children because of the rats. The lawn in front is 7 inches high, and turning brown. Even a visitor is overcome with lassitude, fatigue, domestic despair. All these things could be fixed—but how? How does a woman patch linoleum or plaster? Or bring home a new screen door in a car she hasn't got? Or deal definitively with a naked electric wire? Part of Roxanne's budget goes for insect spray (as much a staple of the urban poor as chicken wings or grits or greens or cheap wine) but the roaches are in the walls and she can't afford an exterminator at $210 a month. If Roxanne were tough or bossy or even calculatingly sexy, she might get someone to help her with these chores, but she is not. **4**

Roxanne's dealings with men—she gives herself in a kind of desperate, joyless romanticism—have changed her life from difficult to unbearable. **5**

Her two youngest children have the same father, a man Roxanne is wildly in love with but rarely sees. He has a family of his own. Roxanne named these two children after him and asked him through the courts for child support, but hasn't otherwise interfered in his personal life. The courts ruled against her, throwing the case out of court for lack of evidence. When she found out, she didn't cry. She'd had too much trouble getting the two little ones down for their naps. Instead, she bent over in her chair until her face almost touched her knees, she sucked on her lips, she clasped her arms around the calves of her legs and stayed that way for some time. Later on that night, alone, she cried.

STUDY QUESTIONS
Organization and Content

1   Which facts in paragraph 1 are the most important for understanding Roxanne?
2   What main elements of character are emphasized in paragraph 2? What does sentence 1, paragraph 3, indicate about Roxanne?
3   Which adjectives in paragraph 3 are most effective for description? What makes them effective?
4   What impression of Roxanne's house do sentences 1–5, paragraph 4, give you? Which details in sentences 7–13 make you see the place most vividly?
5   What is the purpose of sentence 14?
6   How do the adjectives used in the last sentence of paragraph 4 further reveal Roxanne's character? How is the next sentence related to the last sentence of paragraph 4?
7   What effect is produced by sentences 6–9, paragraph 5? What kind of picture does sentence 8 make you see?
8   In your opinion, which of the following terms best apply to Roxanne: desolate, pathetic, weak, sweet, corrupt, gentle, soft, innocent, unsteady, pitiable, ineffective, insipid, unaffected, simple-minded, feckless, stupid?
9   Contrast the portrait of Roxanne with that of Mrs. Gardner.

Sentence Structure

1   In an informal style a writer uses contractions, omits connectives ("he said I should go" instead of ". . . *that* I should go"), and makes sentences grammatically simple so that they sound conversational. Is the sentence style of this selection mainly formal or informal? Give evidence.
2   Which words are repeated throughout paragraph 2 to provide clear transition from one sentence to another?
3   Which detail in sentence 3, paragraph 3, receives the most emphasis? How is emphasis created?

4 *What similar structure do sentences 1–5, paragraph 4, have? Would it be better to vary the sentence pattern or to arrange the five sentences into one sentence? Explain.*

5 *Sentences 9–11, paragraph 4, are short. What effect do they have?*

6 *What is unusual about sentences 7 and 8, paragraph 5? How are they related to sentence 6?*

Diction

1 *You may need to look up* inextricable, stereotype *(paragraph 1),* distinctive *(2),* bravado *(3),* lassitude, definitively *(4).*

2 What does the term "present-tense life" (paragraph 2) imply about Roxanne? Can people live "past-tense" or "future-tense" lives?

3 Do any words in this selection seem extremely formal or extremely colloquial? To what extent is the diction formal, informal, colloquial?

Assignment

Describe and characterize someone you know who has had troubles or reverses—domestic, personal, scholastic, financial, or accidental. Use plenty of vivid details, and try to relate character to situation.

Women at a Well

DORIS LESSING

Two narrow tracks, one of them deepened to a smooth dusty groove by 1
the incessant padding of bare feet, wound from the farm compound to the old well through half a mile of tall blond grass that was soiled and matted because of the nearness of the clustering huts; the compound had been on that ridge for twenty years.

The native women with their children used to loiter down the track, and 2
their shrill laughter and chattering sounded through the trees as if one might suddenly have come on a flock of brilliant noisy parrots. It seemed as if fetching water was more of a social event to them than a chore. At the well itself they would linger half the morning, standing in groups to gossip, their arms raised in that graceful, eternally moving gesture to steady glittering or rusted petrol tins balanced on head-rings woven of grass; kneeling to

From *African Stories* by Doris Lessing. Copyright © 1951, 1953, 1954, 1957, 1958, 1962, 1963, 1964, 1965 by Doris Lessing. Reprinted by permission of Simon & Schuster, a Division of Gulf & Western Corporation.

slap bits of bright cloth on slabs of stone blasted long ago from the depths of earth. Here they washed and scolded and dandled their children. Here they scrubbed their pots. Here they sluiced themselves and combed their hair.

3   Coming upon them suddenly there would be sharp exclamations; a glimpse of soft brown shoulders and thighs withdrawing to the bushes, or annoyed and resentful eyes. It was their well. And while they were there, with their laughter and gossip and singing, their folded draperies, bright armbands, earthenware jars and metal combs, grouped in attitudes of head-slowed indolence, it seemed as if the bellowing of distant cattle, drone of tractor, all the noises of the farm, were simply lending themselves to form a background to this antique scene: Women, drawing water at the well.

STUDY QUESTIONS
Organization and Content

1   What is the purpose of sentence 1?
2   List the details that Lessing mentions in sentence 1. Which words in the sentence create sense impressions?
3   A colon signals the reader to go ahead and find out something. In sentence 1 what is explained after the colon?
4   How does paragraph 2, sentence 2, serve to explain a part of sentence 1?
5   How does the long sentence 3 of paragraph 3 help the description along?
6   In terms of description, how do sentences 4, 5, and 6 of paragraph 2 differ from sentence 3?
7   Which details of sight and sound in paragraph 3 are particularly vivid?
8   Which sentence of paragraph 3 has no descriptive details? Why did the author include this sentence?
9   What kind of picture (or story) does the author try to suggest with ''this antique scene''?

Sentence Structure

1   Sentence 1, sentence 3 of paragraph 2, and sentence 3 of paragraph 3 all have more than fifty words. Which shorter sentences contrast with these long ones and provide variety of sentence length?
2   In paragraph 2, sentence 2, what are the governing words in the participial phrases after the short main clause? Why use the semicolon in this sentence?
3   How is emphasis related to parallel structure in paragraph 2, sentences 4–6?

4 In paragraph 3, sentence 2, what grammatical constructions govern the many details presented?

Diction

1 In paragraph 1 which adjectives especially help you to visualize the scene?
2 To what other creatures are the women compared?
3 Indicate what important descriptive roles the verbal elements (verbs, infinitives, participles) play in paragraph 2?
4 Which words do the most to make you see the grouping of the figures in "this antique scene"?

Assignment

Carefully observe a group of people who form a unit. Then write a description of them. A group of campers, a family away from home, a school team or a club—perhaps waiting for a bus—would make suitable subjects. Vary the length of your sentences. Use verbs and adjectives that will make the reader see and hear.

A Kitchen

JAMES BALDWIN

Their mother, her head tied up in an old rag, sipped black coffee and watched Roy. The pale end-of-winter sunlight filled the room and yellowed all their faces; and John, drugged and morbid and wondering how it was that he had slept again and had been allowed to sleep so long, saw them for a moment like figures on a screen, an effect that the yellow light intensified. The room was narrow and dirty; nothing could alter its dimensions, no labor could ever make it clean. Dirt was in the walls and the floorboards, and triumphed beneath the sink where roaches spawned; was in the fine ridges of the pots and pans, scoured daily, burnt black on the bottom, hanging above the stove; was in the wall against which they hung, and revealed itself where the paint had cracked and leaned outward in stiff squares and fragments, the paper-thin underside webbed with black. Dirt was in every corner, angle, crevice of the monstrous stove, and lived behind it in delirious communion with the corrupted wall. Dirt was in the baseboard that John scrubbed every Saturday, and roughened the cupboard shelves

From *Go Tell It on the Mountain* by James Baldwin. Copyright © 1952, 1953, by James Baldwin. Reprinted by permission of The Dial Press.

that held the cracked and gleaming dishes. Under this dark weight the walls leaned, under it the ceiling, with a great crack like lightning in its center, sagged. The windows gleamed like beaten gold or silver, but now John saw, in the yellow light, how fine dust veiled their doubtful glory. Dirt crawled in the gray mop hung out of the windows to dry. John thought with shame and horror, yet in angry hardness of heart: *He who is filthy, let him be filthy still.* Then he looked at his mother, seeing, as though she were someone else, the dark, hard lines running downward from her eyes, and the·deep, perpetual scowl in her forehead, and the downturned, tightened mouth, and the strong, thin, brown, and bony hands; and the phrase turned against him like a two-edged sword, for was it not he, in his false pride and his evil imagination, who was filthy? Through a storm of tears that did not reach his eyes, he stared at the yellow room; and the room shifted, the light of the sun darkened, and his mother's face changed. Her face became the face that he gave her in his dreams, the face that had been hers in a photograph he had seen once, long ago, a photograph taken before he was born. This face was young and proud, uplifted, with a smile that made the wide mouth beautiful and glowed in the enormous eyes. It was the face of a girl who knew that no evil could undo her, and who could laugh, surely, as his mother did not laugh now. Between the two faces there stretched a darkness and a mystery that John feared, and that sometimes caused him to hate her.

STUDY QUESTIONS

Organization and Content

1   From whose point of view is this description presented? If the observer were a child of three or a man of sixty, would the altered point of view make a difference in the content?

2   In what way does "end-of-winter sunlight," a detail mentioned in sentence 2, influence the description?

3   What is the dominant impression created by this description? What items support this impression?

4   Note the physical point of view in sentences 8 and 9. Where is the eye of the reader led?

5   What change occurs in the presentation in sentence 10? Is the paragraph organized in terms of two main parts, or more?

6   Should the part about the mother be in a separate paragraph or not? Answering this question requires consideration of the question: Does the paragraph have unity?

Sentence Structure

1   Explain how sentence 2 in its second part resembles sentence 1 in structure.

2   If sentence 3 had periods instead of the semicolon and comma, what different effect would be produced?
3   What pattern of verb-plus-prepositional phrases helps Baldwin to get so many details into sentence 4?
4   What subject-verb pattern is repeated in sentences 4–6? What effect does Baldwin secure by this repetition?
5   How does the use of the *and*'s in sentence 11 compare with that in sentences 2, 4, and 12?
6   Do the appositives serve a purpose in sentence 13? Would it be better not to repeat *face* and *photograph*?
7   How does Baldwin put emphasis on *face* in sentences 13–15? Is the word *face* important enough to deserve such emphasis?
8   Point out the parallel clauses in sentences 15 and 16.

Diction

1   The vocabulary is not difficult, but Baldwin uses words with great skill to create a dominant impression or a certain *atmosphere* for his setting. (See *Tone* in Glossary.) Which words through repetition contribute most to this atmosphere?
2   Consider how different the connotations would be if *diseased* replaced *morbid* in sentence 2, and if *reproduced* replaced *spawned* in sentence 4.
3   The verb *be* does not suggest vigor. Writers are often advised to avoid it and use instead verbs of action. In sentences 3–6, however, Baldwin uses *was* several times. Are the sentences weakened by this usage? What is contributed by other verbs, such as *triumphed* and *leaned* (sentence 4), *lived* (5), *roughened* (6), and *crawled* (9)?
4   Baldwin uses some terms which suggest that the thing he is writing about is something else, or is like something else: "like lightning," for example, in sentence 7. His language is "figurative"; that is, he uses metaphors and similes. Identify his figures of speech. Does he use more similes or more metaphors?
5   Should *triumphed* (sentence 4), *lived . . . in delirious communion* (5), *veiled* (8), and *crawled* (9) be regarded as metaphors?
6   What idea is communicated to the reader by *scoured* (sentence 4), *scrubbed* and *cracked and gleaming* (6)?
7   In the latter part of the description both adjectives and verbs are important. Which are the most significant ones in sentences 11, 12, and 14?

Assignment

We move now from descriptions of people to descriptions of places. In describing places, you should use the same general principles as in describing persons.

Imitate Baldwin's paragraph by writing one that describes a room with a person or persons in it and that conveys a dominant impression. Be sure to include abundant details, as Baldwin does.

Use striking adjectives and verbs and some figurative language. As a
subject you might use a bus station, a laboratory, an operating room, a
hospital waiting room, a police station, a barroom, a room prepared for
a party just before the guests arrive or the same room just after the party
is over, a laundromat, or a stadium at the time of a football game.

Similarly, you might convey the dominant impression of a poolroom,
the repair and greasing section of a filling station, a butchering place for
animals or poultry, a room with a dead body and mourners, or a tent
with people during rain.

Supper Time in a Jewish Kitchen

AFLRED KAZIN

Ripeness filled our kitchen even at supper time. The room was so wild
with light, it made me tremble; I could not believe my eyes. In the sink a
great sandy pile of radishes, lettuces, tomatoes, cucumbers, and scallions
broke up on their stark greens and reds the harshness of the world's daily
monotony. The window shade by the sewing machine was drawn, its tab
baking in the sun. Through the screen came the chant of the score being
called up from the last handball game below. Our front door was open, to
let in air; you could hear the boys on the roof scuffing their shoes against
the gravel. Then, my father home to the smell of paint in the hall, we sat
down to chopped cucumbers floating in the ice-cold borscht, radishes and
tomatoes and lettuce in sour cream, a mound of corn just out of the pot
steaming on the table, the butter slowly melting in a cracked blue soup
plate—breathing hard against the heat, we sat down together at last.

STUDY QUESTIONS

Organization and Content

1   What is the main impression created by this paragraph?
2   How important for the impression are *ripeness*, *light*, *monotony*,
    baking, and *heat*?
3   What extent of time is to be assumed between the opening and the
    close of the paragraph? What things occur during that time?
4   What does the paragraph suggest about the kind of dwelling that
    Kazin lived in and the economic position of his parents?

Sentence Structure

1   Why do you think Kazin separated clauses with semicolons in sentences 2 and 6?
2   What effect comes from repeating ''we sat down,'' as Kazin does in the final sentence?
3   Three sentences begin with subordinate elements, and several sentences end with subordinate elements. Has Kazin provided enough variety of sentence structure?

Diction

1   What do these terms contribute to the description: *great sandy pile, stark, scuffing, mound, steaming, cracked blue?*
2   Which words appeal most vividly to the senses?

Assignment

1   In one or two paragraphs describe a family breakfast, supper, or barbecue.
2   Kazin writes of a Jewish city setting. Similarly describe a country kitchen with country food for a country family. Include sensory images with country sounds coming from outdoors.
3   Write a description of a meal in a college cafeteria. Use plenty of vivid and concrete terms to make us see the food and the physical setting.
4   Similarly describe a meal in a fraternity, sorority, or boarding house; a church supper; a picnic or family reunion outdoors; or a luncheon before or supper after a football game.

A Mexican House

ERNESTO GALARZA

Our adobe cottage was on the side of the street away from the arroyo. It   1
was the last house if you were going to Miramar. About fifty yards behind
the corral, the forest closed in.

It was like every other house in Jalco, probably larger. The adobe walls   2
were thick, a foot or more, with patches of whitewash where the thatched
overhang protected the adobe from the rain. There were no windows. The
entrance doorway was at one end of the front wall, and directly opposite the

door that led to the corral. The doors were made of planks axed smooth from tree trunks and joined with two cross pieces and a diagonal brace between them hammered together with large nails bent into the wood on the inside. Next to each door and always handy for instant use, there was the cross bar, the *tranca*. On both sides of the door frame there was a notched stub, mortared into the adobe bricks and about six inches long. The door was secured from the inside by dropping the *tranca* into the two notches.

3   All the living space for the family was in the one large room, about twelve feet wide and three times as long. Against the wall between the two doorways was the *pretil*, a bank of adobe bricks three feet high, three across, and two feet deep. In the center of the *pretil* was the main fire pit. Two smaller hollows, one on either side of the large one, made it a three-burner stove. On a row of pegs above the *pretil* hung the clay pans and other cooking utensils, bottom side out, the soot baked into the red clay. A low bench next to the *pretil*, also made of adobe, served as a table and shelf for the cups, pots, and plates.

4   The rest of the ground floor was divided by a curtain hung from one of the hand-hewed log beams, making two bedrooms. Above them, secured to the beams, was the *tapanco*, a platform the size of a double bed made of thin saplings tied together with pieces of rawhide. The top of a notched pole, braced against the foot of the back wall of the cottage, rested against the side of the *tapanco*, serving as a ladder. Along the wall opposite the *pretil*, in the darkest and coolest part of the house, were the big *cántaros*, the red clay jars; the *canastos*, tall baskets made of woven reeds; the rolled straw *petates* to cover the dirt floor where people walked or sat; and the hoes and other work tools.

5   There was no ceiling other than the underside of the thatch, which was tied to the pole rafters. On top of these, several layers of thatch were laid, making a waterproof cover thicker than the span of a man's hand. The rafters were notched and tied to the ridgepole and mortared on the lower end to the top of the walls. Between the top of the walls and the overhang there was an open space a few inches wide. Through this strip the smoke from the *pretil* went out and the fresh air came in.

6   It was the roof that gave space and lift to the single room that served as kitchen, bedroom, parlor, pantry, closet, storeroom, and tool shed. The slender rafters pointed upward in sharp triangles tied at the peak with bows of darkbrown rawhide that had dried as tight as steel straps. Strings of thatch hung from the ceiling like the fringe of a buggy top, making it appear that the heavy matting of grass did not rest on the rafters but tiptoed on hundreds of threads. It was always half dark up there. My cousins, Jesús and Catarino, and I slept in the *tapanco*. More than a bedroom, to us it was a half-lighted hideaway out of sight of parents, uncles, aunts, and other meddlesome people.

STUDY QUESTIONS
Organization and Content

1   What sort of information about the house does paragraph 1 give us?
2   Which details of the house does Galarza tell about in paragraph 2? At what point does he stop describing the outside of the house and take us inside?
3   What were the proportions of the house? How was it divided? What went on in the *pretil* area? Where were the tools kept? Where was the *tapanco* situated? Who slept there?
4   Going by the description of paragraphs 3 and 4, draw a plan of the house.
5   What things are described in most specific detail in paragraphs 3, 4, and 6?

Sentence Structure

1   Galarza's sentences are not very complicated but they are varied in structure. Contrast the structural patterns of sentence 1, paragraph 1; sentences 2 and 4, paragraph 2; and sentence 2, paragraph 4.
2   Sentence 5, paragraph 2, is quite long. It is a loose sentence. At what point is the sense of the sentence first complete? This sentence is a good illustration of how to use past participles after nouns they modify. What word do *axed* and *joined* modify? How do *pieces* and *brace* function grammatically? What words do *hammered* and *bent* modify?
3   Galarza begins several sentences in paragraphs 3, 4, and 5 with prepositions. Which ones? How do the opening prepositional phrases help to make clear the locations and relations of things within the space of the house?

Diction

1.   Many words have come into the English language from Spanish— for example, *adobe, arroyo,* and *corral* in paragraph 1. Unless you are a Westerner, you may have to look up one or two of them.
2   Galarza italicizes several other Spanish words. Why? Does he explain their meanings?
3   The house was covered with a thatched roof. How is such a roof made? How is the word *thatch* related to *deck*? to *tegument*? to *protect* and *detect*?
4   Which words make you see precise details of color, shape, and size in paragraphs 3, 4, and 6?

Assignment

Describe a room or the interior of a building that contains numerous things. Make the reader see very accurately the arrangement of the things in the space—right, left, above, and below. You might write about a barber shop or a beauty parlor, a stable, a garage, a poolroom, a kitchen, a country store, an antique store, or some other kind of store.

Streets at Night

CARSON McCULLERS

The streets in the middle of the town reminded F. Jasmine of a carnival fair. There was the same air of holiday freedom; and, as in the early morning, she felt herself a part of everything, included and gay. On a Main Street corner a man was selling mechanical mice, and an armless beggar, with a tin cup in his lap, sat cross-legged on the sidewalk, watching. She had never seen Front Avenue at night before, for in the evening she was supposed to play in the neighborhood close to home. The warehouses across the street were black, but the square mill at the far end of the avenue was lighted in all its many windows and there was a faint mill humming and the smell of dyeing vats. Most of the businesses were open, and the neon signs made a mingling of varied lights that gave to the avenue a watery look. There were soldiers on corners, and other soldiers strolling along with grown date girls. The sounds were slurred late-summer sounds—footsteps, laughter, and above the shuffled noises, the voices of someone calling from an upper story down into the summer street. The buildings smelled of sunbaked brick and the sidewalk was warm beneath the soles of her new silver shoes.

STUDY QUESTIONS

Organization and Content

1 What general controlling idea does sentence 1 express? Is sentence 1 the topic sentence of the paragraph? Could it be considered a thesis sentence?
2 Which term in sentence 2 further explains the idea of sentence 1?
3 Which specific details in sentence 3 support the same idea?
4 The observer is a twelve-year-old girl. Which sentence indicates that she is having a new experience? Is the description presented from a moving or a stationary point of view?
5 What use has McCullers made of sounds, smells, and vivid details?
6 Which terms indicate a season of the year?

From *The Ballad of the Sad Cafe: The Novels and Stories of Carson McCullers.* Copyright © 1951 by Carson McCullers. Reprinted by permission of Houghton Mifflin Company.

Sentence Structure

1 Are most of the sentences complex, compound, or simple? Where McCullers uses conjunctions, are they mainly coordinating conjunctions or subordinating conjunctions?
2 Why use a semicolon before *and* in sentence 2 but a comma before *and* in sentence 3? Why is there no punctuation before *and* in sentences 5 and 9?
3 In what positions have the prepositional phrases been placed in sentences 3 and 5? Can any of them be put in other positions?
4 In sentence 8, by what means has *sounds* been made more specific?

Diction

1 What are the roots of *carnival* (sentence 1), *holiday* (2), and *slurred* (8)?
2 Which words in sentence 5 make appeals to the senses?
3 Which terms express an unusual appearance in sentence 6?
4 What impression is communicated in sentence 8 by *slurred* and *shuffled?*
5 What is the reason for the special smell and feel expressed in sentence 9?

Assignment

Turn yourself into a reporter who is writing a feature story designed for the general public, and go for a walk through the industrial, wholesaling, or commercial section of a town or city. A farmers' market, a fish market, docks, a freight station, or a trucking establishment would offer good possibilities for a description similar to that of McCullers in which an observer becomes aware of a succession of sights and other impressions. List details as you see them, and try to use as many details as McCullers did.

A College Campus

RALPH ELLISON

It was a beautiful college. The buildings were old and covered with vines and the roads gracefully winding, lined with hedges and wild roses that dazzled the eyes in the summer sun. Honeysuckle and purple wisteria hung heavy from the trees and white magnolias mixed with their scents in the bee-humming air. I've recalled it often, here in my hole: How the grass turned green in the springtime and how the mocking birds fluttered their tails and sang, how the moon shone down on the buildings, how the bell in the chapel tower rang out the precious short-lived hours; how the girls in bright summer dresses promenaded the grassy lawn. Many times, here at night, I've closed my eyes and walked along the forbidden road that winds past the girls' dormitories, past the hall with the clock in the tower, its windows warmly aglow, on down past the small white Home Economics practice cottage, whiter still in the moonlight, and on down the road with its sloping and turning, paralleling the black powerhouse with its engines droning earth-shaking rhythms in the dark, its windows red from the glow of the furnace, on to where the road became a bridge over a dry riverbed, tangled with brush and clinging vines; the bridge of rustic logs, made for trysting, but virginal and untested by lovers; on up the road, past the buildings, with the southern verandas half-a-city-block long, to the sudden forking, barren of buildings, birds, or grass, where the road turned off to the insane asylum.

STUDY QUESTIONS

Organization and Content

1 Which sentence is the topic sentence of the paragraph?
2 How many different things does Ellison name in this paragraph by using nouns? Which nouns are general, and which specific?
3 Which details are the most concrete?
4 Which terms refer to color, sound, movement, size, and shape?
5 Why should the five sentences of the paragraph be arranged in this order?
6 What do the items named in sentence 3 have in common? Those of the how-clauses of sentence 4?
7 How does the point of view in sentence 5 contrast with that in sentences 1–4?

From Ralph Ellison, *Invisible Man.* Copyright 1952 by Ralph Ellison. Random House, Inc.

8 Should the last detail of the paragraph (the insane asylum) be regarded as literal or symbolic?

Sentence Structure

1 Sentence 2 exemplifies the loose sentence; if it stopped after *old*, it would be complete. How does Ellison add so many more elements after *old?*
2 Contrast the structure of sentences 3 and 4.
3 Sentence 4 has several parallel elements. Indicate them.
4 Sentence 5 is very long and has many parallel elements. What words make the reader aware of the parallelism? Which phrases modify *walked* and which modify *winds?*
5 What is the function of the *with*-phrases in sentence 5? Note how the adjectives (modifiers) are arranged both before and after *cottage.* How does the material between semicolons operate in sentence 5?

Diction

1 Such words as *buildings, vines,* and *roads* are general. What terms does Ellison use to make his description more concrete? Are the adjectives or the verbs more important in making the description concrete?
2 Of the verbs in sentence 4, which are the most effective in suggesting sense impressions?
3 In terms of description what is the difference between "precious short-lived hours" and "bright summer dresses"?
4 Which words in sentence 5 have connotative power in addition to their denotations?

Assignment

Imitate this paragraph by writing a similar one about the campus of your school. Avoid sentimentality and include many details perceptible to the senses. Try to suggest, without speaking of them directly, what feelings the campus arouses in you.

Small-Town Road

ELLINGTON WHITE

. . . I sat there with nothing to do but watch the trucks, big tractor-trailer jobs, ghosting by on Route 49. Luckily a plate glass window had been installed for just that purpose. The window, which occupied the better half of the wall directly behind Octane's heavy shoulders, commanded as impressive a view of the highway as one was likely to find in these flat parts, and I could well imagine the numbers of honeymooners (for Harry ran a little motel in the rear) who had sat in front of this window, awed by the sun dropping behind the cratered mountain of junked cars that had erupted across the road, admiring the latest Galaxies, Comets, and Star Flames streaking dizzily past, and dreaming together of the day, not far off, when they too would turn in their old earthbound Chevy and launch off into outer space. And why not? That's what I asked myself. Why stay here? Here it was Octane and Eubanks and 5 o'clock settling gray and wet over the South. Here it was motels and billboards and the hot jangle of neon bursting red over four lanes of concrete. Here it was a cold drizzle oozing out of low clouds, junk heaps, and raw shoulders pumping mud over the concrete slabs. When the big trucks came over the rise and boomed down the straightaway, they were shawled in spray, like clouds carrying thunder to the coast, and I could see the drivers hunched over their steering wheels, peering ahead through the drizzling mist for the iron signs that marked the city limits of Median, a thirty-mile-an-hour pause in the onward rush to New Orleans, a speed trap and nothing more. Ride the brakes but don't stop. . . . Nobody stopped in Median. Median was one of those towns you pass through on the way to some other town, usually in July at midday, when Main Street is like a glaring white corridor chiseled between granite walls and the only shade is the frayed awning in front of Woolworth's and the only sound is the hum of air-conditioners sucking life into the tired buildings: drifting past the filling stations, past the blistered "Ice Water" signs flapping in the dead dusty air, past the empty high school with shades drawn over the windows and weeds curling over the front steps, you say to yourself, "Thank God I don't live here!"

STUDY QUESTIONS
Organization and Content

1   Where does the observer sit to watch the scene? How does the point of view in this description differ from that in the description by Ellison?

2   Actually White imagines the feelings of other people watching the scene (sentences 3–4). How does he relate his second section (sentences 7–10) to the first one? In what way is the point of view changed in sentence 13?

3   What is the dominant impression created by this description?

Sentence Structure

1   Sentences 3 and 13 are very long. How can White manage such long sentences and communicate clearly with the reader? He does so in part by arranging main units of the sentences in groups of twos and threes and by repeating words that signal parallel constructions. The basic structure of sentence 3 is: "The window . . . commanded a view . . . , and I could· imagine numbers of honeymooners . . . who had sat . . . , awed . . . , admiring . . . , and dreaming. . . ." The less important material is "tucked away" between the main items or added at the end. The basic structure of sentence 13 is

"Median was one of the towns you pass through . . . ,
    when Main Street is like a corridor . . .
    and the only shade is the awning . . .
    and the only sound is the hum . . .
        drifting past filling stations,
            past signs . . . ,
            past the high school . . . ,
            you say . . . , 'Thank God . . . !' "

(The colon in the sentence signifies a continuation leading to a conclusion, which is the idea expressed in the words spoken.) Analyze sentences 7, 8, 9, and 10 similarly, pointing out repetitions and the pairs and trios of basic terms.

2   How much variation in sentence length and rhythm does White have in this passage?

Diction

1   At times White uses words in an unusual way. What does *ghosting* mean, for instance, in sentence 1? (Is there a verb *to ghost?* What would it mean, according to White's usage?) In sentence 8, what appeals to the senses are created by "hot jangle of neon bursting red"? Analyze the operation of this group of words. Does *jangle* belong there?

2 In sentences 7–10, which words are most effective in creating an atmosphere? What sort of atmosphere?
3 Is White justified in using the exaggerated metaphor of "cratered mountain" in sentence 3?
4 Are both of White's similes (sentences 10, 13) equally effective?
5 What does each of the following terms accomplish for descriptive effect in sentence 13: *glaring, frayed, tired, blistered, flapping, dead, empty, weeds curling?*

Assignment

Sit at the window of a little store or restaurant on a road at the outskirts of a town or city, and describe what you see outside. Use vivid language to suggest the kind of environment you are in. Include one long sentence (one hundred words or more) to see how well you can manage it.

Similarly describe a factory as seen by a person sitting in a glassed-in office; or a boat landing or nursing home from a particular point of view.

A New York City Intersection

ANONYMOUS

The southwest windows of my third-floor loft face on one of the most harum-scarum intersections in the city, where Sixth Avenue, Varick Street (Seventh Avenue), West Broadway, and Thompson Street, pinched by the narrowness of Manhattan, dump huge loads of traffic into the already rich mixture of cars and trucks heading east and west on Canal Street between the Manhattan Bridge and the Holland Tunnel. The intersection is really more of an open-air car mall, where stoplights function in a largely advisory capacity, where "WALK" signs are jokes, and where car horns are heard just about non-stop during rush hours and the Feast of San Gennaro. Car horns, and occasional truck horns that lift me clean out of bed on summer nights when I have the windows open, and screeching tires, and the violent hiss of air brakes, and, about twice a year, collisions (last year a guy trying the highly prized and difficult post-green-light turn from Canal onto West Broadway smashed into the window of the luncheonette on the corner; no-

From Notes and Comment in *The New Yorker*. Reprinted by permission; © 1977 the New Yorker Magazine, Inc.

body hurt)—these are mainly what I hear in my apartment. The only human sounds that come through it all are arguments between drivers, and the word "Fireworks," which Italian and Chinese kids shout to passing cars during the week before the Fourth of July. Even at this time of year, I spend a lot of time on my fire escape looking at the cars—I have about a ninety-per-cent accuracy in picking cars from New Jersey—and in the summer I love to watch rain come into the intersection. When rain comes from the west, the sky is often a translucent green, like the glass in my doctor's office door, and the large raindrops hit so hard that you can see the smaller drops that fly off in a circle from the impact, and the cars' windshield wipers switch to superfast with a nerve-racking sound. When rain comes from the east in a very dark thunderhead—something that happens more rarely—you can see the brightness-activated streetlights all the way along Canal pop on one at a time under the advancing storm.

STUDY QUESTIONS

Organization and Content

1 What point of view does the writer use?
2 Are the sense impressions in this description mainly of sight or of sound?
3 What kind of sense appeals does sentence 3 make?
4 How are the sense appeals of sentence 4 different from those of sentence 3?

Sentence Structure

1 Sentence 1 is a loose sentence. Where could it first stop and make complete sense? What modifiers are added after that point to make it so long (Sixty-five words)?
2 Sentence 2 has three parallel *where* clauses. What impression do these three clauses build up?
3 Why does the author use so many *and*'s in sentence 3?
4 How are the last three sentences connected in terms of topic and of grammatical pattern? Which terms provide transition?
5 How do the last two sentences differ in structure (and effect) from sentence 1?

Diction

1 Does the paragraph seem mainly formal or colloquial in style? Consider the effect of *just about, guy, kids, a lot of time, translucent, pop on.*

2   Sentence 1 has two or three metaphors. Identify them. Do you find them effective?

3   In what ways are these words effective: *harum-scarum* (1), *screeching* (3), *smashed* (3), *translucent* (6), *pops* (7)?

4   What does the simile in sentence 6 add to the description?

Assignment

1   Observe a busy intersection, record details of sight and sound, and imitate this paragraph in a similar description.

2   From the window of a dormitory or other campus building, observe activities below, and describe them vividly.

A Sunset in Ethiopia

ROBERT DICK-READ

After our meal we went for a stroll across the plateau. The day was already drawing to a close as we sat down upon a ledge of rock near the lip of the western precipice. From where we sat, as though perched high upon a cloud, we looked out into a gigantic void. Far below, the stream we had crossed that afternoon was a pencil-thin trickle of silver barely visible in the gloaming. Across it, on the other side, the red hills rose one upon another in gentle folds, fading into the distance where the purple thumb-like mountains of Adua and Yeha stretched against the sky like a twisting serpent. As we sat, the sun sank fast, and the heavens in the western sky began to glow. It was a coppery fire at first, the orange streaked with aquamarine; but rapidly the firmament expanded into an explosion of red and orange that burst across the sky sending tongues of flame through the feathery clouds to the very limits of the heavens. When the flames had reached their zenith, a great quantity of storks came flying from the south. They circled above us once, their slender bodies sleek and black against the orange sky. Then, gathering together, they flew off into the setting sun, leaving us alone in peace to contemplate. One of the monks who sat with us, hushed by the intensity of the moment, muttered a prayer. The sun died beyond the hills; and the fire withdrew.

From *Sanamu: Adventures in Search of African Art* by Robert Dick-Read. E. P. Dutton & Co., Inc., New York, 1964, pp. 228–229. Reprinted by permission of Curtis Brown, Ltd.

STUDY QUESTIONS
Organization and Content

1 Like many other compositions, this one may be divided into introduction, body, and conclusion. At what points would you mark off these sections?
2 The author is concerned here with both space and time. At what points does he indicate positions in space?
3 With what words does he indicate the passing of time?
4 In the latter part of the description, what moving things does Dick-Read describe in contrast to the sunset?

Sentence Structure

1 Do most of Dick-Read's sentences begin with the subject or with introductory subordinate material?
2 Dick-Read uses many transitional devices. Point out where he repeats words so that we can pass easily from one sentence to the next—for example, ''from where we sat'' in sentence 3 after ''as we sat'' in sentence 2.
3 Show where he also uses pronouns to refer to nouns in preceding sentences.
4 Contrast the grammatical patterns of sentences 2, 3, and 4.
5 Explain how the author gets so much subordinate material into the latter part of sentences 5 and 7.
6 Each sentence of sentences 8–12 has a different pattern. Contrast these five varying patterns.

Diction

1 Look up *plateau*. What other words come from the same root?
2 Look up *precipice*. What adjective, with what different meanings, is closely connected with it?
3 Look up *void, gloaming, aquamarine, firmament, zenith, contemplate*.
4 In sentence 4, which specially vivid words show how the stream looked?
5 Besides color-words, what other terms does Dick-Read use to describe the sunset in sentence 7?
6 Which words give contrasting impressions of the storks?
7 Why are the last three verbs suitable?

Assignment

Describe a sunset or a sunrise from some particular spot from which you observe it. Organize your description into introduction, body, and conclusion.

Jungle Night, Ecuador

ANNIE DILLARD

1   A nightjar in deep-leaved shadows called three long melodic notes, and hushed. The men with me talked softly in clumps: three North Americans, five Ecuadorians who were showing us the jungle. We were holding cool drinks, sipping, and idly watching a hand-sized tarantula seize moths that came to the lone bulb on the generator shed beside us.

2   It was February, the middle of summer. Great green fireflies spattered lights across the air and illumined for seconds, now here, now there, the pale trunks of enormous, solitaire trees. Cicadas ground out their long noise. Beneath us the brown Napo was rising, in all silence; it coiled up the sandy mud bank and tangled its floating foam in vines that trailed from the forest and roots that looped the shores.

3   Each breath of night smelled sweet, more moistened and sweet than any kitchen, or cradle, or garden; each star in Orion seemed to tremble and stir with my breath. At once, in the thatch house across the clearings behind us, one of the Jesuit priests, filled with unknown feelings, lifted his alto recorder and played, played a wordless song, lyric, in a minor key, that twined over the village clearing, that caught in the big trees' canopies, muted our talk on the bankside, and wandered over the river, dissolving downstream.

STUDY QUESTIONS

Organization and Content

1   In this description the author presents mostly details of sound and sight. Which sentences in each paragraph deal with sounds that the author heard? Which ones deal with visual images? Does the description appeal to any other senses?
2   Which words make us aware of colors? of shapes? of movements?
3   How does the author indicate the position of things in the setting in relation to the people? Which things are closest? which farthest away?
4   Why are the three paragraphs placed in the order that they have?

Sentence Structure

1   Would you place a comma after *notes* in sentence 1? If you left it out, how would the effect of the sentence be different?

From "Jungle Peace" by Annie Dillard, in *Holiday,* September 1975, p. 24. Reprinted by permission of the author and her agent, Blanche C. Gregory, Inc. Copyright © 1975 by Annie Dillard.

2   What is the function of the colon after *clumps* in sentence 2?
3   Point out the parallel triple verbs in the predicate of sentence 3. How does the author add details after the third verb?
4   In sentence 2, paragraph 2, what is the object of *illumined?* Show how adverbial material is placed between the verb and its object.
5   Explain the variety of sentence length in paragraph 2.
6   Point out the parallel grammatical pattern at the end of sentence 4, paragraph 2.
7   What words are repeated, for clearness, parallel construction, and emphasis, in sentence 1, paragraph 3?
8   What material comes before the subject in sentence 2, paragraph 3? What material is tucked away between the subject and verb? Show how the author uses modifiers at the end of sentence 2 and arranges the material in parallel patterns.
9   These sentences are carefully, and beautifully, composed. To appreciate their structure and rhythm, read aloud the long sentences of paragraphs 2 and 3.

Diction

1   Look up *nightjar, tarantula* (paragraph 1), *illumined, cicadas* (2), *Orion, Jesuit, recorder* (3).
2   If you heard a nightjar in this country, what would you call it?
3   Which words are especially vivid and effective in sentence 2, paragraph 2? in sentence 3?
4   Which words in sentence 4, paragraph 2, make you see the most precise word-pictures?
5   The author cannot, of course, make us hear the music that the priest played. What does she try to do instead? Do the nouns, adjectives, or verbs produce the most effect in sentence 2, paragraph 3?
6   In this selection the sounds of words are significant. Point out examples of alliteration, both consonance and assonance.

Assignment

Describe a night scene, bringing out details of sound and color as Annie Dillard does. Write carefully composed sentences like hers.

Arrival at Mexico City

JOAN COLEBROOK

1   So to Mexico again (with the back of the winter still unbroken, with New York City quieted by blizzards, with even the airport activities slowed while industrious snow-removing machines creep over the tarmac). When we reach Mexico City the wide streets are still filled with activity; children play by the embankments; lights hang in a haze of trees—creating a mood as close to twilight as is ever seen in this southern country. Yet not far away there are all the signs of the encroachment of the technological paralysis. That *malaise* which is evident in all the big centers of the world is evident here too (with more than seven million people in this great Mexican valley, that is three million more than during my visit in 1965). Not to mention a fog which spreads to hide the brilliant sun, and is created by half a million motor vehicles, and more than fifty thousand industrial plants.

2   Yet in spite of pollution the old charm lingers. An Indian woman seated on the edge of the pavement is quite obviously in the way of those who pour out of the big airport doors. Her head leans against one of the cement uprights; her bare feet are in the gutter. Her pinkish *reboso* echoes the burnished glow on her face, as bright as the bunch of orange and red gladiolas which lies abandoned in her lap. Around her feet the traffic makes a slight detour. Behind her the sky fades into violent colors. . . . She is fast asleep!

3   On the very edge of the city, morning comes with its usual highland brilliance. A man on a horse passes slowly, accompanied by a boy on foot who carries a willow branch. The rider slouches, only a dark hawk-like profile can be seen under the wide *sombrero*. The boy behind walks with that air of rural innocence which has not yet disappeared from the capital. Slowly they pass; Mexico of the nineteenth century proceeding across the landscape of the twentieth.

4   But that scene on the outskirts (where the lava plains still lie half empty, and tracks still wind amongst the houses) is soon forgotten in the heart of the city. Here traffic pours four cars deep along the great avenues. The smell of cheap gasoline hangs over the intersections. Planes fly low over houses and shops. Street markets are so crowded that it is hard to push along the aisles. Hotels are filled with global conventions; *Club de Leones; Wine-growers de Bretagne.*

5   The poverty seems less omnipresent. The white-clad peon is not so much in evidence; workmen are beginning to dress like small shop-owners. Heavy furniture is more often moved by truck than upon the shoulders of *cargadores;* if one sees anything carted through the streets it is likely to be a spot-

From *Innocents of the West: Travels through the Sixties,* © 1979 by Joan Colebrook, Basic Books, Inc., Publishers, New York.

less white porcelain toilet. Even the respectable eagle-eyed housekeeper in her black dress, clutching her bunch of keys as she is followed by a little servant girl lost in a spotless white apron and carrying a huge basket, is becoming outdated. In fact, women are beginning to bleach and dye their hair, to paint their finger-nails, to drive cars. This city, which for so long retained its charming provinciality and was for so long noted for its sparkling mornings, has at last passed the limits of health and safety and is becoming as worldly, as difficult (and soon perhaps will be as "indifferent") as Paris, London, New York.

STUDY QUESTIONS
Organization and Content

1 Note the contrasts in this description. In what terms are New York City and Mexico City contrasted in paragraph 1? What different impressions are created by the contrasting paragraphs 2–3 and the paragraphs 4–5? Would it be correct to say that the description is mainly organized on the principle of contrast?
2 On the other hand, what similarities does the author point out?
3 What specific "signs of the encroachment of the technological paralysis" does she mention?
4 What part do human beings play in the middle section of the description?
5 What kind of details does Colebrook emphasize in paragraph 4?
6 What representatives of old ways and new ways are described in paragraph 5?
7 What colors and shapes does Colebrook emphasize in paragraph 2?
8 Which person is described in most detail—the sleeping woman, the rider, or the housekeeper?
9 Does Colebrook use a moving or a stationary point of view?

Sentence Structure

1 Why do you think the sentences are written in the present tense?
2 The first and last sentences of paragraph 1 are not complete statements. How do you think they could best be completed? What effects does their incompleteness produce?
3 What parallel structures can you point out in sentence 1?
4 In paragraph 4 why does Colebrook use the same structure in several successive sentences?
5 What is the sentence pattern in paragraph 5, sentences 2 and 3? What is the function of that pattern?
6 Show how in paragraph 5, sentence 4, Colebrook arranges the modifiers of *housekeeper* and *girl* to balance these two main parts of the sentence without creating an identical paralleling of elements.

Diction

1   If you need to, look up *encroachment,* malaise, *omnipresent, provinciality.*
2   Would you call Colebrook's diction unusual, original, extreme, vivid, powerful, or what? Consider *industrious* (paragraph 1, sentence 1), *haze* (paragraph 1, sentence 2), *burnished, echoes* (paragraph 2, sentence 4), *violent* (paragraph 2, sentence 6), *hawk-like* (paragraph 3, sentence 3), *lost* (paragraph 5, sentence 4).

Assignment

1   Has your home town changed since you were small, so that different things, more mechanical and citified, have taken the place of simpler, more earthy things (shopping malls, for instance, rather than small, privately owned stores)? Imitate the Colebrook description, pointing out these changes plus the old-time elements (including characters) that still are in evidence.
2   Write a description bringing out the atmosphere of a town or city that struck you as different from what you were used to. Use plenty of concrete details to make your reader aware of the difference.
3   When you first arrived at the campus of your college, you were probably impressed by ways in which the college was different from your high school as well as by ways in which it was similar. By means of concrete descriptive material, make your reader see and feel these differences and likenesses.
4   Describe a main congregating place on your campus, such as a mall outside a large classroom building or the area outside the Union, say at ten o'clock in the morning; and bring in contrasting description of the scene at the same time of day in your home town or place in the country. Emphasize auditory sense appeals as well as visual ones.

China from a Train Window

HARRISON E. SALISBURY

First impressions . . . I leaned back against the lace antimacassar, neatly **1**
pinned to the blue upholstery of the train seat. It was a clean train, decorated in blue and gray, lace curtains at the window, many excited Japanese
tourists taking pictures of each other, and at one end, a rather poor painting
of the famous new bridge across the Yangtze at Nanking.

I turned my eyes to the window and watched China . . . emerald-green **2**
countryside, the emerald of rice paddies (I thought of the Emerald City in
the land of Oz), terraces in the red earth climbing every hillside; gray water
buffalo in the ponds and paddies, knee-high corn, women in conical straw
hats transplanting the rice; new orchards on the hillsides, new pine stands,
and in some places people setting out the trees; fields of cabbage, beans,
peas, squash, melon and cucumbers; walled gray-brick villages, each with a
two- or three-story tower. Grain elevators? Or watchtowers?

I lost track of time as field succeeded endless field, then looked at my **3**
watch with a start. We had traveled for an hour and a half through the
countryside and I had yet to see a car or a truck or a tractor or any kind of
farm machinery more complex than a shovel. I had not even seen a road,
only narrow paths wandering through the fields, curving around the paddies, linking village to village. The countryside lay quiet, verdant, planted to
the last inch; the villages seeming to grow out of the very fields, the people
moving slowly across the horizon at their traditional tasks, backs bent as
they set out the rice, backs bent as they set out the new young trees, backs
bent as they pulled their barrows along the narrow paths.

As I watched a man trundle his barrow through the field, I realized that I **4**
had done more than simply walk across the plank boards of the little bridge
over Shumchun River, passing from one country into another. I had walked
across an invisible line that took me from one century to another. On the
Lo Wu side I was in the 20th century, the 20th century of industrialism, of
tin cans, of paper wrappings, of gasoline engines, of urgent motors, of blaz-
ing billboards, of crashing sounds—the world of waste and garbage and lit-
ter and junk, the land of machines and hurry and hustle.

Now from the window of a 19th-century railroad car I looked out at the **5**
17th century. There was nothing in this cavalcade of villages, this checker-

board of rice paddies, this world of men and women and animals and simple tools, hand made, hand wielded, that would startle the eye of a traveler to China in 1672 or even 1572. The people wore the same conical hats, the same simple blue trousers and formless jackets that march across those willow pattern dishes of grandmother's day that introduced most of us to the land of China. The rice grew in the same way, its green as brilliant as ever. The water buffalo had not changed. The meticulous orchards and precise terraces had been transferred from some ancient scroll.

STUDY QUESTIONS

Organization and Content

1   Were Salisbury's first impressions favorable or not?
2   In paragraph 2 Salisbury says he "watched China." With what (and how many) different details does he make us see China? Which of them appeal to our senses in terms of color and shape?
3   Since Salisbury is riding on a train, he is using a moving point of view. But does the moving point of view really influence the description?
4   Why does paragraph 3 have to come after paragraph 2? paragraph 4 after paragraph 3?
5   What principle of organization has the author used?
6   What key words contrast in sentences 1 and 2 of paragraph 4?
7   With what concrete details does Salisbury represent "the 20th century of industrialism" in paragraph 4? What contrasting idea does he make us see in paragraph 5?

Sentence Structure

1   Notice the ellipsis periods in the first sentences of paragraphs 1 and 2. What are they intended to represent?
2   Most of paragraph 2 is put into one sentence, a sentence of ninety words. In what pattern did Salisbury construct this sentence? How did he set off its main parts?
3   In sentence 2, paragraph 3, how do the three *or*'s give emphasis? How does Salisbury emphasize the main idea of sentence 3, paragraph 3?
4   What three participles are used in parallel construction to modify *paths* in sentence 3, paragraph 3? Where are they placed in the sentence?
5   Sentence 4, paragraph 3, has an interesting pattern. What three terms first describe the countryside? Then what nouns follow in sentence 4 to give us a more specific picture of the countryside as the train passes through it?
6   What pattern of parallel modifiers does Salisbury repeat at the end of sentence 4? What word do they modify?

7   In sentence 3, paragraph 4, which word is often repeated to give
     a pattern of parallel phrases?
8   Which three words are objects of the preposition *in* in sentence 2,
     paragraph 5? What word does the final *that*-clause modify?
9   In sentence 3, paragraph 5, how does repetition help to empha-
     size the idea expressed?
10   How do sentences 4–6, paragraph 5, differ in make-up from the
     sentences that come before?

Diction

1   Look up *antimacassar* (paragraph 1)—it has an unusual origin—
     paddies, conical (2), *succeeded, verdant, traditional* (3), *trundle,
     urgent* (4), *cavalcade* (check the origin), *wielded, meticulous, pre-
     cise, scroll* (5).
2   What impression do you get from *narrow* and *wandering* in sen-
     tence 3, paragraph 3?
3   What feelings are aroused by the connotations of the words after
     industrialism in sentence 3, paragraph 4? Which words of para-
     graph 5 have contrasting connotations?

Assignment

Describe the appearance of a landscape as you travel over it by
airplane, bus, or automobile—or train, if you happen to ride on a
train. Include plenty of precise details to make your reader visualize the scenes you observe.

Guaymas, Sonora

JOAN DIDION

It had rained in Los Angeles until the cliff was crumbling into the surf   1
and I did not feel like getting dressed in the morning, so we decided to go
to Mexico, to Guaymas, where it was hot. We did not go for marlin. We
did not go to skin dive. We went to get away from ourselves, and the way
to do that is to drive, down through Nogales some day when the pretty
green places pall and all that will move the imagination is some place difficult, some desert. The desert, any desert, is indeed the valley of the shadow
of death; come back from the desert and you feel like Alcestis, reborn. After

Reprinted by permission of Farrar, Straus and Giroux, Inc. from *Slouching towards
Bethlehem* by Joan Didion. Copyright © 1961, 1964, 1965, 1966, 1967, 1968 by Joan
Didion.

Nogales on Route 15 there is nothing but the Sonoran desert, nothing but mesquite and rattlesnakes and the Sierra Madre floating to the east, no trace of human endeavor but an occasional Pemex truck hurtling north and once in a while in the distance the dusty Pullman cars of the Ferrocarril del Pacifico. Magdalena is on Route 15, and then Hermosillo, where the American ore and cattle buyers gather in the bar at the Hotel San Alberto. There is an airport in Hermosillo, and Hermosillo is only eighty-five miles above Guaymas, but to fly is to miss the point. The point is to become disoriented, shriven, by the heat and the deceptive perspectives and the oppressive sense of carrion. The road shimmers. The eyes want to close.

2   And then, just past that moment when the desert has become the only reality, Route 15 hits the coast and there is Guaymas, a lunar thrust of volcanic hills and islands with the warm Gulf of California lapping idly all around, lapping even at the cactus, the water glassy as a mirage, the ships in the harbor whistling unsettlingly, moaning, ghost schooners, landlocked, lost. That is Guaymas. As far as the town goes, Graham Greene might have written it: a shadowy square with a filigree pergola for the Sunday band, a racket of birds, a cathedral in bad repair with a robin's-egg-blue tile dome, a turkey buzzard on the cross. The wharves are piled with bales of Sonoran cotton and mounds of dark copper concentrates; out on the freighters with the Panamanian and Liberian flags the Greek and German boys stand in the hot twilight and stare sullenly at the grotesque and claustrophobic hills, at the still town, a curious limbo at which to call.

3   Had we really been intent upon losing ourselves we might have stayed in town, at a hotel where faded and broken turquoise-blue shutters open onto the courtyard, where old men sit in the doorways and nothing moves, but instead we stayed outside town, at the Playa de Cortés, the big old hotel built by the Southern Pacific before the railways were nationalized. That place was a mirage, too, lovely and cool with thick whitewashed walls and dark shutters and bright tiles, tables made from ebony railroad ties, pale appliqued muslin curtains, shocks of corn wrapped around the heavy beams. Pepper trees grew around the swimming pool, and lemons and bananas in the courtyard. The food was unremarkable, but after dinner one could lie in a hammock on the terrace and listen to the fountains and the sea. For a week we lay in hammocks and fished desultorily and went to bed early and got very brown and lazy. My husband caught eight sharks, and I read an oceanography textbook, and we did not talk much. At the end of the week we wanted to do something, but all there was to do was visit the tracking station for an old space program or go see John Wayne and Claudia Cardinale in *Circus World,* and we knew it was time to go home.

STUDY QUESTIONS
Organization and Content

1   In this selection we find a combination of descriptive and narrative elements. Didion does not tell of many events that happened; but she and her husband did a few things. Point out both story elements and descriptive details. Is any one paragraph purely narrative or purely descriptive?
2   How does Didion make us aware of a sequence of happenings in time?
3   She uses much material that is very specific. Does she shift at any time to the general?
4   The selection does tell of a journey. How far in the narrative does paragraph 1 take us? paragraph 2? paragraph 3?
5   Which details in paragraph 1 create an impression of the Sonoran desert?
6   Which details in paragraph 2 provide impressions of Guaymas? Didion says, ''Graham Greene might have written it.'' The settings of Graham Greene's novels are often called ''seedy.'' It is instructive to consider the *selection* of *few* details that Didion makes in paragraph 2, sentence 3.
7   How does she contrast the two hotels?
8   What made the two travelers decide to go home?
9   Does this piece have a beginning, a middle, and a conclusion?

Sentence Structure

1   Note the conversational style of sentence 1, with clauses connected by *and* and *so*. Are there similar sentences throughout the selection?
2   Which sentences of paragraph 1 are shortest? How much variety of sentence length and structure do you find in paragraphs 1 and 2?
3   Which grammatical elements are parallel in paragraph 2, sentences 1 and 3, and in paragraph 3, sentences 1 and 2? Note that these parallel parts of the sentences contain many details.
4   Why does Didion use a colon in paragraph 2, sentence 3?

Diction

1   You may need to look up *Alcestis, mesquite, hurtling, shriven* (paragraph 1), *mirage, filigree, claustrophobic, limbo* (2), *desultorily* (3).
2   What atmospheric effects does Didion get with *dusty* (paragraph 1, sentence 6), *lunar thrust* and *glassy as a mirage* and *moaning* (paragraph 2, sentence 1), *limbo* (paragraph 2, sentence 2), *racket of birds* (paragraph 2, sentence 3)?
3   Which adjectives make us see colors in paragraph 3?

Assignment

1   Imitate Didion in three mainly descriptive paragraphs with a little narration, telling how you visited some place that had a special atmosphere. Use sentences of varied length and structure with numerous concrete details.
2   Similarly tell of a visit to two hotels or apartments where you stayed which had contrasting atmospheres.
3   Perhaps your family has taken vacations repeatedly in some place or area such as the coast or the mountains. With plenty of description tell of your trip there, what you did, and what the place was like.

Theft and Flight

DANIEL DEFOE

1   Wandering thus about, I knew not whither, I passed by an apothecary's shop in Leadenhall Street, where I saw lie on a stool just before the counter a little bundle wrapped in a white cloth; beyond it stood a maid-servant with her back to it, looking towards the top of the shop, where the apothecary's apprentice, as I suppose, was standing upon the counter, with his back to the door, and a candle in his hand, looking and reaching up to the upper shelf for something he wanted, so that both were engaged mighty earnestly, and nobody else in the shop.

2   This was the bait; and the devil, who I said laid the snare, as readily prompted me as if he had spoke, for I remember, and shall never forget it, 'twas like a voice spoken to me over my shoulder, "Take the bundle; be quick; do it this moment." It was no sooner said but I stepped into the shop, and with my back to the wench, as if I had stood up for a cart that was going by, I put my hand behind me and took the bundle, and went off with it, the maid or the fellow not perceiving me, or any one else.

3   It is impossible to express the horror of my soul all the while I did it. When I went away I had no heart to run, or scarce to mend my pace. I crossed the street indeed, and went down the first turning I came to, and I think it was a street that went through into Fenchurch Street. From thence I crossed and turned through so many ways and turnings, that I could never tell which way it was, nor where I went; for I felt not the ground I stepped on, and the farther I was out of danger, the faster I went, till, tired and out of breath, I was forced to sit down on a little bench at a door, and then I began to recover, and found I was got into Thames Street, near Billingsgate. I rested me a little and went on; my blood was all in a fire; my heart beat as

From *The Fortunes and Misfortunes of the Famous Moll Flanders* (1722).

if I was in a sudden fright. In short, I was under such a surprise that I still knew not whither I was going, or what to do.

After I had tired myself thus with walking a long way about, and so eagerly, I began to consider and make home to my lodging, where I came about nine o'clock at night. 4

STUDY QUESTIONS

Organization and Content

1 This is a famous episode in *The Fortunes and Misfortunes of the Famous Moll Flanders*—her first theft. What part of the action does Defoe put in each of the four paragraphs?

2 Is the material organized in a regular sequence of points in time? Where does the climax of the episode come?

3 From whose point of view is the episode narrated? How does Defoe distribute the emphasis on action, Moll's moral feelings, and her physical sensations?

4 Where and how does Defoe make us feel excitement and suspense?

5 Are there any descriptive elements in this selection?

Sentence Structure

1 Paragraph 1 consists of a single sentence. How long is it? Where is the main point of division in it, and how is that point indicated?

2 Point out the seven clauses of sentence 1.

3 Sentence 1 is essentially a pair of loose sentences; the essential element of the first one is "I passed by an apothecary's shop." Show how Defoe has added material—especially prepositional phrases—to fill out the statement and make Moll's experience vivid.

4 This episode is written in a colloquial style. What things, especially in paragraph 2, indicate a speaking voice and a conversational tone?

5 What is the effect of the semicolon after *bait* in sentence 1, paragraph 2? In that sentence how does Defoe put strong emphasis on the statements in quotation marks? Compare the effect of these statements with that of sentence 5, paragraph 3.

6 How does Defoe's use of *and* in paragraph 2 and in sentences 3 and 4, paragraph 3, contribute to a sense of tension and rapid action?

7 How do the rhythm and balance of the final sentence fit the close of the episode?

Diction

1 Defoe is noted for his effective use of simple diction—short, concrete words. Point out the concrete nouns in paragraphs 1 and 2.
2 Are there any abstract terms in the four paragraphs? For concreteness, compare this selection with the one by Galarza or White.
3 Does the effect of this selection depend more on verbs or on adjectives?

Assignment

Imitate Defoe by narrating an incident in which the protagonist is frightened. Perhaps an accident or emergency would be best for this. Write rather colloquially, using concrete diction, and try to achieve an effect of rapid action.

Nocturnal Pursuit

FLANNERY O'CONNOR

1 As Rayber lay watching the window darken, he felt that all his nerves were stretched through him like high tension wire. He began trying to relax one muscle at a time as the books recommended, beginning with those in the back of his neck. He emptied his mind of everything but the just visible pattern of the hedge against the screen. Still he was alert for any sound. Long after he lay in complete darkness, he was still alert, unrelaxed, ready to spring up at the least creak of a floor board in the hall. All at once he sat up, wide awake. A door opened and closed. He leapt up and ran across the hall into the opposite room. The boy was gone. He ran back to his own room and pulled his trousers on over his pajamas. Then grabbing his coat, he went out of the house by way of the kitchen, barefooted, his jaw set.

2 Keeping close to his side of the hedge, he crept through the dark damp grass toward the street. The night was close and very still. A light went on in a window of the next house and revealed, at the end of the hedge, the hat. It turned slightly and Rayber saw the sharp profile beneath it, the set thrust of a jaw very like his own. The boy was stopped still, most likely taking his bearings, deciding which direction to walk in.

3 He turned again and again. Rayber saw only the hat, intransigently ground upon his head, fierce-looking even in the dim light. It had the boy's own defiant quality, as if its shape had been formed over the years by his

personality. It had been the first thing that Rayber had seen must go. It
suddenly moved out of the light and vanished.

Rayber slipped through the hedge and followed, soundless on his bare 4
feet. Nothing cast a shadow. He could barely make out the boy a quarter of
a block in front of him, except when occasionally light from a window outlined him briefly. Since Rayber didn't know whether he thought he was
leaving for good or only going for a walk on his own, he decided not to
shout and stop him but to follow silently and observe. He turned off his
hearing aid and pursued the dim figure as if in a dream. The boy walked
even faster at night than in the daytime and was always on the verge of
vanishing.

Rayber felt the accelerated beat of his heart. He took a handkerchief out 5
of his pocket and wiped his forehead and inside the neck of his pajama top.
He walked over something sticky on the sidewalk and shifted hurriedly to
the other side, cursing under his breath. Tarwater was heading toward
town. Rayber thought it likely he was returning to see something that had
secretly interested him. He might discover tonight what he would have
found by testing if the boy had not been so pig-headed. He felt the insidious
pleasure of revenge and checked it.

A patch of sky blanched, revealing for a moment the outlines of the 6
housetops. Tarwater turned suddenly to the right. Rayber cursed himself for
not stopping long enough to get his shoes. They had come into a neighborhood of large ramshackle boarding houses with porches that abutted the
sidewalks. On some of them late sitters were rocking and watching the
street. He felt eyes in the darkness move on him and he turned on the hearing aid again. On one porch a woman rose and leaned over the banister. She
stopped with her hands on her hips, looking him over, taking in his bare
feet, the striped pajama coat under his seersucker suit. Irritated, he glanced
back at her. The thrust of her neck indicated a conclusion formed. He but-
toned his coat and hurried on.

The boy stopped on the next corner. His lean shadow made by a street 7
light slanted to the side of him. The hat's shadow, like a knob at the top of
it, turned to the right and then the left. He appeared to be considering his
direction. Rayber's muscles felt suddenly weighted. He was not conscious of
his fatigue until the pace slackened.

Tarwater turned to the left and Rayber began angrily to move again. 8
They went down a street of dilapidated stores. When Rayber turned the
next corner, the gaudy cave of a movie house yawned to the side of him. A
knot of small boys stood in front of it. "Forgot yer shoes!" one of them
chirruped. "Forgot yer shirt!"

He began a kind of limping lope. 9

The chorus followed him down the block. "Hi yo Silverwear, Tonto's 10
lost his underwear! What in the heck do we care?"

He kept his eye wrathfully on Tarwater who was turning to the right. 11

When he reached the corner and turned, he saw the boy stopped in the middle of the block, looking in a store window. He slipped into a narrow entrance a few yards farther on where a flight of steps led upward into darkness. Then he looked out.

12   Tarwater's face was strangely lit from the window he was standing before. Rayber watched curiously for a few moments. It looked to him like the face of someone starving who sees a meal he can't reach laid out before him. At last, something he *wants*, he thought, and determined that tomorrow he would return and buy it. Tarwater reached out and touched the glass and then drew his hand back slowly. He hung there as if he could not take his eyes off what it was he wanted. A pet shop, perhaps, Rayber thought. Maybe he wants a dog. A dog might make all the difference. Abruptly the boy broke away and moved on.

13   Rayber stepped out of the entrance and made for the window he had left. He stopped with a shock of disappointment. The place was only a bakery. The window was empty except for a loaf of bread pushed to the side that must have been overlooked when the shelf was cleaned for the night. He stared, puzzled, at the empty window for a second before he started after the boy again. Everything a false alarm, he thought with disgust. If he had eaten his dinner, he wouldn't be hungry. A man and a woman strolling past looked with interest at his bare feet. He glared at them, then glanced to the side and saw his bloodless wired reflection in the glass of a shoe shop. The boy disappeared all at once into an alley. My God, Rayber thought, how long is this going on?

14   He turned into the alley, which was unpaved and so dark that he could not see Tarwater in it at all. He was certain that any minute he would cut his feet on broken glass. A garbage can materialized in his path. There was a noise like the collapse of a tin house and he found himself sitting up with his hand and one foot in something unidentifiable. He scrambled up and limped on, hearing his own curses like the voice of a stranger broadcast through his hearing aid. At the end of the alley, he saw the lean figure in the middle of the next block, and with a sudden fury he began to run.

STUDY QUESTIONS

Organization and Content

1   In Flannery O'Connor's novel *The Violent Bear It Away*, Tarwater, a boy of fourteen, comes from the country to see his Uncle Rayber in the city. Tarwater dislikes the city, but he is curious about it. Rayber wants him to stay there, but he fears that Tarwater may run away. How does the author create tension and suspense in paragraph 1? How is suspense kept up as the story continues?

2   Note that the "most likely" of sentence 5, paragraph 2, shows that

the experience is communicated from Rayber's point of view. Where are we told what Rayber sees? thinks? What changes of feeling does he have as he follows Tarwater?

3 In paragraph 3 Tarwater's hat has a symbolic quality; that is, it represents something. What does Rayber feel that it symbolizes or represents?

4 Where do we find out Rayber's purpose in following the boy?

5 Is there any conflict or are there difficulties that have to be overcome in the course of the episode?

6 What physical sensations does Rayber experience in paragraph 5? in paragraphs 7 and 14? What feelings does he have in paragraph 6?

7 Why are paragraphs 9 and 10 so short? How does the paragraphing help us to imagine the action?

8 Which parts of the narrative are the most humorous? Do they make us laugh with Rayber or at him?

9 What do we find out about R yber? What kind of man is he?

Sentence Structure

1 In any story of pursuit there must be a connection between the pursuer and the one he follows. What influence will this connection have upon the sentences? What words are the subjects of the majority of the sentences here?

2 Do most of the sentences begin with the subject or not? How does the sentence pattern of sentence 1, paragraph 8, indicate the relationship between the two characters? Point out other examples of this pattern.

3 The final sentence of paragraph 1 is a good example of economical and emphatic writing. Explain how predication is reduced. What do the last three words tell us?

4 In sentence 3, paragraph 2, how does the author place emphasis on Tarwater's hat?

Diction

1 Define *intransigently* (paragraph 3), *verge* (4), *insidious* (5), *blanched, abutted* (6), *materialized* (14).

2 Which verb elements in sentences 4–11 in paragraph 1 show action and movement?

3 Explain the descriptive quality each of the following terms has: *least creak* (paragraph 1), *sharp* (2), *lean* (7), *scrambled up, limped on* (14).

4 What word in sentence 1, paragraph 3, helps to communicate the most imformation about Tarwater's hat and his character?

5 Why does the author at times use general terms—*something sticky* (paragraph 5), *something unidentifiable* (paragraph 14)? Would more exact terms be more effective? Explain your answer.

6 The author uses *suddenly* several times and *abruptly* once. How do these words affect the progress of the narrative?

7 The selection contains a few similes. Point out the similes and determine if there is any difference in the effect of those in paragraphs
   1, 4, 12, and 14.
8 What words in the selection help us to visualize Rayber? How would
   you describe Rayber's physical appearance? How would you describe his character?

Assignment

1 Relate an episode in which one person follows another, observing
   and not entirely understanding, or perhaps disapproving of, what
   the second one is doing. Use specific terms and vivid descriptive
   language.
2 Put yourself in the place of a romantic boy who is attracted to a girl
   and cannot help following her. Show the sequence of his actions,
   and also tell how he feels and what he thinks. Or do the same for a
   girl who cannot resist the temptation to follow a boy and observe
   him.
3 Or similarly tell how a detective "shadows" some person.

Hooking a Muskellunge

JOHN KEATS

1   When the weather cleared we returned to the river and to the three pleasures that had been primarily responsible for our purchase of the island. The
first of these was fishing, the original attraction of the St. Lawrence for the
first vacationers. In the mornings Chris and I would cast from the dock and
often enough have a good bass or pike cleaned, boned, cut into pieces, and
ready to be shaken in a bag of seasoned flour by the time the coffee was done
and the bacon crisp. After breakfast we would go out on the water to combine the pleasure of fishing with the other two principal pleasures—exploring and swimming. We would troll slowly downriver along the edges of
weedbeds, turning the boat to drag the big Skinner spoons in and out of
coves and beside deep-water rocks that seemed to promise large fish lying in
the shadow. We could have taken more fish if we had anchored over a deep
hole in the river floor and still-fished with live minnows, but we trolled because we loved to savor, slowly, the constantly changing shapes of stones
and trees and water as the islands slid by. In those days, when many of the
islands had no houses on them, we would put ashore on a deserted island to

swim, build a fire, and cook the fish we had caught for lunch, then troll slowly home in red sunsets that made black silhouettes of island pines.

Whenever we trolled thus, our persistent hope was to land a fish such as Will described. You can see them lying under skim ice in the shallows in the spring, hanging in clear water beneath a windowpane of ice, predators built for speed and armed with rows of long, sharp, double-edged teeth, their fins gently moving. These are what you hunt in summer: the enormous pike and their even larger cousins the muskellunge. The record catch on rod and reel was a muskellunge that weighed more than sixty-nine pounds and was caught some thirteen miles upriver from our island. When you see them in the shallows in the spring they are spawning and you may not fish for them then. At this time of year, however, hungry men to whom need is more compelling than any game law shoot or spear them as they lie. **2**

These fish feed near shore at dawn and dusk, so lore says, but we always hoped, and so we trolled baits astern whenever we were on the water. One bright afternoon, when Margaret and I were returning from Rockport with bread and milk, trolling as we moved along the edge of the cliffs below McGoogan's Point, the river exploded ahead of us. **3**

"Did you see that!" I shouted. **4**

Of course, facing astern, she had not seen it. **5**

But in the next moment she was fairly pulled from her seat on the thwart, desperately hanging onto a rod almost snatched from her hands. **6**

"Bottom!" she said. "Back up. I'm on bottom! No, it isn't! It's moving!" **7**

The bottom of the river, if that is what she had, was moving rapidly and steadily out toward the channel away from the cliffs. **8**

"I don't know if I can hold him," she said. "Oh, I've got a fish! I've got a fish!" **9**

Just how long she would have it seemed an interesting question. The vision I had, when the river exploded, was of a vast dark shape at the center of the explosion. Margaret was fishing with her grandfather's old steel trolling rod. There was no star drag on this rod, just a leather thumb tab. You were supposed to apply pressure on this tab as the line came off the reel, enough pressure to slow the fish and hold him so that he would exhaust himself fighting the whip in the rod but not so much as to break the line. The line was made of black cotton and, when new, whenever that may have been, was supposed to support a weight of twelve pounds. **10**

I had shut the motor off, but we, too, were moving out toward the channel and against the current. As the line began to slant up out of the water, Margaret raised the rod tip up and back, reeling as fast as she could, guiding the line in even loops with her left thumb. Angling consists of maintaining an angle formed by rod and line. When that huge, slab-sided fish came boiling out of the water, walking for a moment on his thrashing tail and shaking that great, toothed head, showing us those silver sides with the dark, **11** circular blotches on them, Margaret succeeded in keeping that angle and the line taut.

12   And away he went down again, now speeding beneath the bows of the boat, with Margaret scrambling to keep the line from fouling beneath.

13   Again and again he jumped, shaking his great head, then flashed under the stern to send Margaret piling over me to keep the line from the motor. All this went on for more than half an hour before Margaret had him swimming slowly near the surface, drawing him ever closer to the boat.

14   Magnified by the water, that fish looked nearly as long as the oar. The next problem would be landing him. Some fishing guides carry .22-caliber Colt Woodsman pistols to shoot muskies at boatside. Most carry gaffs. The ones who carry pistols are those who do not want to run the risk of having their arms broken when a heavy muskellunge, thrashing beside the boat, breaks the gaff handle free from the guide's grasp and cracks his arm with it. One way to land a muskie is to work him into the shallows, go over the side yourself, and beach him. Guides recommend this. But no matter how you land a muskellunge, all the guides advocate hitting him over the head at once, and they all carry something heavy, such as a jemmey or a tire iron, for this purpose. You no more want a live muskellunge flopping around in your boat than you would want a live barracuda. There are all those grinning teeth, and, apart from them, there is a great deal of power in that smashing tail.

15   With the fish coming toward us, rolling now on the water with his air bladder full and his power momentarily spent, I began to consider the problem. I had no pistol, no gaff, no net (and there was no hand net that would ever hold this fish), and no crowbar. All we had in the boat was a loaf of bread and a quart of milk. Nor was there any beach; we were on a cliff shore.

16   "Easy," I told her. "Just bring him along easy. You're doing fine. Here he comes."

17   I pulled gently on the line while Margaret as carefully reeled. I wanted to get hold of the copper-wire leader. With the leader in one hand, I would close my other hand over the top of his head, crushing in on the gill plates, and, with both hands at once, swing him in over the gunwales. Then I'd hit him with an oar.

18   "Oh, he's huge," Margaret said.

19   He was a great, dark-backed, orange-finned, silver-flanked muskellunge, the largest fish I had ever seen at boatside. He was larger than our son. His head was as big as a football.

20   "Just keep him coming like that," I told her. I could feel Margaret trembling; her reeling was just the least bit jittery.

21   "The leader is all the way down his throat," I told her. "All right, now I've got him!"

22   Since I could not grasp the copper leader, I held the line while I grabbed

the fish over the back of the head, squeezed, and with both hands lifted him out of the water.

That heavy tail smashed against the gunwale with a force that shook the boat. My hand skidded on the slippery wet gill plates, and as the head slipped through my fingers the weight of the fish broke the line. I grabbed for him again as he lay for an instant beside the boat in the water.   **23**

Margaret sat on the thwart and cried.   **24**

Somebody once told us that the fish that gets away is the best one of all, because he keeps getting bigger each time you tell the story. I disagree. The muskellunge that Margaret caught that day, fought for more than half an hour, played beautifully, and brought perfectly to the side of the boat never got away. Instead, I lost it. Nothing will ever make up for that, and I will always see that wonderful fish, a trophy fish if ever there was one, lying in the water for the instant it took to recover before it slowly and then more rapidly sank swimming down out of sight in deep water.   **25**

STUDY QUESTIONS

Organization and Content

1   This is an account of a personal experience, partly description but mostly narration. The first part is an introduction. Where does the introduction end and the story proper begin?

2   What differences of verb-tenses and of type of material do you notice between the introduction and the story?

3   Where does the climax of the story come? After the climax, how long a conclusion does Keats have?

4   Point out the places where Keats indicates the sequence of time points when the different parts of the whole action take place.

5   At what point in the narrative does the conflict seem fiercest? When is the suspense greatest?

6   Keats uses dialogue—gives us the exact words spoken—in paragraphs 4–9 and 16–21. What effect does the dialogue have?

7   Some paragraphs, such as 10 and 14, provide necessary information. Do they seem too much of an interruption of the story? Should, or could, Keats have given this information somewhere else?

8   In which paragraphs do you find the most vivid description?

9   What does Keats do in paragraph 13 that makes it particularly significant? Why is paragraph 24 so short? What is its special purpose?

Sentence Structure

1   Most of the sentences in paragraph 1 are loose sentences with considerable material added on after the basic grammatical meaning has been completed. Identify, in sentence 2, the use of the apposi-

tive; in sentence 3, additional verbs and phrasal material; in sentence 4, infinitive phrase and appositive; in sentence 5, participial phrase plus prepositional phrases and an adjective clause.

2 In contrast, point out in sentence 7 the introductory subordinate elements and the use of verbs and infinitives toward the end.

3 Keats varies his sentence movement a good deal. Notice, for instance, the leisurely, informal style of sentence 1, paragraph 3; the periodic sentence 2 that follows it—with the dramatic climax held back till the end; and the very short sentences of paragraphs 4 and 5. Which of these sentences is closest in structure to sentence 4, paragraph 11?

4 Keats sometimes alternates short sentences and longish sentences with parallel verbs. Point out examples of this technique of variation in paragraphs 14 and 15.

5 Comment on sentence variety in paragraphs 21–24.

6 A sentence that ends a paragraph or a theme should be carefully constructed. Analyze the structure and effect of Keats's final sentence.

Diction

1 Look up these words if you do not know them: *troll* (sentence 5, paragraph 1), *savor* (6:1), *silhouettes* (7); *persistent* (sentence 1, paragraph 2), *predators* (2:2); *lore* (sentence 1, paragraph 3); *gaffs* (sentence 4, paragraph 14), *advocate, jemmey* (8:14); *gunwales* (sentence 3, paragraph 17); *trophy* (sentence 5, paragraph 25).

2 Which are the most emphatic or precise verbs in paragraphs 3, 11, 12, 13, 23?

3 Which words show us precise details in paragraphs 1, 2, 14, 19?

Assignment

Using some description and giving essential background information, write the story of some dramatic experience you have had—fishing or hunting, exploring, mountain climbing, spelunking, racing, fire fighting, scuba diving, skiing, or the like.

Check Point

1

At this point you will have written enough description to be aware of the importance of sharp observation. You also will have practiced organizing paragraphs that create a dominant impression, and will have described scenes from both a stationary and a moving point of view and not only according to patterns of spatial arrangement but also according to a sequence of time. Your appreciation and control of sentence construction should have improved. You will, in addition, have had the opportunity to write simple narratives with elements of suspense and climax. You should by now place a high value on exact words. Above all, you will have learned how valuable specific details are in effective description and narration. As you practice the types of writing that are to follow, you will need to remember constantly the importance of details.

SECTION TWO

Exposition

One of the most important and most often used types of writing is explanation. People are constantly being requested or urged to explain something or other. Explain what was done; explain what it was like; explain how it operates; explain the sequence of happenings; explain what it means; explain how it developed; explain how you felt; explain your position; explain what you think; explain yourself!—these demands for explanations crowd upon us all, day after day. These same demands account for the frequency and the vast importance of explanatory writing—which, in discussions of composition, is more commonly called *exposition*.

Though it may certainly deal with things that may be observed by means of the senses, exposition appeals more, however, to the mind than to the senses. Understanding, achieved by the mind, rather than the immediate experience conveyed by the senses, is the chief goal of the expository writer. It is not so much the look or smell or feel of things that the reader gains from exposition as an idea of how they originated, how they developed, how they are organized, how numerous or how complicated they are, how they are related to other things, how significant they are, or what they mean. Description has to do with concrete phenomena and concrete experiences; exposition very often goes beyond the concrete into the region of abstractions, the realm of ideas.

Providing instruction and meeting the needs of the human race for knowledge and understanding—these are the purposes of exposition. Everything found in encyclopedias, handbooks, and dictionaries is exposition. Most of the nonfiction articles in our magazines, and practically all the articles in scientific journals and other scholarly publications, come under the head of exposition. An infantry manual, a handbook explaining the basic movements of square dancing, a pamphlet on methods of insect control—all are examples of exposition, as are such works as a textbook of surgery or a grammar of the French language.

Expository writing concerns itself with practical matters; all the reports that provide information for executives, members of Congress, mayors, deans, military officers, school superintendents, diplomats, stock analysts, and prime ministers—all these systematic accumulations of data that help in getting the world's work done are pieces of expository writing. Therefore, it may be stated that exposition is practical writing. But, though exposition deals with every practical matter in the world, it is not limited to practical affairs in the workaday sense of the term. The writer of exposition may present ideas on the most theoretical matters too. Books on physics or philosophy, on metaphysics or evolution, highly theoretical, are exposition; but, of course, they are written to satisfy practical demands for understanding in all these areas.

Whatever may be the subject of exposition, the writing itself must be systematic and well organized. The simplest type of exposition is an *enumeration*, a very common and useful way of developing expository paragraphs. Many explanations simply comprise a list of details (with or without actual numbers) to show what something is like or how something is done.

More complex methods of exposition are *analysis* and *definition*, which involve classification and division. Whether one is explaining the functioning of an airplane or of a frog, he or she will have to do some analyzing, that is, tell what the parts are and how they are related for purposes of functioning. Likewise, if a student is defining a frog, he or she must first classify it: obviously it does not belong in the class of vegetables or any nonanimal group. After it has been properly classified, the student must show how it is different from other members of the same class; he or she must explain what points of difference separate frogs from toads and salamanders.

In all expository writing it is advisable to use examples, analogies, *comparisons*, and *contrasts*, particularly when the subject is an abstract one. Readers will be able to understand an unfamiliar subject better if it is somehow related to a thing with which they are already familiar. The concept of relativity, for example, can be approached by means of the illustration of two trains moving at different speeds. Understanding is helped too by systematic comparisons and contrasts: two different groups may be compared or contrasted, two different periods, or people, or theories, or methods of agriculture, or government, or medical treatment. The reader is very likely to learn, to be enlightened, by reading a thoughtful comparison. A comparison or contrast, based on various points of resemblance or difference, will have been made possible by an act of analysis.

All of these matters will become clearer as the apprentice writer studies the examples given in the following sections of the text. Though some of the selections in the section on description have contained a small amount of exposition, the readings in the present section contain very little that is not expository.

Enumeration

Writers of exposition must understand their material thoroughly enough to be able to organize it clearly according to some scheme that the reader can follow and understand. We have already noted that the simplest type of exposition is enumeration: a certain number of things exist or are our concern. These are the things, or the parts, or the steps: one, two, three, four. Much the same is the arrangement of items in chronological order: one, two, three, four, from the earliest to the latest. When we are dealing with a systematic arrangement of things in space rather than in time, we can take them up according to a spatial order: one, two, three, four from right to left or from left to right, from top to bottom or from bottom to top. Such an arrangement may seem rather arbitrary, but it has the great virtue of being clear. A reader will hardly get lost during the explanation.

Reasons for Moving to a Small Town

SLOAN WILSON

1   A few years ago my wife and I bought a house in Ticonderoga, N.Y., a town with a population of 5,000, which is about 90 miles north of Albany. Because we had spent most of our lives in New York City and Miami, Fla., a lot of our friends were astonished. Why had we done it?

2   We had three big reasons: (1) We hoped that a country village would offer a fear-free friendly atmosphere that would be good for our seven-year-old daughter and for us in our middle age. (2) We hoped that a small town could offer a combination of the conveniences of city life and the beauties of the nearby lakes and mountains. (3) We hoped that life in a small town would be vastly cheaper than existence in a big city or suburb, where inflation, taxes, tuition and bills of all kinds kept snowballing every year.

STUDY QUESTIONS
Organization and Content

1   What caused Wilson's friends to be astonished?
2   What is the relation of sentence 3, paragraph 1, to sentence 2?
3   What is the relation of paragraph 2 to sentence 3, paragraph 1?
4   How is paragraph 2 organized?
5   What reasons does Wilson give for moving to a small town? Answer in the fewest possible words.

Sentence Structure

1   In sentence 1, what is the relation of *town* to *Ticonderoga?* What word does the *which*-clause modify?
2   The beginning and the end of a sentence are positions of strong possible emphasis. How does Wilson get emphasis on *astonished* at the end of sentence 2? A sentence constructed in this manner, with the emphasis at the end, is called a periodic sentence.
3   With what words does Wilson begin each statement of his three reasons? Why begin in that way?

Diction

1   What is the origin of *astonished?* Is it a stronger word than *astounded* or *surprised?*
2   In paragraph 2, what does *atmosphere* mean as Wilson uses it? What is the opposite of a *fear-free* atmosphere?
3   What does *conveniences* mean in sentence 2, paragraph 2?
4   In sentence 3, paragraph 2, Wilson does not say *life* in a big city, but *existence.* Do the two words have the same meaning or not?
5   *Snowballing* as Wilson uses it is a vivid, imaginative word. Explain why.

Assignment

1   Perhaps you know exactly where you would like to live. If so, enumerate your reasons for wishing to live there.
2   Enumerate your reasons for choosing a certain course of study.
3   Enumerate your reasons for selecting a certain sport (or other college activity) to which to give your time.

"The Old Days"

A TEACHER TODAY

A recent letter writer to The Bee complained about "mediocre" teaching, 1
pointing out how well teachers in the "old days" could teach classes of 60
students. That may be true. Now let's take a look at a few other things that
were different in the "old days."

In the old days, children did not spend more time in front of the TV than 2
in the classroom. They were not deluged with material possessions. Children did not expect constant entertainment in school. Work was not a
stranger to them. In the old days, children respected adults.

In the old days, teachers were allowed to fail children when they did not 3
meet adequate standards. Teachers were allowed to discipline students ade-
quately. Principals had more power to suspend or expel repeated trouble-
makers, and parents accepted their share of the discipline.

In the old days, parents read to their children. Children did not come 4
home to an empty house after school. Parents saw that children did their
homework. Children cared what grades they received.

In the old days, liquor and drugs were not common in school. Adminis- 5
trators required students to appear at school decently dressed and groomed.
And in the old days, children and teachers did not have to fear for their
safety at school.

STUDY QUESTIONS

Organization and Content

1 What is the purpose of paragraph 1?
2 Which aspect of the topic does the writer take up in each of the four
other short paragraphs?
3 Is there any reason for the order of the paragraphs? Could paragraph 5 just as well replace 2 or 3 in the order? Has the writer tried
to work up to any sort of climax?
4 Would the discussion be more effective if the writer were to explain
how conditions are today?
5 For the technique of handling an enumeration how does this piece
differ from the one by Sloan Wilson?

From *The Fresno Bee,* December 10, 1976, Fresno, California.

Sentence Structure

1   Most of the sentences are short. What effect does such a succession of short sentences have? Do most of the sentences begin with the subject or with some other sentence element?
2   Would the discussion be better if the writer had used greater variety of sentence length and structure?
3   How do paragraphs 2–5 begin? Why do they begin thus?
4   In paragraph 5 how does the writer round off the enumeration?

Diction

1   Does the diction seem to fit a mainly formal or mainly colloquial style?
2   *Mediocre, deluged, adequate,* and *discipline* have interesting origins. Are they all from the Latin?
3   How is *deluged* related to *lavish* and *discipline* to *disciple?*

Assignment

1   Enumerate the ways in which you find college different from high school.
2   If you have moved from the city to the country or from the country to the city, enumerate the differences you have discovered in the life patterns of city and country dwellers.
3   Enumerate the changes in the pattern of your life during summers, now that you are no longer a child.
4   Enumerate differences between the pioneer American and the American of today.

Methods of Developing Great Minds

GILBERT HIGHET

No, we can never tell how great minds arise, and it is very hard to tell **1** how to detect and encourage them when they do appear. But we do know two methods of feeding them as they grow.

One is to give them constant challenge and stimulus. Put problems be- **2** fore them. Make things difficult for them. They need to think. Produce things for them to think about and question their thinking at every stage. They are inventive and original. Propose experiments to them. Tell them to discover what is hidden.

The second method is to bring them into contact with other eminent **3** minds. It is not enough, not nearly enough, for a clever boy or girl to meet his fellows and his teachers and his parents. He (or she) must meet men and woman of real and undeniable distinction. That is, he must meet the immortals. That brilliant and pessimistic scoundrel Plato died just over 2,300 years ago, but through his books he is still talking and thinking and leading others to think; and there is no better way, none, for a young man to start thinking about any kind of philosophical problem—human conduct, political action, logical analysis, metaphysics, aesthetics—than by reading Plato and trying to answer his arguments, detect his sophisms, resist his skillful persuasions, and become both his pupil and his critic. No one can learn to write music better than by studying *The Well-tempered Clavier* of Bach and the symphonies of Beethoven. A young composer who does so will not, if he is any good, write music like Bach and Beethoven. He will write music more like the music that he wanted to write. A man may become a routine diplomat by following the rule book and solving every problem as it comes up, but if he is to grow into a statesman he must read his Machiavelli and consider the lives of Bismarck and Lincoln and Disraeli. The best way toward greatness is to mix with the great.

Challenge and experiment; association with immortal minds: These are **4** the two sure ways of rearing intelligent men and women. And these two opportunities for greatness are, or ought to be, provided by schools and colleges and universities.

From Gilbert Highet, "The Unpredictable Intellect," in *Man's Unconquerable Mind.* New York: Columbia University Press, 1954.

STUDY QUESTIONS
Organization and Content

1   Paragraph 1 has two sentences. Explain the function of each sentence. What is the function of the paragraph?
2   Which are the topic sentences of paragraphs 2 and 3?
3   Highet uses several sentences in paragraphs 2 and 3 in order to illustrate the topic idea. What is the difference in the illustrative material of the two paragraphs?
4   What books by Plato and Machiavelli would stimulate the minds of young people? Why should "Bismarck and Lincoln and Disraeli" be grouped together?
5   What is the function of paragraph 4?
6   In one well-written sentence, explain how this selection functions as an example of enumeration.

Sentence Structure

1   What is the effect of the successive short sentences that the author uses in paragraph 2?
2   Show how parallel phrasing and repetition provide both emphasis and good linking among sentences of paragraph 2.
3   In what way has Highet gained emphasis in sentence 2, paragraph 1; sentences 2 and 5, paragraph 3?
4   In sentences 3 and 4, paragraph 3, certain words are placed in emphatic positions. Which words are they?
5   Sentence 5, paragraph 3, is long. Is it simple, compound, or complex? Draw a diagram illustrating the parallel structure that is used in the sentence.
6   Good writers repeat important words for emphasis. Which words are thus repeated in the last part of paragraph 3?
7   Why did Highet use the semicolon and the colon in sentence 1, paragraph 4?

Diction

1   What is the difference between a *challenge* and a *stimulus*?
2   Is there a difference between *eminence* and *distinction*?
3   Which two areas of philosophy are represented by *metaphysics* and *aesthetics*?
4   Distinguish among *sophism, philosophy,* and *sophisticate.*

Assignment

Enumerate, with illustrations: methods of developing character; physical strength; agility; sound health; an appreciation of music; an interest in reading, art, geography, mathematics, or science.

Ways in Which Women Are Segregated

PATRICIA O'BRIEN

There are many ways in which society segregates women alone, ways 1
based on other unarticulated presumptions of moral infirmity: women alone
are many times not allowed to rent apartments, open charge accounts, or be
comfortable at social events where everyone comes in pairs. They are viewed
with suspicion if they live with other women; ignored if they are old; and if
they are divorced, their morals are monitored by self-appointed watchdogs.
Restaurants will refuse to seat them or do so only reluctantly; country clubs
will not accept memberships from single businesswomen who are therefore
closed off from an important informal setting for conducting business that
many men consider essential. But the attitudes which are particularly hurt-
ful in a practical sense are those which affect the way a woman alone is able
to earn her living or spend her money.

Some companies refuse to hire women who are the sole support of their 2
families, the corporate reasoning being they would be unreliable on the job
if a family crisis came up. Yet studies have shown that women alone often
have better working records with less absenteeism than men, precisely because they have a responsibility to support their families that cannot be ignored. There are many of them. Of the more than 5.5 million widowed, divorced, or separated women working in 1968, almost all held jobs because it
was financially necessary. Most of them take what they can get. They are
usually unable to afford school or training before they go to work and are
therefore limited in the job market. . . .

Women alone are considered poor credit risks by a number of companies 3
and department stores. "I tried to get an account at three department stores;
one of them refused, explaining I was a bad risk, and the other two refused
without explanation," complained a young divorced woman making $15,-
000 a year. "A man making half what I make with six kids to support can
get a charge account—but not me."

STUDY QUESTIONS
Organization and Content

1   The author says that society segregates women alone in many ways. How many ways does she enumerate? Does she number the items in her list?
2   Why is *but* significant in sentence 4?
3   How are paragraphs 2 and 3 related to sentence 4, paragraph 1?
4   What is the topic sentence of paragraph 2? What relation do the other five sentences of paragraph 2 have to the topic sentence? What is paragraph 2 trying to prove?
5   What is the topic sentence of paragraph 3? What kind of evidence supports the topic idea?
6   Explain why the order of the three paragraphs is a logical sequence.

Sentence Structure

1   Why does the author use a second *ways*—an appositive—in sentence 1? What signal is given by the colon after *infirmity*?
2   Why does the author not list all the ways in one sentence?
3   What functions do the semicolons perform in sentences 2 and 3?
4   What word and pronouns standing for it are repeated throughout sentence 1 so as to give the paragraph good transitions and coherence? (Look up *coherence*.)
5   Is the same technique of repetition used in paragraphs 2 and 3?
6   Why does sentence 2, paragraph 2, begin with *yet*?

Diction

1   Look up *segregated, unarticulated, presumptions, infirmity, monitored, reluctantly, essential.*
2   What is the Latin root of *segregates*? How does it operate in *gregarious*?
3   What is the Latin root of *unarticulated*? Name several other words in which this root appears.
4   What is the origin of *corporate*? What is meant in sentence 1, paragraph 2, by ''corporate reasoning''?
5   Which words in sentence 3, paragraph 3, give it a colloquial tone? (Be sure you know what *colloquial* means.)

Assignment

1   Enumerate ways in which women are treated differently from men at your college; or vice versa.
2   Enumerate ways in which life becomes different for people when they reach legal adulthood at 21—or 18 in some states.

American Intellectual Traits from the Frontier

FREDERICK JACKSON TURNER

From the conditions of frontier life came intellectual traits of profound importance. The works of travelers along each frontier from colonial days onward describe certain common traits, and these traits have, while softening down, still persisted as survivals in the place of their origin, even when a higher social organization succeeded. The result is that to the frontier the American intellect owes its striking characteristics. That coarseness and strength combined with acuteness and inquisitiveness; that practical, inventive turn of mind, quick to find expedients; that masterful grasp of material things, lacking in the artistic but powerful to effect great ends; that restless, nervous energy; that dominant individualism, working for good and for evil, and withal that buoyancy and exuberance which comes with freedom—these are traits of the frontier, or traits called out elsewhere because of the existence of the frontier. Since the days when the fleet of Columbus sailed into the waters of the New World, America has been another name for opportunity, and the people of the United States have taken their tone from the incessant expansion which has not only been open but has even been forced upon them. He would be a rash prophet who should assert that the expansive character of American life has now entirely ceased. Movement has been its dominant fact, and, unless this training has no effect upon a people, the American energy will continually demand a wider field for its exercise.

STUDY QUESTIONS

Organization and Content

1   Is sentence 1 the topic sentence of the paragraph? Sentence 3 says much the same thing as sentence 1. But what specific little differences of idea have been introduced?
2   According to sentence 2 where did Turner find out about the "striking characteristics" of the American intellect?
3   This paragraph illustrates how a writer may use enumeration in a broader discussion. How many American intellectual traits does Turner list?
4   How does he separate them in the sentence where they appear? How does his technique of enumeration differ from that of Sloan Wilson?

From *The Significance of the Frontier* by Frederick Jackson Turner.

5   What is the "tone" that Turner mentions in sentence 5, and what produced it?

Sentence Structure

1   Notice Turner's variety of sentence structure. Which sentences begin with phrases or dependent clauses, which with subjects? Which are compound sentences with clauses connected by *and*?
2   How did Turner arrange his material in sentence 3 so as to end the sentence with *characteristics?* How did he thus create good transition?

Diction

1   If you need to, look up *profound, expedients, buoyancy, exuberance,* and *incessant.*
2   How does *profound* differ in meaning from *striking* and *dominant?*

Assignment

1   Enumerate causes of student activism or of student apathy on your campus; causes of the generation gap; or causes of young people's unconventionality (or their conventionality).
2   Examine yourself and enumerate the traits (mental and physical) that you have inherited from your parents and/or grandparents.
3   Enumerate the characteristics of freshmen, sophomores, seniors, athletes, students in engineering, students in journalism, students in art, or professors.
4   What is your home town like? Why is it this way? Enumerate its outstanding features and account for them.

Japanese Characteristics

FOSCO MARAINI

(Eric Mosbacker, trans.)

Summing up the experience of many years in Japan, I should say that there 1
are at least five important Japanese characteristics which throw light on
their success in the world, the modern world which they did not help to
create.

The first is their sense of communion with nature. As we shall see later, 2
the relations between man and his environment in the Far East are profoundly different from our own. Matter is not regarded as something inert
and passive to be dominated, but as life, to be understood, loved, possessed.
This, of course, is not consciously present in the mind of an operator using
a machine-tool in an engineering shop, and if you questioned him about it
he would probably be at a loss for an answer, but, like all other men, he is
much more than he is consciously aware of. In each one of us there lives the
civilization in which we were brought up; behind that workman there are
thousands of years of mystic relationship with things, the subtleties of a
profoundly monist philosophy, all the poetry of a popular religion according to which the divine suffuses everything, of an art which regards matter
as a sister, not as a slave. These realities, on the level of an entire people,
count; they give the Japanese, whether designer, director, artist, or simply
workman, a lead of several lengths over others.

The second characteristic, closely connected with the first, is the extraor- 3
dinary manual skill, particularly in little things, widespread among Japanese
of all regions and all classes. Examine an eighteenth-century *linrō* (medicine
box), a sixteenth- or seventeenth-century *tsuba* (sword guard), a plate, any
lacquered object, a wicker basket, above all a sword blade; consider the skill
and care with which boats, wooden boxes, lanterns, cheap paper-and-bam-
boo umbrellas are made, and you will immediately appreciate that this standard of workmanship, when harnessed to modern industry, is equivalent to
a fabulous gold mine on which to draw. For centuries the level of excellence
required for native products has been such that these skills have become second nature. Examining the work of western craftsmen after one has grown
used to Japanese standards is like passing one's hand over articles of furniture chopped with an axe after caressing the work of a first-class cabinetmaker. To get some idea of Japanese standards, one must think of Swiss
watches, Italian Renaissance armour, certain English furniture and clothing;
bearing in mind, however, that in Japan the high standard of craftsmanship

applies not only to expensive products, but also to cheap articles of everyday use.

4   The third characteristic is the traditional specialization of the classes. In Japan the feudal system was abolished in 1868; only the day before yesterday, so to speak. For three centuries Japanese society had been rigidly stratified. At one extreme were the 262 *daimyo* (great names) and their families; at the other the *eta*, social pariahs condemned to what in a society under Buddhist influence were such degrading tasks as tanning hides and butchery. In between, starting from the top, came the Samurai (warriors, about 7 percent of the population), *hyakushō* (peasants, about 85 percent), *shokunin* (craftsmen, about 2 percent) and *shonin* (traders, about 3 percent). [N. Skene Smith, *Tokugawa Japan*, Tokyo, 1937, p. 31.] It should be noted that traders were at the bottom of the scale, only a little way above the pariahs; a fact which explains the low Japanese commercial morality which prevailed, particularly during the long period at the end of the nineteenth century and the beginning of the twentieth, when the descendants of the best families preferred the professions or state employment to commerce or industry. There is still something degrading associated with money in Japan, and this often leads to hypocritical behaviour of the kind which with us is associated with sex. To return to class divisions; being so close to a past of specialization imposed from birth leads to ready acceptance of the limitations imposed by the requirements of modern industry. In the brief space of three or four generations there has been no time to develop a complete human nature, a rounded personality; thus a working life confined to the perpetual repetition of a few movements tends less strongly to stimulate resentment; it harmonizes with the atmosphere of family memories handed down by word of mouth; and that makes the condition seem more tolerable.

5   Some of the characteristics of the Japanese of which everyone has heard should also be remembered—their frugal and Spartan habits. These are favoured by the fact that life is organized in such a way that the fundamental human needs are satisfied both cheaply and pleasingly. Housing, food, clothes, baths, are all much cheaper than they are with us; a man can be surrounded by beautiful objects without much expense. Luxury, as I have already remarked, is regarded as vulgar. Even middle-class habits are Spartan. People get up early, put up patiently with cold, and are not demanding in such matters as food, dress, and entertainment.

6   Finally, there is a group of characteristics which I perhaps should have put first, characteristics that are to be noted in all fields of Japanese life; the lack of outstanding personalities, the natural need to collaborate, the docility of groups to their leader. . . . One of the things which strikes foreigners, particularly Latins, most vividly is that when you meet the Japanese you rarely have the impression of meeting an outstanding personality, with an above-average intelligence, though when you meet Japan (the product of some labour, a work of art, an event) you are so often carried away by the

warmest admiration. With us it is nearly always individuals who are interesting, brilliant, or witty, while collectively they are a poor thing. In Japan the reverse is true, and the whole is superior to the sum of its parts. Japanese of real talent may perhaps be few, but evidently the system carries them to the top; the others follow and the organism works.

STUDY QUESTIONS
Organization and Content

1   What is the function of paragraph 1? Compare it with paragraph 1 of O'Brien.
2   To what phase of Japanese life does Maraini's list of characteristics apply?
3   What terms does Maraini use to indicate his enumeration?
4   In paragraph 2, what is the relation of sentence 3 to sentence 2? Explain the important contrast brought out in sentence 3.
5   In sentence 5, paragraph 2, Maraini lists four elements that influence a Japanese workman. Identify them.
6   Sentence 5 has a simile: "an art which regards matter as a sister, not as a slave." How effective is this simile? Try to express in nonfigurative terms what this simile, with its connotations, expresses. To do so, how many words do you require?
7   Sentence 2, paragraph 3, lists ten things. What do they exemplify? What is the difference between the four items after the semicolon and those that precede it?
8   With what simile does Maraini express the difference between Japanese craftsmanship and Western craftsmanship?
9   Why did Maraini select certain products of Switzerland, Italy, and England to mention in sentence 5, paragraph 3? What relation does sentence 5 have to sentence 2 in the same paragraph?
10   What is the significance of the Japanese feudal system in its relation to modern industry?
11   How are sentences 4 and 5, paragraph 5, related to the topic discussed in that paragraph?
12   How is paragraph 5 related to Maraini's main point about the Japanese? paragraph 6?
13   What is the meaning of "the system" and "the organism" in paragraph 6? Are these terms metaphors or not?
14   In paragraph 6, Maraini mentions characteristics which he says he "perhaps should have put first." Is there a justification for the order of characteristics that he uses? Do you think there is a better order than his?

Sentence Structure

1   What is the arrangement of the dependent material and the independent material in the sentence which constitutes paragraph 1?

2   Point out the elements that are balanced and parallel in sentence 3, paragraph 2, and those that depart from parallelism to provide variety. What would be the effect of placing *and* before *possessed?*

3   To what extent has Maraini used varied sentence structure in paragraph 2 by using sentences of different types—simple, compound, and complex?

4   What are the main terms in the series of elements listed in sentence 5, paragraph 2?

5   Sentences 5 and 6, paragraph 2, use semicolons. Why?

6   To what extent is sentence 1, paragraph 3, symmetrically arranged? How has Maraini handled interrupters here?

7   In sentence 5, paragraph 3, and in sentences 2 and 3, paragraph 4, semicolons appear. For what different purposes are they used? Which of these sentences is a balanced sentence?

8   Why does sentence 4, paragraph 4, have inverted order?

9   A transitional phrase is used after a digression in sentence 7, paragraph 4. What is it? Where did the digression begin?

10   Sentence 8, paragraph 4, has several parts separated by semicolons. What does each part contribute to the thought of the sentence?

11   Both sentences 1 and 2, paragraph 6, are fairly long. Which one exhibits the greater dexterity in the managing of complex sentence materials?

Diction

1   In case you need to, look up *inert, mystic, subtleties, monist, popular, suffuses, feudal, stratified, pariahs, frugal, Spartan, vulgar, collaborate, docility.*

2   Is there any etymological connection between *mystic* and *mysterious, feudal* and *feud?*

3   Learn the roots of *popular, suffuses, stratified, collaborate.* In what other words do these roots appear?

4   Explain how each of the following metaphors functions in the discussion: *lives* (sentence 5, paragraph 2), *lead* (sentence 6, paragraph 2), *gold mine* (sentence 2, paragraph 3). Which one has the most force and is the most imaginative?

5   Why is *caressing* (sentence 4, paragraph 3) an especially effective word?

Assignment

1   Imitate Maraini by enumerating characteristics of the American or some variety of the American, such as the New Englander, Southerner, or Californian.

2   If you are acquainted with any of the following groups, similarly write on the Italians, Jews, Armenians, Negroes, Indians, Puerto Ricans, Latin Americans, Mexicans, Russians, Scandinavians, English, or Germans.

3   Like Maraini, list the characteristics of one of these groups which pertain to one phase of life, such as art, craftsmanship, or business.

4   Enumerate characteristics of aged people, children, or adolescents; of freshmen, sophomores, or seniors; or of the typical student at your college.

5   Enumerate characteristics of football fans, "jocks," "good ole boys," or tourists.

Analysis

Another method of exposition, somewhat different from the mere listing of details, is called *analysis.* In making a list, one may wish simply to set down a record of something: for example, these are the properties of calcium phosphate, these are the laws passed by the legislature last week, these are the typical activities of the Prince of Wales. On the other hand, one may wish to explain what conclusions one has reached by thinking about some subject in an analytical way. The process of analysis is a process of taking something apart——not ripping it apart and throwing the parts about helter-skelter but taking it apart in a thoughtful, systematic manner so that one can see the parts clearly and understand how they are related to each other. It is rather like "factoring" a problem. Analysis is one of the chief ways by which the human mind deals with the world. The mind can seldom understand anything immediately as a whole; it cannot "take in" an undivided subject very conveniently. It does not feel satisfied that it has properly done its work of thinking unless it knows that it has divided what ever *can* be divided or has classified whatever *can* be classified. So writers, when they explain something by the method of analysis, "think out" the subject; they divide a thing into parts, or they arrange items according to some scheme of classification.

Analysis by Partition

It would be difficult to explain the construction or the operation of an airplane, for example, without mentioning the different parts of the airplane. Merely listing all the parts (as if one were making up a catalogue of supplies) will not help a reader to understand the construction or operation of an airplane. A writer will have to cut up the airplane, as it were——that is, show what chief functioning areas an airplane designer must take into consideration: the power plant, the fuselage, the guiding apparatus, the landing gear, the instruments. Then, of course, the writer can subdivide and explain what the parts of each main area are and how they relate to each other. Thus, we may see that analysis, as a form of expository writing, goes beyond enumeration although it also makes some use of enumeration.

Analysis by Classification

The process of analysis as it might be applied to the topic of *an airplane* has just been illustrated. But suppose that the topic is *airplanes.* In this case the writer will take the subject apart in a different fashion——by means of classification. The writer will tell about airplanes according to types: such as heavy, medium, and light; or fighters, bombers, passenger planes, and cargo planes; or propeller-driven planes, turboprop planes, and jet-propelled planes. When one is classifying, the important rule to follow is to use principles that are logically parallel for the "files" or "bins" of classification. There would be an illogical hodgepodge if it were stated, "Airplanes fall into the following classification: jet-propelled, passenger, and medium." The three principles of method of propulsion, function, and weight would be mixed up. Such illogical classifying would not help readers; it would only confuse them. Classification, then, must be made according to logical principles.

Uses of Analysis

Both of these methods of explanation, analysis by partition and analysis by classification, are very commonly used. When we are discussing topics such as those mentioned above or explaining, for example, how something is made, we will use analysis. Analysis of a process is a frequently used type of exposition: for example, how steel is produced, how paper is made, how oil pipelines are welded, how to weave a rug, or how to care for a shotgun— these are typical topics for treatment by analysis.

Process Analysis

Writers of process analysis do one of two things: either they give directions, that is, tell readers how they should do a thing; or they provide information, that is, explain how a thing is generally done or has been done. Usually a definition of the process is not needed, but if it is, it should be kept short. The process itself must be taken apart, step by step, and each step must be explained. The writer must take up one step at a time, and be sure to provide clear transition from one step to another. Because in general the writer must follow an order of steps in time, he or she may need to use enumeration. But if the process is complicated and things are going on simultaneously, the writer will need to indicate general phases of the process and then show subdivisions within each phase. In such situations, making an outline is often helpful.

　　The writing apprentice will readily realize how enormous is the field of exposition by analysis. It is, therefore, extremely important that the writer train to be efficient in this type of writing.

Smoking Animals out of a Tree

GERALD M. DURRELL

The smoking of a tree is quite an art and requires a certain amount of practice before you can perfect it. First, having found your tree and made sure that it is really hollow all the way up, you have to make sure whether there are any exit holes farther up the trunk, and if there are, you have to send a man up to cover them with nets. Having done this, you drape a net over the main hole at the base of the tree, and this has to be done in such a way that it does not interfere with the smoking process and yet prevents anything from getting away. The important thing is to make sure that this net is secure: there is nothing quite so exasperating as to have it fall down and envelop you in its folds just as the creatures inside the tree are starting to come out. With all your nets in position you have to deal with the problem of the fire: this, contrary to all proverbial expectations, has to be all smoke and no fire, unless you want your specimens roasted. A small pile of dry twigs is laid in the opening, soaked with kerosene, and set alight. As soon as it is ablaze, you lay a handful of green leaves on top, and keep replenishing them. The burning of these green leaves produces scarcely any flame but vast quantities of pungent smoke, which is immediately sucked up into the hollow interior of the tree. Your next problem is to make sure that there is not too much smoke, for, if you are not careful, you can quite easily asphyxiate your specimens before they can rush out of the tree. The idea is to strike the happy medium between roasting and suffocation. Once the fire has been lit and piled with green leaves, it generally takes about three minutes (depending on the size of the tree) before the smoke percolates to every part and the animals start to break cover.

STUDY QUESTIONS

Organization and Content

1   In this paragraph the author, a zoological collector who has made several expeditions to Africa, analyzes the process of smoking animals out of a tree. Into how many steps does he divide the process? Are any of the steps subdivided into smaller operations?

2 Make an outline of the paragraph with the usual indications of divisions: I, A, B, 1, 2; II, and so forth.
3 What is the function of the first and last sentences?
4 To what extent does Durrell use enumeration?

Sentence Structure

1 By what means does Durrell provide transitions between the steps of the process he is analyzing?
2 Are Durrell's sentences generally formal or colloquial in style? Consider how complicated they are and whether the elements are mainly coordinate or subordinate.
3 What functions do the colons have in sentences 4 and 5?
4 Which sentences begin with subordinate elements? Are there enough of them to provide variety of sentence structure, or does the construction pattern of the sentences seem monotonous?

Diction

1 Look up *replenishing, pungent, suffocation, percolate.*
2 What is the relation between *replenish* and *plenty, pungent* and *point, percolate* and *colander?* Is there any difference between *asphyxiation* and *suffocation?*
3 Is Durrell's diction suitable to a formal style or a colloquial style?

Assignment

Write one analytical paragraph showing the steps in a simple process. Some suggestions: changing a tire, setting lines to catch fish, barbecuing a steak, making a dress, tuning up an engine, organizing a picnic or a party, building a fire in a fireplace, sawing down a tree for firewood, collecting honey from a beehive, trapping lobsters, steaming clams, washing a dog.

Crow Indian Country

ARAPOOISH, CROW CHIEF

Arapooish, Crow chief, in late summer of 1833, spoke in eulogy of his be-
loved country to Robert Campbell of the Rocky Mountain Fur Company. The
Crow dynasty extended from the Black Hills to the Rocky Mountains.

1 The Crow country is a good country. The Great Spirit put it exactly in the right place; while you are in it you fare well; whenever you are out of it, whichever way you travel, you fare worse. . . . The Crow country is exactly in the right place. It has snowy mountains and sunny plains, all kinds of climate and good things for every season. When the summer heats scorch the prairies, you can draw up under the mountains, where the air is sweet and cool, the grasses fresh, and the bright streams come tumbling out of the snowbanks. There you can hunt the elk, the deer, and the antelope, when their skins are fit for dressing; there you will find plenty of white bear and mountain sheep.

2 In the autumn, when your horses are fat and strong from the mountain pastures, you can go into the plains and hunt the buffalo, or trap beaver on the streams. And when winter comes on, you can take shelter in the woody bottoms along the rivers; there you will find buffalo meat for yourselves, and cottonwood bark for your horses; or you may winter in Wind River Valley, where there is salt weed in abundance.

3 The Crow country is exactly in the right place. Everything good is to be found there. There is no place like Crow country.

STUDY QUESTIONS

Organization and Content

1 According to what elements of excellence has the Crow chief analyzed the Crow country? What factors of geography, of climate, and
of resources has he brought out?
2 What is the relation of sentence 4, paragraph 1, to sentence 3?
3 What are sentences 5 and 6 intended to show?
4 What further parts of the analysis are explained in paragraph 2?
5 What is the purpose of the very brief paragraph 3?

Sentence Structure

1 How is sentence 2, paragraph 1, arranged so as to balance positive
and negative ideas?

Virginia Irving Armstrong. *I Have Spoken: American History through the Voices of the*
Indians. Copyright © 1971. Swallow Press: Chicago.

2 What sequence of things in sentence 4 gives support to the statement in sentence 3?

3 Point out the repetition of phrase and the balance of ideas in sentence 6.

4 Sentence 2, paragraph 2, has three main parts. How are they varied in grammatical structure?

5 Point out the difference between paragraphs 2 and 3 in regard to sentence length and variety of sentence structure.

Diction

1 Which words in this selection are the most concrete?

2 Are there any abstract terms?

3 Which terms produce the most vivid sense impressions?

Assignment

Write a brief analysis of your community or your college in terms of its excellence or its deficiencies. You may wish to concentrate on a single phase of life there: sport, education, recreation, business, or personal development, for example.

Childhood Experiences of Women Who Succeed in Business

MARGARET HENNIG AND ANNE JARDIM

In their study of the women enrolled in the M.B.A. program at Harvard Business School in the year 1963–64, Hennig and Hackman found that there was a particularly strong and regular pattern to the family histories of their subjects: twenty out of twenty-five were either eldest or only children; five were not first-born but on examination their experiences were essentially similar to those of a first-born child. This was so for a variety of reasons: the death of the eldest brother or sister, a large age difference between the subject and an older child, or changes in the family, for instance divorce, which moved the younger child into the position of an only child. All had

had extremely close relationships with their fathers and had been involved in an unusually wide range of traditionally masculine activities in the company of their fathers, beginning when they were very young. They believed that they had been given unusually strong support by their families in following their own interests regardless of the sex-role attributes of those interests. Finally, they thought that they had developed a very early preference for the company of men rather than of women.

STUDY QUESTIONS
Organization and Content

1   Much information about groups of people is obtained by means of questionnaires. But before the answers to the questions can be put to any use, they have to be analyzed—classified according to some plan that will reveal common factors among the people in the group. How many common factors among the twenty-five women studied by Hennig and Hackman seemed significant to them?
2   What seems important about the relation of these women to their parents and about their interests and activities?
3   What would you predict about the career of a girl who was sixth in a family of seven and whose father had to spend much time away from home?

Sentence Structure

1   Why do the authors use colons in sentences 1 and 2? In sentence 1 what is the relation of the two parts of the sentence that come after the colon? In sentence 2 how is the material after the colon grammatically different from that in sentence 1?
2   How many of the sentences begin with elements other than the subject?
3   What transitional device is used throughout this paragraph?
4   Why do the authors begin the last sentence with *finally*?
5   Examine this short paragraph to see how much sentence variety it has.

Diction

1   What is meant by ''traditionally masculine activities''? By ''sex-role attributes''? Give some examples.
2   How concrete or abstract is the language in this selection?
3   Are there vivid images created by the language? Why or why not?

Assignment

1 Does any group of students on your campus seem to have characteristics in common—perhaps sorority girls, fraternity men, or independents? Modeling your paper on the paragraph above, write an analysis of the reasons for their being or not being in Greek organizations.

2 Inquire among a group of your friends or fellow classmates to find out their reasons for coming to college. (You might limit the group to members of the same sex.) Then, following the method of Hennig and Jardim, classify these reasons in one paragraph.

3 Do mathematics or physics majors differ appreciably from art or architecture majors, or do humanities majors and pre-law students differ appreciably from pre-medicine students and majors in biology, zoology, or botany? Identify and then analyze the common traits possessed by one of these groups of students.

Types of College Students

THEODORE H. WHITE

Students divide themselves by their own discriminations in every generation, and the group I ran with had a neat system of classification. Harvard, my own group held, was divided into three groups—white men, gray men and meatballs. I belonged to the meatballs, by self-classification. White men were youngsters of great name; my own class held a Boston Saltonstall, a New York Straus, a Chicago Marshall Field, two Roosevelts (John and Kermit), a Joseph P. Kennedy, Jr. The upper classes had another Roosevelt (Franklin, Jr.), a Rockefeller (David, with whom I shared a tutor in my sophomore year), a Morgan, and New York and Boston names of a dozen different fashionable pedigrees. Students of such names had automobiles; they went to Boston deb parties, football games, the June crew race against Yale; they belonged to clubs. At Harvard today, they are called "preppies," the private-school boys of mythical "St. Grottlesex." 1

Between white men above and meatballs at the bottom came the gray men. The gray men were mostly public-high-school boys, sturdy sons of America's middle class. They went out for football and baseball, manned the *Crimson* and the *Lampoon,* ran for class committees and, later in life, for school committees and political office. They came neither of the aristocracy 2 nor of the deserving poor, as did most meatballs and scholarship boys. Caspar Weinberger, of my class of 1938, for example, was president of the *Crimson* and graduated magna cum laude; he later became Secretary of Health, Education and Welfare, but as an undergraduate was a gray man from California. John King, of the same class of 1938, was another gray man; he became governor of New Hampshire. Wiley Mayne, an earnest student of history, who graduated with us, was a gray man from Iowa, later becoming congressman from Sioux City. He served on the House Judiciary Committee that voted to impeach Richard Nixon—with Wiley Mayne voting to support the President. The most brilliant member of the class was probably Arthur M. Schlesinger, Jr., who defied categorization. Definitely no meatball, Schlesinger lacked then either the wealth or the savoir-faire of the white men. Indeed, Schlesinger, who was to go on to a fame surpassing that of his scholar father, was one who could apparently mingle with both white men *and* meatballs. In his youth, Schlesinger was a boy of extraordinary sweetness and generosity, one of the few on campus who would be friendly to a Jewish meatball, not only a liberal by heredity, but a liberal in practice. Since Wiley Mayne, Arthur Schlesinger and I were all rivals, in an indistinct way, in the undergraduate rivalry of the History Department, I followed their careers with some interest. Mayne was a conservative, tart-tongued and stiff. I remember on the night of our Class Day dance, as we were all about to leave, he unburdened himself to me on "Eastern liberals who look down their long snob noses on people like me from the Midwest." Over the years Mayne grew into a milder, gentler, warmer person until in his agony over Nixon, wrestling with his conscience on whether to impeach or not, he seemed to be perhaps the most sensitive and human member of the Judiciary Committee. Schlesinger, by contrast, developed a certainty about affairs, a public tartness of manner associated with the general liberal rigidity of the late sixties that offended many—and yet, for all that, he remained as kind and gentle to old friends like myself, with whose politics he came profoundly to disagree, as he had been in boyhood. Both Schlesinger and Mayne, the liberal and the conservative, were always absolutely firm in their opinions. I, in the years starting at Harvard, and continuing in later life, wandered all through the political spectrum, and envied them both for their certainties.

3   I find some difficulty in describing what a "meatball" was. Meatballs were usually day students or scholarship students. We were at Harvard not to enjoy the games, the girls, the burlesque shows of the Old Howard, the companionship, the elms, the turning leaves of fall, the grassy banks of the Charles. We had come to get the Harvard badge, which says "Veritas," but really means a job somewhere in the future, in some bureaucracy, in some institution, in some school, laboratory, university or law firm.

STUDY QUESTIONS

Organization and Content

1 According to White, how did the division of Harvard students into three groups come about?
2 What are the bases of the three-group division?
3 Why do you think that White gives much more space to the second group than to the other two groups? Why so relatively little space to the last group?
4 What kinds of specific illustrations of the three kinds of Harvard students does White provide?
5 Compare and contrast the three history majors.
6 Does paragraph 3 serve as a good conclusion to the classification?

Sentence Structure

1 Both sentences 4 and 5, paragraph 1, contain lists of items. Explain the difference in their grammatical pattern.
2 Point out the transition in paragraph 2 from sentence 1 to sentence 2.
3 Sentences 5–12, paragraph 2, have similarities of structure. Which of them are the most complicated? Show how White has used appositives and subordinate clauses to control numerous modifiers in several of these sentences.
4 Sentences 16 and 17, paragraph 2, are long. Point out the internal participial modifiers (interrupters) in both sentences.
5 Identify the two kinds of parallel elements in paragraph 3, sentences 3 and 4.

Diction

1 You may need to look up *discriminations, pedigrees* (they both have interesting etymologies), and *savoir-faire.*
2 *Veritas* is Latin for truth. How is it related to *verity* and *very?*

Assignment

1 Classify the members of your college class or your fraternity or sorority into groups as White did. Use individuals and their typical interests, ambitions, and activities.
2 Similarly classify teachers in your high school or college.
3 Similarly divide the people in your home town into social classes.
4 If they are distinctive enough, similarly describe the communicants of different churches in your home town.

Reasons for City Changes

EMRYS JONES

Change does not affect the whole of society in the same way or at the same time. Generally speaking changes are more common in an urban than in a rural context, for two reasons. The first is that rural society must set itself in equilibrium with a physical, natural environment which if it changes at all does so very slowly indeed. The whole rhythm of life of a peasant community is tied to summer and winter, to day and night, to planting and harvesting. Urban society has divorced itself from this pattern. In towns and cities we are regimented by clocks and time zones. Our lives may be dominated by television series which have a Newtonian regularity, but this is a pattern of our own devising, a change brought about by society, and conceivably it could be changed again. Secondly, the city may be regarded as the centre of innovation—begging the question of the link between the urban process and innovation being a causal one. From earliest times the city has been the symbol of increasing organizational and social complexity. Commerce, class structure, industrialization, increasing communications, are all inextricably part and parcel of the life of a western city. To some extent the control of some of these processes involves planning. In the western world change is overwhelmingly urban change, and planners are products of the city.

STUDY QUESTIONS

Organization and Content

1 What is the function of sentence 1? Of sentence 2?
2 What analytical division is the organizing principle in sentences 3–12?
3 How is the urban-rural contrast organized in sentences 3–7?
4 What similarity of ideas provides transitional linkage between sentences 7 and 8?

Sentence Structure

1 How does Jones arrange sentence 2 so as to get easy transition to sentence 3?
2 Show how parallel phrasing in sentence 4 nicely develops the idea of "rhythm of life."

From Emrys Jones, "The Future Habitat," in *Man and His Habitat: Essays Presented to Emyr Estyn Evans,* Ed. R. H. Buchanan, Barnes & Noble Books, New York, 1971.

3 Sentence 7 is the longest in the paragraph. Explain how Jones has used four clauses and an interruptive appositive to organize sentence 7.

4 How are the four subjects of sentence 10 linked to the preceding sentence?

Diction

1 Jones uses a number of words with Latin roots, for example, *urban* and *rural*. Explain the relation between *urban* and *urbane*; *rural* and *rustic*; *context, text*, and *thatch*; *innovation, novelty*, and *new*.

2 *Peasant* and *inextricably* have interesting origins. Look them up.

3 Jones says that television series may "have a Newtonian regularity." What work of Sir Isaac Newton gives point to this allusive statement?

4 Be sure that you understand "begging the question" (sentence 8).

Assignment

1 If you are aware of changes in the life of your community, analyze the reasons for them in one substantial paragraph.

2 Explain what chief causes account for differences between communities that you have known or between different styles of living in your community.

3 Similarly explain why some place where you have lived was agreeable or disagreeable. You might analyze such things as its situation, atmosphere, arrangement, and particular facilities.

Factors in Business Success

ROY LEWIS AND ROSEMARY STEWART

1   Business considered as a game has been developed far more seriously in America than in Europe, and the rules have been more scientifically worked out. Adaptability, mobility, and sociability are three of the most important requisites for success when the game is played the American way. A successful businessman must always appear to be a regular guy, and his wife must always be one of the girls. They must not seem to be too different, too fashionable, or too clever. They must do what their peers do; live in the same type of neighborhood, wear the same type of clothes, enjoy the same amusements, and bring up their children in the same permissive way. According to *Fortune*, one rule transcends all others:

> Don't be too good. Keeping up with the Joneses is still important; but where in pushier and more primitive times it implied going substantially ahead of the Joneses, today keeping up means just that: keeping up. One can move ahead, yes—but slightly, and the timing must be exquisite. "We will have a grand piano," says one wife, "when we are ready for it"—which is quite different from "when we can afford it."

2   A successsful businessman and his wife must also be mobile; they must be willing to move their neighborhood and to change their friends when promotion requires it. According to Warner and Abegglen, mobility is one of the key characteristics of the big-business leaders. They describe those mobile men as being able "to a singular degree, to devote all their available energies to the solution of immediate and practical goals." The man on the make must also have a capacity for keeping a substantial emotional distance from people, which permits him to detach himself and move on.

3   One of the factors in success in any country is knowing the right people, but this assumes special importance in the U.S. because business is so closely integrated into the community. An ambitious man anywhere should cultivate useful acquaintances, but when work and leisure are separate, a man can have what friends he likes. Where his friends tend also to be colleagues, he is likely to be judged by the company he keeps, and he must therefore be more circumscribed in his social life....

Great emphasis is placed in American companies, and, indeed, in Ameri- 4
can society generally, on easy human relations. The American businessman
must appear both friendly and accessible, qualities which are symbolized by
the universal use of first names and by the ever-open office door. The British
businessman will normally keep his office door shut, but in most American
companies, the office door must be left open to show that you are always
accessible. This holds true no matter how great the din outside, nor how
disturbing constant interruption may be. No wonder some American businessmen come to their office before everyone else or work at home—otherwise they would have no opportunity to think! In a British company, the
secretary is the watchdog who guards her manager's privacy and with whom
all arrangements must be made before the sanctum can be penetrated. But
in many American companies, you can walk straight in through the boss's
open door. One large company, which is a particularly ardent supporter of
the ever-open-door policy, found that the occupants of the executive suite,
all of whose rooms opened onto a central hall, were too-often interrupted.
Their solution was not to shut the door or to have a secretary arrange ap-
pointments, but to take the names off the doors so that callers who did not
know their man by sight would be baffled.

STUDY QUESTIONS
Organization and Content

1 The "rules" mentioned in sentence 1, paragraph 1, apply to
what? What three rules have to be followed?
2 Which of the requisites for success do sentences 3–10, paragraph 1, apply to?
3 How do sentences 4 and 5, paragraph 1, contrast?
4 What is the purpose in the discussion of the quotations that the authors use in paragraphs 1 and 2? Note the ways in which the
quotations are introduced and identified as quotations.
5 What part does paragraph 2 play in the analysis?
6 Why is mobility an important quality for an ambitious businessman
to have?
7 Why is the point made in sentence 4, paragraph 2, significant in
the discussion of mobility?
8 Which factor in the analysis is taken up in paragraphs 3 and 4?
9 Show what ideas are contrasted in sentences 2 and 3, paragraph
3.
10 What contrast between American and British businessmen is indicated in paragraph 4? Which group has the advantage over the
other?
11 In paragraph 4, what two qualities represent sociability?
12 Make a two-level outline of this selection. That is, use Roman numerals for main headings and capital letters for subheadings.

Sentence Structure

1   What kind of sentence is sentence 1—simple, compound, or complex? What two aspects of business as a game does it express?

2   What elements in the discussion are emphasized at the beginning and the end of sentence 2? Similarly, what terms are placed at the beginning and the end of each clause in sentence 3?

3   What parallel grammatical construction is used in sentence 4? Point out the parallel verbs in sentence 5.

4   In sentence 1, paragraph 2, two concrete illustrations bring out the idea of "mobile." How are these illustrations arranged in the sentence?

5   In sentence 1, paragraph 3, how is the *but*-clause related to the clause before it? How is the *because*-clause related to the *but*-clause?

6   Note how the interrupting material between commas is placed in sentence 1, paragraph 4. Which words in this sentence receive greatest emphasis?

7   What type of sentence is sentence 3, paragraph 4? Why is it a good sentence to show contrast? In the two clauses of the sentence which words receive greatest emphasis?

8   Note that in sentence 8, paragraph 4, there are two interrupters placed between commas. What parts of the sentence do they separate?

Diction

1   Look up *mobility, peers, transcends, exquisite* (paragraph 1), *circumscribed* (3), *accessible, din, sanctum, penetrated, ardent, baffled* (4).

2   Some terms in this selection are used with rather special meanings: for example, "a *regular* guy" and "one of the *girls*" in paragraph 1, "*useful* acquaintances" in paragraph 3, and "*easy* human relations" in paragraph 4. How would you explain the meanings of these terms?

Assignment

1   Analyze the factors that lead to success in high school or college courses.

2   Analyze the factors producing what you consider the ideal home.

3   Analyze the factors that make your college or university a successful educational enterprise. Use two or three quotations if you can.

The Typical
Science Fiction Film

SUSAN SONTAG

The typical science fiction film has a form as predictable as a Western, and   1
is made up of elements which, to a practiced eye, are as classic as the saloon
brawl, the blonde schoolteacher from the East, and the gun duel on the deserted main street.

One model scenario proceeds through five phases.   2

(1) The arrival of the thing. (Emergence of the monsters, landing of the   3
alien spaceship, etc.) This is usually witnessed or suspected by just one person, a young scientist on a field trip. Nobody, neither his neighbors nor his
colleagues, will believe him for some time. The hero is not married, but has
a sympathetic though also incredulous girl friend.

(2) Confirmation of the hero's report by a host of witnesses to a great act   4
of destruction. (If the invaders are beings from another planet, a fruitless
attempt to parley with them and get them to leave peacefully.) The local
police are summoned to deal with the situation and massacred.

(3) In the capital of the country, conferences between scientists and the   5
military take place, with the hero lecturing before a chart, map, or black-
board. A national emergency is declared. Reports of further destruction. Authorities from other countries arrive in black limousines. All international
tensions are suspended in view of the planetary emergency. This stage often
includes a rapid montage of news broadcasts in various languages, a meeting
at the UN, and more conferences between the military and the scientists.
Plans are made for destroying the enemy.

(4) Further atrocities. At some point the hero's girl friend is in grave dan-   6
ger. Massive counter-attacks by international forces, with brilliant displays
of rocketry, rays, and other advanced weapons, are all unsuccessful. Enormous military casualties, usually by incineration. Cities are destroyed and/or
evacuated. There is an obligatory scene here of panicked crowds stampeding
along a highway or a big bridge, being waved on by numerous policemen
who, if the film is Japanese, are immaculately white-gloved, preternaturally
calm, and call out in dubbed English, "Keep moving. There is no need to
be alarmed."

(5) More conferences, whose motif is: "They must be vulnerable to some-   7
thing." Throughout the hero has been working in his lab to this end. The

final strategy, upon which all hopes depend, is drawn up; the ultimate weapon—often a super-powerful, as yet untested, nuclear device—is mounted. Countdown. Final repulse of the monster or invaders. Mutual congratulations, while the hero and girl friend embrace cheek to cheek and scan the skies sturdily. "But have we seen the last of them?"

STUDY QUESTIONS
Organization and Content

1   What is the function of the one-sentence paragraph 1? paragraph 2? What general idea is stated in paragraph 1?
2   What predictable ("classic") elements of the Western film are mentioned?
3   Into how many parts is a typical science fiction film divided?
4   How does Sontag present these parts? In which paragraphs?
5   Why (paragraph 5) are "all international tensions . . . suspended"? In concrete terms, what happens?
6   Who finally saves the world from the "monsters" and by what means?
7   What doubt is expressed at the end?

Sentence Structure

1   What are the two parts of sentence 1? How are the three elements added to the second part?
2   In the enumeration of "phases," Sontag uses several incomplete sentences. What effect do they have? Are they a kind of "shorthand"?

Diction

1   Look up *classic, emergence, colleagues, host, fruitless, parley, planetary, casualties, incineration, evacuated, obligatory, preternaturally, repulse, sturdily.*
2   What languages were these words taken from?—*scenario, montage, motif.* Which ones keep their foreign pronunciation?
3   Give the roots, and their meanings, of *incredulous, atrocities, immaculately, vulnerable.*
4   What is the source of *panicked?* of *tensions* (how is it related to *thin?*).

Assignment

1   Analyze some other type of film.
2   Analyze a football or baseball game, following the pattern provided by Sontag.
3   Similarly, analyze a fraternity or sorority pledge drive.

Merits of Democracy

E. M. FORSTER

Democracy is not . . . less hateful than other contemporary forms of government, and to that extent it deserves our support. It does start from the assumption that the individual is important, and that all types are needed to make a civilisation. It does not divide its citizens into the bossers and the bossed—as an efficiency-regime tends to do. The people I admire most are those who are sensitive and want to create something or discover something, and do not see life in terms of power, and such people get more of a chance under a democracy than elsewhere. They found religions, great or small, or they produce literature and art, or they do disinterested scientific research, or they may be what is called "ordinary people," who are creative in their private lives, bring up their children decently, for instance, or help their neighbours. All these people need to express themselves; they cannot do so unless society allows them to do so, and the society which allows them most liberty is a democracy.   1

Democracy has another merit. It allows criticism, and if there is not public criticism there are bound to be hushed-up scandals. That is why I believe in the Press, despite all its lies and vulgarity, and why I believe in Parliament. Parliament is often sneered at because it is a Talking Shop. I believe in it *because* it is a talking shop. I believe in the Private Member who makes himself a nuisance. He gets snubbed and is told that he is cranky or ill-informed, but he does expose abuses which would otherwise never have been mentioned, and very often an abuse gets put right just by being mentioned. Occasionally, too, a well-meaning public official starts losing his head in the cause of efficiency, and thinks himself God Almighty. Such officials are particularly frequent in the Home Office. Well, there will be questions about them in Parliament sooner or later, and then they will have to mind their steps. Whether Parliament is either a representative body or an efficient one is questionable, but I value it because it criticises and talks, and because its chatter gets widely reported.   2

3   So Two Cheers for Democracy: one because it admits variety and two because it permits criticism.

STUDY QUESTIONS
Organization and Content

1   In paragraph 1, sentences 1–3, what main point does Forster make? What somewhat different aspect of his topic does he take up in sentences 4–6?
2   Give an example of "an efficiency-regime." In a country with a different type of government, what arrangement might there be instead of "the bossers and the bossed"?
3   What does Forster see as the value of permitting self-expression in a society?
4   Point out the transition from paragraph 1 to paragraph 2.
5   What is the value of criticism of governmental policies by elected representatives of the people?
6   How do Press and Parliament (or Congress in the United States) fit together to promote honest government?
7   What is the function of the final paragraph?

Sentence Structure

1   What transitional device does Forster use in paragraph 1, sentences 2 and 3?
2   How does he create grammatical parallelism in sentence 5?
3   What key word is emphasized in sentence 6? By what means is it emphasized?
4   Forster does not write very complicated sentences though some of his sentences are fairly long. In paragraph 2, the longish sentences 6, 9, and 10 have similar patterns. Describe them.

Diction

1   In the British system of government a Private Member is a member of Parliament who is not a Cabinet minister, and the Home Office is an administrative department for certain domestic matters.
2   A scientist who does "disinterested scientific research" has what sort of attitude?
3   Be sure you know what *vulgarity* means as Forster uses it.

Assignment

1   In order to show its chief merits, analyze the curriculum you are studying or a course you are taking.
2   Similarly analyze your college or university.
3   Similarly analyze your fraternity or sorority or other organization that you believe to have value.

The Duration of Human Relationships

ALVIN TOFFLER

Sociologists like Wirth have referred in passing to the transitory nature of **1** human ties in urban society. But they have made no systematic effort to relate the shorter duration of human ties to shorter durations in other kinds of relationships. Nor have they attempted to document the progressive decline in these durations. Until we analyze the temporal character of human bonds, we will completely misunderstand the move toward super-industrialism.

For one thing, the decline in the *average* duration of human relationships **2** is a likely corollary of the increase in the number of such relationships. The average urban individual today probably comes into contact with more people in a week than the feudal villager did in a year, perhaps even in a lifetime. The villager's ties with other people no doubt include some transient relationships, but most of the people he knew were the same throughout his life. The urban man may have a core group of people with whom his interactions are sustained over long periods of time, but he also interacts with hundreds, perhaps thousands, of people whom he may see only once or twice and who then vanish into anonymity.

All of us approach human relationships, as we approach other kinds of **3** relationships, with a set of built-in durational expectancies. We expect that certain kinds of relationships will endure longer than others. It is, in fact, possible to classify relationships with other people in terms of their expected duration. These vary, of course, from culture to culture and from person to person. Nevertheless, throughout wide sectors of the population of the advanced technological societies something like the following order is typical:

Long-duration relationships. We expect ties with our immediate family, **4** and to a lesser extent with other kin, to extend throughout the lifetimes of the people involved. This expectation is by no means always fulfilled, as rising divorce rates and family break-ups indicate. Nevertheless, we still theoretically marry "until death do us part" and the social ideal is a lifetime relationship. Whether this is a proper or realistic expectation in a society of high transience is debatable. The fact remains, however, that family links are expected to be long term, if not lifelong, and considerable guilt attaches to the person who breaks off such a relationship.

5   *Medium-duration relationships.* Four classes of relationships fall within this category. Roughly in order of descending durational expectancies, these are relationships with friends, neighbors, job associates, and co-members of churches, clubs and other voluntary organizations.

6   Friendships are traditionally supposed to survive almost, if not quite, as long as family ties. The culture places high value on "old friends" and a certain amount of blame attaches to dropping a friendship. One type of friendship relationship, however, acquaintanceship, is recognized as less durable.

7   Neighbor relationships are no longer regarded as long-term commitments—the rate of geographical turnover is too high. They are expected to last as long as the individual remains in a single location, an interval that is growing shorter and shorter on average. Breaking off with a neighbor may involve other difficulties, but it carries no great burden of guilt.

8   On-the-job relationships frequently overlap friendships, and less often, neighbor relationships. Traditionally, particularly among white-collar, professional and technical people, job relationships were supposed to last a relatively long time. This expectation, however, is also changing rapidly, as we shall see.

9   Co-membership relationships—links with people in church or civic organizations, political parties and the like—sometimes flower into friendship, but until that happens such individual associations are regarded as more perishable than either friendships, ties with neighbors or fellow workers.

10   *Short-duration relationships.* Most, though not all, service relationships fall into this category. These include salesclerks, delivery people, gas station attendants, milkmen, barbers, hairdressers, etc. The turnover among these is relatively rapid and little or no shame attaches to the person who terminates such a relationship. Exceptions to the service patterns are professionals such as physicians, lawyers and accountants, with whom relationships are expected to be somewhat more enduring.

11   This categorization is hardly airtight. Most of us can cite some "service" relationship that has lasted longer than some friendship, job or neighbor relationship. Moreover, most of us can cite a number of quite long-lasting relationships in our own lives—perhaps we have been going to the same doctor for years or have maintained extremely close ties with a college friend. Such cases are hardly unusual, but they are relatively few in number in our lives. They are like long-stemmed flowers towering above a field of grass in which each blade represents a short-term relationship, a transient contact. It is the very durability of these ties that makes them noticeable. Such exceptions do not invalidate the rule. They do not change the net fact that, across the board, the *average* interpersonal relationship in our life is shorter and shorter in duration.

STUDY QUESTIONS

Organization and Content

1 Toffler's main objective is to explain the kind of human society that is likely to develop out of the present one. Transience and speed are the key terms among the influences (especially urban influences) that will produce the society of the future. Explain how Toffler's analysis of human relationships in terms of their duration is connected with his main objective.

2 According to paragraph 2, why is the average length of human relationships shorter now than it used to be?

3 According to paragraph 3, what kind of analysis has Toffler made? To what sort of society does it apply?

4 What is the purpose of paragraph 5?

5 What principle of organization has Toffler used in paragraphs 4–10? What are his main divisions? Where do subdivisions appear? Make an outline (I, A, B, and so on) of paragraphs 4–10.

6 What is the purpose of paragraph 11? Explain the simile in sentence 4. What is the function of Toffler's final sentence?

Sentence Structure

1 By what transitional devices are sentences 1–3 linked?

2 How do the majority of Toffler's sentences begin—with clauses as introductory modifiers, with brief introductory modifiers (phrases or single words), or with the subject?

3 In paragraphs 3 and 4 there are at least six parenthetical elements. Are most of them at the beginning, tucked inside, or at the end of a sentence? Why did Toffler place them where he did?

4 Explain the differences in the functions of the dashes in sentence 1, paragraph 7, sentence 1, paragraph 9, and sentence 3, paragraph 11.

5 In paragraph 10 how has Toffler set up lists of persons in sentences 3 and 5?

6 What terms furnish links among the last four sentences (paragraph 11)? To what word do these terms refer?

Diction

1 Perhaps you should check the meanings of *transitory, temporal* (paragraph 1), *feudal* (2), *transience* (4), and *invalidate* (11).

2 Toffler uses a number of words formed by combinations, such as *built-in* (paragraph 3), *break-ups* (4), *on-the-job, white-collar* (8), and *turnover* (10). Do these words make Toffler's style seem highly colloquial? Are there synonyms for these words that he could have used just as well?

Assignment

1 Toffler's analysis is a general one. Make a similar classification but much more specific, classifying specific individuals you have interacted with, according to the duration of each interaction.
2 Classify dwellings on streets near your home on the basis of their age, style of construction, or size.
3 Analyze the music that you hear in a certain period (perhaps a week) according to a principle that you determine.
4 Analyze the members of your fraternity or sorority according to some principle that is significant.
5 Analyze the different means of gaining knowledge that a student can use, or different types of recreation that are available to a student on your campus.

Lithography

CALVIN TOMKINS

1   Lithography is believed to have been perfected about 1798, by Alois Senefelder, a Bavarian printer, who thought of his invention as a cheap way to print literary and music manuscripts. Senefelder's method was vastly more efficient than any of the others; it soon proved, in addition, to have enormous appeal for artists.

2   Lithography is based on the mutual antipathy of oil and water. In the classic technique, the lithographer draws with a greasy substance on a smoothly ground block of limestone; the stone is moistened with water, which the greasy markings reject; then printer's ink is applied to it, adhering to the greasy, drawn portions and being rejected by the moist, blank portions; a sheet of paper pressed down on the surface absorbs the ink, and the result is a reversed impression of the original drawing on the stone. With subsequent inkings, the process can be repeated through many impressions before the drawing wears out. For an artist, the method offers a great many advantages. No complicated tools or technologies must be mastered: he draws directly on the stone (the word "lithography" comes from the Greek *"lithos,"* or "stone," and *"graphein,"* "to write or draw"), using either a special lithographic crayon or an oily compound called tusche, which he applies with a brush. In fact, if he chooses, he can even make his drawing on lithographic transfer paper, which is then pressed down on the stone, leaving a reversed image—one that is re-reversed to its original state when the stone is printed. (Whistler often used this method.) Lithography

From "The Moods of the Stone" by Calvin Tomkins in *The New Yorker*. Reprinted by permission; © 1976 The New Yorker Magazine, Inc.

enables the artist to achieve tones from the densest black to the most delicate shades of gray, and by using more than one stone he can employ a wide
and subtle range of color. For this reason, lithography is considered the
most painterly of the print techniques. The technical manipulation of the
process—the "cookery" involved in graining the surface of the stone to pre-
pare it for the artist; the etching of the artist's design with a weak acid solution, so that it will last through multiple impressions; the inking of the
stone and the actual job of putting it through the press; and the adjustment
and alteration of the various steps until a proof has been pulled that satisfies
the artist—is all done by a professional printer who is a specialist.

STUDY QUESTIONS
Organization and Content

1   What three significant points are brought out in paragraph 1?
2   In the analysis of lithography how many steps in the process are
    first indicated?
3   What alternative methods are then mentioned?
4   Why is this process of printing drawings advantageous to artists?
5   What role in the process is played by the professional printer of lith-
    ographs?
6   Has Tomkins organized his material in a clear and reasonable way?

Sentence Structure

1   Note that in sentence 1 Tomkins uses the passive voice for a state-
    ment about a general belief. Thus *Senefelder* comes after the verb.
    How does this arrangement affect the main emphasis in the sen-
    tence?
2   How has Tomkins arranged sentence 2 for balance and emphasis?
3   By what means does he include so much material in the long sen-
    tence 2 of paragraph 2?
4   How and why does he introduce a bit of etymology where he does?
5   What transitional elements appear in paragraph 2, sentences 6 and
    9?
6   What material does Tomkins place between dashes in the last sen-
    tence? In that sentence what is the subject of *is done*?

Diction

1   Learn the meanings of the roots of *antipathy* (paragraph 2, sen-
    tence 1) and of *sympathy*.
2   Tomkins uses *impression* in a specialized, technical sense. Look it
    up.

3 What does *painterly* (paragraph 2, sentence 9) mean? In art criticism how does it contrast with *linear*?
4 Explain the meaning of "a proof has been pulled."
5 Is this selection especially difficult because Tomkins has used too many technical terms? Could he have avoided the use of such terms?

Assignment

Analyze a process and explain the steps required. Some suggestions:
1 Making a fish pond.
2 Spraying fruit.
3 Painting a house or a room.
4 Constructing or operating a chicken house.
5 Preparing a flower bed, from the first step to the blooming of the flowers.
6 Developing film into good photographs.
7 Painting a picture either with oil paints or with watercolors.

Results of Exterminating Hawks

BY LAVOISIER LAMAR

1   With the idea of protecting chickens and game birds, the owner of the Crocksville *Weekly Messenger* in the spring of 1933 wrote an editorial urging all farmers in the community to wage a relentless war on what he called "chicken hawks." In the same paper a coalition of social organizations announced that they would contribute twenty-five cents for each dead hawk brought to the town garbage incinerator. During the next ten months the sound of gunfire in the countryside and even in the city became so common that people stopped being conscious of it. Dead hawks poured into the incinerator in a steady stream. Quarter dollars poured out of the Hawk Fund (as it was called) so fast that the bounty had to be reduced to ten cents a hawk. By the spring of 1934 the *Weekly Messenger* could proclaim in big black headlines: ALL HAWKS EXTERMINATED! Poultry farmers who in the past years had lost no more than eight to ten baby chicks each to the raids of hawks cheered this virtuous accomplishment.

2   Meanwhile in meadows, under barns, behind woodpiles, mother rats and mother mice brought into the Crocksville community many thousands of

From *Pattern and Purpose in Writing* by Lavoisier Lamar.

baby rats and baby mice. The same thing happened with rabbits, skunks, squirrels, grass-hoppers, and snakes. In normal years the populations of all these creatures would have been severely reduced by the attacks of hawks, and especially by that variety of hawk known as the chicken hawk. The truth is that chicken hawks rarely eat chickens. Once in a while an individual hawk will learn to kill chickens. In general, however, this type of hawk feeds on rodents and insects.

But from 1933 to 1936 there were no hawks in the Crocksville commu- 3 nity. All of the creatures mentioned above increased in enormous numbers. Rats ate corn in the fields and in the corn cribs; mice raided the pantries in the homes; rabbits devoured vegetable gardens; skunks killed more chickens than hawks had; squirrels seriously reduced the crop of pecans; grasshoppers attacked young plants; and snakes bit cotton pickers. No one would have connected all of these things with the disappearance of hawks if it had not been for an outbreak of typhus fever spread by the fleas on the rats.

When this happened the alarmed community sought help. Health offi- 4 cers and game wardens convinced the leaders of the community that they must not only fight the rats but must also encourage the hawks. It took five years of editorials in the *Weekly Messenger* and many hours of discussion in the corner drugstore. But now, Crocksville people *like* hawks. They even protect them.

STUDY QUESTIONS
Organization and Content

1 What motive did the newspaper owner have for the "war" he encouraged?
2 What two causal factors are mentioned in paragraph 1?
3 What immediate effects did they have? What later effects?
4 In paragraph 2 what other results are we told about?
5 What is the importance of sentence 3 in paragraph 2?
6 What light is thrown on paragraph 1 by paragraph 2, sentences 4–6?
7 Explain the connection, for the cause-effect sequence, among sentences 1, 2, and 3 of paragraph 3.
8 What climactic effect finally occurred?
9 How does paragraph 4 function in the analytical account of the Crocksville situation?
10 This cause-effect sequence is also a series of events in time. Where and how has Lamar made you aware of the time-sequence? From beginning to end how much time elapsed?

Sentence Structure

1   Point out the many transitional connections that Lamar has created in his four paragraphs.
2   Why does he begin so many sentences in paragraphs 1 and 2 with prepositional phrases?
3   What is the effect of repetition and parallelism in paragraph 1, sentences 4 and 5, and of the series of parallel elements in paragraph 2, sentences 1 and 2?
4   Sentence 3 of paragraph 3 is rather long. Explain how it is organized. (Check its relation with paragraph 2.) Does it have a climactic order?
5   Sentence 4, paragraph 3, is a loose sentence, but it has a special effect as we get to the end of it. Explain the effect.
6   Show how balanced elements in paragraph 4, sentences 2 and 3, are effective.
7   Why does Lamar end paragraph 4 with such extremely short sentences? Do they work well? Explain why or why not.

Diction

1   Is *relentless* linguistically related to *Lent* or *violent?*
2   Look up the roots of *incinerator, exterminated, rodents, alarmed.*

Assignment

Lamar's analysis of anti-hawk measures and their results moves from cause to effect, with the result that effects, coming toward the end, receive the main emphasis. Using Lamar's technique, analyze some social or educational situation in terms of causes and effects. For example:

1   What effects come from paying entertainers, athletes, lawyers, physicians, or plumbers such high salaries and fees?
2   From a system of unemployment benefits or of medicare and medicaid payments?
3   From building multi-lane highways?
4   From government controls on rent?
5   From the great increase in the number of college students; or from the great increase in world population?
6   From watching television?
7   From using drugs?
8   From instituting student evaluations of teachers?
9   From poor preparation for college?
10 From having a winning (or losing) football team?
11 From overemphasis on football?

Essential Requirements for Bird Flight

JEAN DORST

I. C. J. Galbraith, trans.

Despite extensive variations birds present a remarkable structural unity, all 1
being built on the same general plan. This unity in diversity is a result of
their common evolution as flying animals. Their most important features
are adaptations to the conquest of the air. Their present success, following
an explosive radiation in the Tertiary, can be explained in terms of this fundamental adaptation. By annual migrations they have been able to exploit
important resources, despite great fluctuations in physical conditions and
the availability of food. Every aspect of their biology, and especially their
ways of obtaining food and raising their young, is profoundly affected by
their ability to move rapidly in all three planes of space.

The acquistion of such highly-specialized powers of locomotion has de- 2
manded modifications to the general vertebrate plan. All other attempts by
vertebrates to master aerial space, such as by the flying reptiles of the Secondary and Tertiary epochs, have miscarried and left no survivors.

The first essential property is lightness. Every anatomical and physiologi- 3
cal feature tending towards useless weight has been suppressed in birds—for
example a chewing structure in the head; the intake of low-energy foods
which take a long time to be digested; the accumulation of food reserves;
and viviparous reproduction. Every part, even the bones, is lightened to the
limit. Thus the specific gravity of a duck, a "heavy" bird, is only 0.6,
whereas that of most vertebrates is about 1.0.

The second property is streamlining. Birds must be able to slip through 4
the air offering the least possible resistance. Every projection is suppressed.
The legs can be retracted into the plumage, like the undercarriage of a modern aeroplane, or stretched out horizontally. The head, neck and body are
shaped to part the air and ensure a smooth airflow. The muscular and visceral masses are concentrated near the centre of gravity of the whole animal,
while the propulsive organs are lightened so as to reduce the energy wasted
on inertia when they move.

The third property is strength. A bird travels through a fluid which pro- 5
vides no effective buoyancy. A fish needs to use its muscles only for propulsion, since its weight is balanced by that of the water in which it floats
without effort. A bird on the other hand must work, not only to move
forward but to keep itself airborne. It must therefore have strong and effi-

From *The Life of Birds, Vol. I,* by Jean Dorst. Columbia University Press.

cient muscles attached to a rigid skeleton. The rigidity of the skeleton, the strength of the musculature, and the lightness of the flying surfaces made up of feathers, combine to satisfy this demand.

6   Most quadrupeds, whether reptiles or mammals, move on all four limbs, so that they are supported in the same way during movement as when at rest. In contrast a bird is supported in flight by its wings, and hence by its thoracic cage, whereas when resting support comes from the legs to the pelvic girdle. The distribution of weight is different in the two configurations, and the layout of the skeletal and muscular support must be able to meet both situations.

7   The last property is the possession of an "engine" capable of powering the mechanism. This must work at high efficiency in order to convert energy without introducing useless weight. The circulatory, respiratory, and digestive systems of birds are remarkably efficient, with a high performance, and a bird's metabolic rate is always very high.

STUDY QUESTIONS

Organization and Content

1   Though birds do show many differences of shape and behavior, from hummingbirds to eagles, for example, why do they have so much sameness of structure?

2   In paragraph 2 Dorst reminds us that birds are vertebrates though their evolution demanded ''modifications to the general vertebrate plan.'' Why is this information necessary to his exposition? What is the function of the very brief paragraph 2?

3   In paragraph 3, sentence 2, notice the enumeration. What is the purpose of the list?

4   According to Dorst, why do birds lay eggs?

5   How does Dorst develop paragraph 4?

6   Why do birds have to have such strong muscles?

7   What special difference between birds and four-footed animals does Dorst point out in paragraph 6?

8   What does Dorst mean by the ''engine'' of a bird? Why does he place ''engine'' in quotation marks?

9   Make a two-level outline of this analysis.

Sentence Structure

1   Note similar sentence pattern in paragraph 1, sentences 2–4; paragraph 2, sentence 1; paragraph 3, sentence 1; paragraph 4, sentences 1–5; and numerous other sentences. Why do you think this sentence pattern appears so often?

2   Sentences 5 and 6, paragraph 1, have a similar basic structure.

What grammatical element lacking in sentence 5 does sentence 6 have?

3   In paragraph 3, sentence 2, how is the list of items introduced, and how are the items separated?

4   In paragraph 5, sentence 4, how does Dorst bring out a contrast? What other transitional term appears in the next sentence?

5   Point out parallel structure in paragraph 5, sentence 6.

Diction

1   You may need to look up *fluctuations* (paragraph 1), *viviparous* (3), *visceral* (4), *metabolic* (7).

2   How long ago was the Tertiary epoch?

3   *Radiation* (paragraph 1) is an example of a word used in a somewhat technical sense by a biologist. What do you understand "explosive radiation" to mean in paragraph 1? Could a writer just as well use *chest* as *thoracic cage*? Are both terms really metaphors?

Assignment

1   Analyze the qualifications necessary in a person who wishes to win scholastic honors; win athletic honors; be a leader in student organizations; succeed in a particular area such as mathematics, literature, science, engineering; or be an effective minister or priest.

2   Analyze some kind of work, such as studying, showing the essential activities that a person must perform in order to study effectively; or the basic operations involved in preparing a meal, planting a tree, or making a garden.

3   Assume that you are a city planner or a person about to run for political office, and make an analysis of the essential needs of your community.

The Work of the Manager

PETER F. DRUCKER

1   Every manager does many things that are not managing. He may spend most of his time on them. A sales manager makes a statistical analysis or placates an important customer. A foreman repairs a tool or fills in a production report. A manufacturing manager designs a new plant layout or tests new materials. A company president works through the details of a bank loan or negotiates a big contract—or spends dreary hours presiding at a dinner in honor of long-service employees. All these things pertain to a particular function. All are necessary, and have to be done well.

2   But they are apart from that work which every manager does whatever his function or activity, whatever his rank and position, work which is common to all managers and peculiar to them. The best proof is that we can apply to the job of the manager the systematic analysis of Scientific Management. We can isolate that which a man does because he is a manager. We can divide it into the basic constituent operations. And a man can improve his performance as a manager by improving his performance of these constituent motions.

3   There are five such basic operations in the work of the manager. Together they result in the integration of resources into a living and growing organism.

4   A manager, in the first place, *sets objectives*. He determines what the objectives should be. He determines what the goals in each area of objectives should be. He decides what has to be done to reach these objectives. He makes the objectives effective by communicating them to the people whose performance is needed to attain them.

5   Secondly, a manager *organizes*. He analyzes the activities, decisions and relations needed. He classifies the work. He divides it into manageable activities. He further divides the activities into manageable jobs. He groups these units and jobs into an organization structure. He selects people for the management of these units and for the jobs to be done.

6   Next a manager *motivates and communicates*. He makes a team out of the people that are responsible for various jobs. He does that through the practices with which he manages. He does it in his own relation to the men he manages. He does it through incentives and rewards for successful work. He does it through his promotion policy. And he does it through constant communication, both from the manager to his subordinate, and from the subordinate to the manager.

7   The fourth basic element in the work of the manager is *the job of measure-*

Pp. 343–344 from *The Practice of Management* by Peter F. Drucker. Copyright, 1954, by Peter F. Drucker. Reprinted by permission of Harper & Row, Publishers, Inc.

ment. The manager establishes measuring yardsticks—and there are few factors as important to the performance of the organization and of every man in it. He sees to it that each man in the organization has measurements available to him which are focused on the performance of the whole organization and which at the same time focus on the work of the individual and help him do it. He analyzes performance, appraises it and interprets it. And again, as in every other area of his work, he communicates both the meaning of the measurements and their findings to his subordinates as well as to his superiors.

Finally, a manager *develops people.* Through the way he manages he makes **8** it easy or difficult for them to develop themselves. He directs people or misdirects them. He brings out what is in them or he stifles them. He strengthens their integrity or he corrupts them. He trains them to stand upright and strong or he deforms them.

Every manager does these things when he manages—whether he knows it **9** or not. He may do them well, or he may do them wretchedly. But he always does them.

STUDY QUESTIONS
Organization and Content

1 What is the purpose of paragraph 1? What is its topic sentence? How many examples support the topic idea? Why does Drucker begin the last two sentences with the emphatic *All?*

2 What signal tells us that paragraph 2 contrasts with paragraph 1? What is the basis of the contrast? How does Drucker define "analysis of Scientific Management"?

3 Why is paragraph 3 so short? What do paragraphs 4–8 have in common? What purpose does paragraph 9 serve, and why is it so short?

4 Explain in one sentence the pattern of Drucker's discussion of the work of the manager.

5 With what terms has Drucker enumerated the parts of his analysis? How has he emphasized the key terms of his explanation?

6 Paragraph 8 introduces an aspect of the manager's work not mentioned in the other paragraphs. What is it? Why include it in paragraph 8?

Sentence Structure

1 A large majority of Drucker's sentences belong to one of three types. Are most of his sentences simple, compound, or complex?

2 How many sentences belong to the subject-verb-complement type?

3 What do the answers to these two questions indicate about Drucker's style of writing?

4   By what method of transition does Drucker link most of his sentences?
5   Would you call Drucker's style of writing formal or colloquial? Compare it with the style of See, Defoe, and Maraini.

Diction

1   Look up *constituent, integration, organism, determines, incentives, integrity.*
2   What is the relation between *constituent* and *constitution, integration* and *integrity, determines* and *terminal?*
3   Is there a difference between *incentives* and *rewards?*
4   Is Drucker's vocabulary difficult to understand? Is it mainly abstract or concrete? Is there any relation between the vocabulary and the sentence style?

Assignment

Write a short theme in which you analyze the "basic constituent operations" of—for example—a teacher, a student, a housewife, a soldier, a salesperson, a police officer, a cook, a bus driver, a minister, or a priest.

Mistakes Engineers Make

SAMUEL C. FLORMAN

1   Since technology cannot be abandoned, the next logical step is to see what can be done to avoid repetition of technological mistakes that have been made in the past. Toward this end, let us consider the types of mistakes that engineers have made, and the reasons for them.

2   First, there are the mistakes that have been made by carelessness or error in calculation. Occasionally a decimal point is misplaced, the mistake is not picked up on review, and a structure collapses or a machine explodes. Human error. It happens rarely, and much less frequently now than in times past.

3   More often, failure results from lack of imagination. The Quebec Bridge collapsed while under construction in 1907 because large steel members under compression behaved differently than the smaller members that had

Pp. 32–33 from *The Existential Pleasures of Engineering* by Samuel C. Florman, St. Martin's Press, Inc.

been tested time and again. The Tacoma Narrows Bridge failed in 1940 because the dynamic effect of wind load was not taken into account. Although designed to withstand a static wind load of fifty pounds per square foot, the bridge was destroyed by harmonic oscillations resulting from a wind pressure of a mere five pounds per square foot. We do not have to be too concerned about bridge failures anymore. (In 1869 American bridges were failing at the rate of 25 or more annually!) But the problem of reasoning from small to large, and from static to dynamic, is symbolic of the difficulties we face in designing anything in a complex, interdependent, technological society. The Aswan Dam is an example. As a structure it is a success. But in its effect on the ecology of the Nile Basin—most of which could have been predicted—it is a failure.

Finally, there are the mistakes that result from pure and absolute igno-   4
rance. We use asbestos to fireproof steel, with no way of knowing that it is any more dangerous to health than cement or gypsum or a dozen other common materials. Years later, we find that the workers who handled it are developing cancer.

Human error, lack of imagination, and blind ignorance. The practice of   5
engineering is in large measure a continuing struggle to avoid making mistakes for these reasons.

STUDY QUESTIONS

Organization and Content

1 Is this an analysis by division or by classification?
2 What is the purpose of paragraph 1?
3 How many types of engineering errors does Florman point out? Name them.
4 How does he develop paragraphs 2–4? Why is paragraph 3 more fully developed than the other paragraphs?
5 How does paragraph 5 relate to paragraph 1?

Sentence Structure

1 From the way paragraph 1, sentence 1, is constructed, what do you think Florman was discussing in his preceding sentence?
2 In paragraph 2, sentence 3 is incomplete. What does it lack? Is Florman doing the same thing at the beginning of paragraph 5?
3 Point out advantages of using parallel structures in paragraph 2, sentence 1; paragraph 3, sentence 7; paragraph 4, sentence 1.
4 Indicate parallel patterns in paragraph 3, sentences 9 and 10. Indicate also the contrast between them and the suitable emphasis in both.

Diction

1 If you need to, look up *dynamic, harmonic oscillations, ecology* (paragraph 3).
2 What do *pure* and *absolute* mean (4)?
3 Is Florman's vocabulary more, or less, difficult to understand than Dorst's or Drucker's?

Assignment

1 Analyze the abilities and performance of the best student you know, and explain in three or four paragraphs why he does so well. Be sure to use specific examples to show just how this student arranges and conducts his life.
2 Treat in the same way the poorest student you know.
3 Have you ever failed in some undertaking? If you have, analyze the reasons for your failure.

Typical Day-Time Activities in "Eastville"

ELENA PADILLA

1   In New York City on Manhattan Island there is a neighborhood which we shall call Eastville. It is a slum, and as in many another slum of urban America, the people who live there can trace their ancestry, recent or remote, to all the four corners of the earth. But in Eastville many are newcomers not only to this city, but also to this country. This makes the neighborhood distinctive. Among these are large numbers of Puerto Ricans. . . .

2   Eastville is more than just a place where people live. It is like a community where people find much of their social life, have many of their friends, where their churches and a large number of business enterprises in which they can buy the things they need are located. . . . The people of Eastville nonetheless must leave the neighborhood for many of the essentials of life. They have to seek work outside it, frequently in Brooklyn, the Bronx, and Long Island, for the few small factories and the businesses in and around the neighborhood provide very little employment for its residents. While grammar and junior high school children attend school in or near the neighborhood, high school students have to travel by subway or bus to distant points in the city for their education. . . .

3   The street-life of Eastvillers follows distinctive and routine patterns. From

From *Up from Puerto Rico.* N.Y.: Columbia University Press, 1958.

dawn or before, regardless of the weather, a stream of young and middle-aged adult men and women carrying lunch boxes can be seen walking quickly out of the neighborhood on their way to work. This stream continues until eight or eight-thirty. The people go either in groups of two or three, or individually. Among those who pass through Second Street, some stop at Mrs. Penny's newspaper stand, which is improvised out of an empty wooden grocery box. She sells the *Mirror,* the *News* and *El Diario de Nueva York.* Mrs. Penny hands a paper to a customer who pays her for it and continues on his way. Apparently she makes no error as to who reads what. Occasionally she asks about a sick child, or something else pertaining to the customer, who, while walking away, briefly replies. Mrs. Penny's business practices are not unusual for Eastville, for, with the exception of the large supermarket, buyer and storekeeper are involved in a more than business relationship; they are friends and neighbors. The storekeeper knows his customers' tastes and is acquainted with their lives. Both exchange personal questions and information as they transact their business. In addition, the storekeeper provides credit which contributes to making the relationship between him and his patrons one of trust, understanding, and mutual obligation.

After eight or eight-thirty, the children start out to school. Among the teen-age crowds there are various groups. Second-generation Puerto Rican girls, and those who have lived in New York most of their lives, usually go together with boys, either recent migrants, second-generation, or those who migrated as small children. In some of these groups, particularly those in which there are colored Puerto Ricans, are American Negro girls and boys who attend the same schools. These groups are different in composition and overt behavior from those of recent migrants. They speak English among themselves. Their clothes, kind of conversation, and social manners distinguish them from recent migrant children of the same age and social class. They blend into comparable teen-age groups in American society. In winter they wear woolen skirts, socks, long athlete's sweaters with letters, and sports coats and jackets. Only by knowing them and their families personally would one know whether they were Puerto Ricans. Recent migrant girls especially are more noticeable, however. Ordinarily, they walk to school by themselves or in small groups, and are rarely accompanied by boys. They wear cottons and rayons the entire year round, sweaters, and princess or other fitted coats in winter. Also to be seen are the crowds of Italian boys, recently arrived Puerto Rican boys, and American Negro boys. Those who go to school alone, whether boys or girls, are generally the ones who are also seen alone on other occasions, or in the company of their brothers, sisters, or parents, but seldom with friends. In Eastville friends are considered by some as sources of evil, and a significant sector of Eastville life has to do with protection of oneself and of those one loves from becoming "bad."

5   Junior high school children follow a somewhat different pattern: among these the groups are formed by children of the same sex. Girls and boys are seldom seen together unless they are brothers and sisters. The Puerto Rican girls especially are accompanied by other Puerto Rican girls, or else by their brothers. This is particularly true of those who have arrived recently, and seldom does one see such a girl with one who has been born or brought up in New York, unless she is the daughter of a relative or friend with whom the parents maintain a close social relationship.

6   Of children attending grammar school, the youngest, who are starting their first year, are accompanied by an adult, older brothers or sisters, or older children known to the parents. The older boys and girls who do not have to be taken care of in the street, or who do not have to look after younger children, go by themselves or in small groups of two or three, boys and girls not mixing. Among recently arrived Puerto Ricans one sees many of the nonemployed mothers accompanying their daughters to grammar school regardless of the girls' age. Some of these mothers then stand by the school buildings while the classes are in session, others go away, returning to pick up the children when the classes are dismissed. These parents regard their presence as necessary to protect their daughters from men and boys, to prevent other children from beating them up, and to protect the younger children from the added hazard of traffic accidents.

7   After the school crowd has gone in the morning, housewives emerge into the streets, some to undertake the shopping for the day, some "to catch the sun," others "just to breathe." Those receiving welfare aid remain upstairs on the days the investigator is expected. From this time of morning until one o'clock in the afternoon the bets on the numbers are also placed, on the sidewalk, in the stores, and on the stoops.

8   At noon the children start coming home from school. Even those who have had lunch at school return to their block. Some of those who attend morning classes in double-session schools then commence their play in the alleys and the streets with people of various ages. In Eastville groups of playmates at times involve children of six to adults of nineteen or twenty who, during warm weather, play together such games as baseball, punch ball, and handball. In games requiring teamwork, ethnic barriers do not operate, particularly for those who speak English. One also sees horseplay in the street among groups of children of more or less the same age. Peer groups, however, may range from children in middle childhood to teenagers and young adults. Grammar school boys also play other seasonal games—top spinning during June and marbles in the early spring. Teenagers visit the candy stores where they listen to their favorite tunes. One may see a conversation among eight or ten adolescents broken off suddenly by the movement of all of them into the candy store where someone has dropped a nickel in the jukebox to play a rock 'n' roll tune, such as *The Ship*

of Love, Sexy Ways, or *Good Night, Good Night Sweetheart,* which rated high with Eastville youth. Recent migrant girls from Puerto Rico are seldom seen in these groups or even standing on the sidewalks or stoops by themselves. Rather, they are at home.

In the afternoon the street is also a place of recreation for adult men and recent migrant boys. Various groups sit here and there over a game of checkers, cards, or dominoes. The corner of Second Street, for instance, is a spot where young American Negro men stand watching passers-by and a game of checkers in which American Negro players participate. On Fifth Street there is a spot next to an alley where Puerto Rican men play cards or dominoes. Down Avenue B a group of old Italian men play checkers next to a restaurant, where one can see aged Italian immigrants meeting for coffee. Other games also run on during these hours of the day and beyond: for example, in some bodegas—Puerto Rican grocery stores—games of dominoes are played continuously for hours and hours, even late into the night. Then there are the illegal gambling hideouts from which the public is barred.

After three o'clock in the afternoon one rarely sees an adult woman in the street. By this time cooking for the evening meal has started, and most children are out of school. The streets then are flooded with children of all ages, playing, singing, and shouting, while some, however, just gaze longingly from their windows at the streets and alleys below. Employed men and women also start returning to the neighborhood, and many take a bit of time to stop and chat for a short while in the street. By six or seven o'clock in the evening, dinner over, mothers and housewives are again on the sidewalks, perched perhaps on top of garbage can covers, chatting with neighbors who have also come down to watch the children. It is not uncommon to see a number of small Puerto Rican, American Negro, and other children, two or three years old, all being cared for by a five- or six-year-old girl of any ethnic group. On the other hand, one may also see a number of children whose mothers maintain a close watch to prevent children of other ethnic groups from playing with them and who warn them not to play with "Puerto Ricans" or "Italians" or "Negroes" because these are "bad" and will harm them. As night falls, particularly during summer, one of the avenues of Eastville is so jammed with people of all ages, including babies in carriages, that it is very difficult to walk there at all. Even at midnight on a summer night the stores of Eastville are open, the jukeboxes are blaring loudly, the men are gambling and chatting in the social and athletic clubs, cars drive by, children play and sing, men and women and whole families sit on stoops telling stories and drinking soda pop. North of Fifth and south of First Street, Eastville fades. Beyond its borders there are no crowds in the streets, and the whole tone of life—day and night—conditions, and standards of living are different.

STUDY QUESTIONS
Organization and Content

1   How long an introduction does Padilla have before she begins her analysis?
2   In analyzing her material, what principle or principles of organizaton has she used?
3   What point is brought out by the part about Mrs. Penny in paragraph 3?
4   Into what groups does Padilla divide school children in paragraph 4?
5   Point out the details with which she supports the idea in paragraph 4, sentence 5.
6   What contrast is indicated in paragraph 4, sentences 11–13?
7   What things do the ''Eastville'' parents do to protect their children?
8   What recreational activities do the people of ''Eastville'' engage in?
9   The final paragraph is the longest. Into what subdivisions would you divide it?
10 Make a two-level outline of the analysis.

Sentence Structure

1   Notice that sentence 1, paragraph 1, opens with phrasal modifiers, and thus the *there is* construction allows the first clause to end with *neighborhood*. Explain how this structure affects the emphasis at the end of the whole sentence.
2   In sentence 2 where are the interruptive modifiers placed?
3   Why does sentence 3 begin with *but*? What parts of sentence 3 are in balance? What contrast is indicated by the balanced parts? By what means does Padilla throw strong emphasis on *country*?
4   Is there enough sentence variety in paragraph 1?
5   In paragraph 3, sentence 10, notice how the thought proceeds from the specific to the general. The short clause at the end of the sentence is for what purpose?
6   In paragraph 4 what means of transition leads us into sentence 1? How does Padilla then make a transition to sentence 2? What means of transition links together sentences 6–10?
7   In paragraph 5, sentence 1, what is the purpose of the clause after the colon?
8   Notice the author's smooth handling of six different clauses in paragraph 5, sentence 4. Which of them are dependent clauses?
9   Point out the parallel grammatical structure in paragraph 6, sentences 1–2. What different type of parallel structure do you find in sentence 5?
10 What necessary transition does the author use in paragraph 7, sentence 1?
11 Does paragraph 8 have a sufficient variety of sentence structure?

12   What are the functions of the colon and the dashes in paragraph 9, sentence 6?

13   In paragraph 10, sentence 5, note the reduced predication of *dinner over*, and the participial phrases at the end. How are the two interrupters worked into sentence 8?

14 · How does Padilla succeed in including so many details in sentence 9? What is the effect of this sentence? What contrasting effect do the last two sentences give?

Diction

1   In paragraphs 1 and 3 Padilla uses *distinctive*. Does it have a different meaning from *distinct* and *distinguished*?

2   In paragraph 8 what sort of barriers are *ethnic* barriers, and what sort of groups are *peer* groups?

3   What is the origin, and what is the literal meaning, of *adolescents* (8)?

4   Which verbs do you think are most effective in paragraph 10?

Assignment

One can observe the activities of many groups of people in different settings. Like Padilla, you might analyze daytime activities on certain blocks or along certain streets of a town; activities of guests at a big party; members of a family at a family reunion or big family dinner; children on a playground; or people at a camp or a beach.

Raymond Chandler's Characters

FRANK MacSHANE

Nearly all his early stories adhere to certain conventions. The private detective is not employed to unravel a mystery or reveal the murderer of the corpse that appears on page one, as in the tales of ratiocination so popular in England. Chandler's detectives become immediately involved in an active world of crime and have to steer a tricky course between the criminals and the police (who are sometimes the same) as well as be circumspect about the women. Chandler experimented with a number of detectives before he settled on Marlowe. Some of the stories are told through an anonymous first person; some are characters observed by the omniscient author. But whether named or not, John Dalmas, Ted Carmady, Johnny DeRuse, Pete Anglish, and Sam Delaguerra are all tough, independent men, aware that society has gone wrong, who try to deflect the corruption a little bit by saving one or two innocent people, usually women who are being blackmailed. The type is set in the first story: "The man in the powder-blue suit—which wasn't powder-blue under the lights of the Club Bolivar—was tall, with wide-set gray eyes, a thin nose, a jaw of stone. He had a rather sensitive mouth. His hair was crisp and black, ever so faintly touched with gray, as by an almost diffident hand. His clothes fitted him as though they had a soul of their own, not just a doubtful past. His name happened to be Mallory."

2   In Chandler's work the private detective is usually disliked, or at most tolerated, by the police. His very existence is an implied criticism of their incompetence, corruption, or both. The "private eye" as portrayed by Chandler is a fictional hero in the central tradition of American literature. Like so many rebellious and individualistic characters in the novels of Hawthorne, Melville, Cooper, and Mark Twain, he lives by his own code of morality and is at odds with prevailing standards of behavior. The Robin Hood tradition is one of the oldest in all fiction, and its popularity rests on the skeptical view most people have of human institutions.

3   On the other hand, the detective is not the most important character in Chandler's early work. He is there mainly as narrator and as someone through whom other, far more interesting characters may be seen. These cover the whole range of society, far more so than in the ordinary story that has a fixed setting and class of people. The gangsters range from brutal thugs to polished sophisticates. Those who do the kicking and gouging, the pistol whipping, torturing, and blackjack sapping are usually ignorant hulks with picturesque names like Moose Magoon and Big Chin Lorentz. Mentally deficient, they just follow orders, but Chandler recognizes their humanity. In "Mandarin's Jade" one of the gangsters comes to a bad end, and the detective comments: "He wasn't funny any more or tough, or nasty. He was just a poor simple dead guy who had never known what it was all about."

4   The men who hire these hoodlums generally live in the shadowy middle world of crime. They sell pornography or drugs, are gamblers or fake spiritualists; they run doubtful clinics or crooked veterinary hospitals. A large number are nightclub operators or owners. As heir to the speakeasy of Prohibition, the nightclub is a natural arena for Chandler's dramas. It is a place where night is turned into day and where people reveal the undersides of their nature. People from all levels of society mingle there. Chandler's nightclub proprietors vary in elegance and style: some are fairly squalid; others are too clever to get their hands dirty. Most of them are typed, wearing dinner jackets and dark glasses, with a pistol in the desk drawer in the

back office. Most of them are Italian or Mexican with names like Zapparty, Benny Cyrano, and Canales. Although they give orders to the hoodlums and goon squads, they are really not much above them. They are caught in the middle like Soukesian in "Mandarin's Jade," who "looked like a man who had something to do he didn't relish, but was going to do it all the same."

The police have a similar hierarchy. The tough cops may be honest or dis- 5 honest, but all rely equally on force to get what they want. Above them there are some hard-working chief inspectors and detectives, but there are also others, usually with ambition, who become as corrupt as the crooks, making deals for their own advantage. At this point, the corruption is mainly personal. Above comes the level of politics, which, like everything else in Chandler's world, has both its legal and illegal aspects. In "Finger Man" the murder is arranged by a political manipulator, Frank Dorr, who peddles influence and lives off graft from gamblers and others on the fringe of legitimate society. "Politics—even when it's a lot of fun—is tough on the nerves," Dorr says. "You know me. I'm tough and I get what I want. There ain't a hell of a lot I want any more, but what I want—I want bad. And ain't so damn particular how I get it." In another story, "Spanish Blood," the criminal turns out to be the police commissioner, but there is nothing to be done about it. "Downtown," the detective explains, "they like it the way it is. It's swell politics." Though rarely so overt, Chandler's cynicism about society is a pervasive element in his stories. All a decent man has is his individual code of honor. As for society, it offers little to cheer about. At the end of "Smart-Aleck Kill" the detective and the police captain are sitting together. "What'll we drink to?" asks the captain. "Let's just drink," answers the detective.

But Chandler is not interested so much in social justice as in people, even 6 if, like the women, they play somewhat conventional roles. Since there can be no real romance between the detective and the women of the story, because the detective must remain professionally apart and personally uninvolved, the women are mainly decorative. Most of them are beautiful and glamorous, tall, willowy blondes or girls, like Rhonda Farr in "Blackmailers Don't Shoot," with the telltale "eyes of cornflower blue" and "the sort of skin an old rake dreams of"—a phrase lifted incidentally (and probably unconsciously) from his prewar story about the London duchess who had "such skin as an old roué dreams of on his deathbed." Most of these girls require protection: they have got caught up in somebody else's troubles and are victims. "She was just a nice girl in a jam—and she didn't even know she was in a jam," says Marlowe in "Red Wind." Some of the girls are just drifters. Francine Ley, for example, is mixed up with a lot of marginal characters, and although not mischievous herself, she picks up their habits. She is amoral, a pretty girl who is playing with fire and doesn't know how to act. Others are sentimental and warm-hearted, but almost all of them are infected by the atmosphere of crime in which they live. In this cat-and-mouse world they are always afraid, for they are caught up in the drama as much as the men are. The detective helps wherever possible. In "Pickup on Noon Street" he finds the innocent girl he had been looking for everywhere, and when they meet, "the girl stared back at him. Slowly all the fear went out of her face."

7   Chandler is enough of a feminist to allow some of his women to be crooks, and no one is tougher than Carol Donovan in "Goldfish." She is "a very pretty black-haired, grey-eyed girl" and carries a .32. Even her partner in crime says, "She's too damn rough, Marlowe. I've seen hard women, but she's the bluing on armor plate." Finally, there is the pert, capable kind of girl who doesn't need help but needs love instead. Carol Pride is such a girl, with "a tired, pretty little face under fluffed-out brown hair, a rather narrow forehead with more height than is considered elegant, a small inquisitive nose, an upper lip a shade too long and a mouth more than a shade too wide. Her eyes could be very blue if they tried. She looked quiet, but not mousy-quiet. She looked smart, but not Hollywood smart."

8   Chandler's characters are really not fully developed in these stories. His avoidance of type figures makes his people seem real, but there are too many characters in each story for any one to be especially memorable. Many are vivid enough, however, to give the impression that they seem to be trying to grow.

STUDY QUESTIONS
Organization and Content

1   Make a two-level outline of this analysis.
2   Is there a thesis sentence in this selection?
3   What different kinds of Chandler's characters does MacShane discuss?
4   According to MacShane, Chandler's detectives resemble what American fictional characters rather than what British characters?
5   Why are Chandler's detectives likely to be less interesting than other characters in his stories?
6   How does Chandler generally present the police? What is their attitude toward the Chandler detective?
7   What do the quotations at the end of paragraphs 1, 3, 5, and 6 illustrate?
8   Why are Chandler's women characters "mainly decorative"? Enumerate the types into which MacShane divides them.
9   What principle of organization does MacShane use in writing this analysis?
10   Does MacShane develop his paragraphs with enough details to give support to his ideas?

Sentence Structure

1 To what extent does MacShane use elements of parallel structure in the sentences of paragraphs 1 and 3? Does he use fewer elements of this kind in paragraphs 4 and 5?
2 Indicate the ways in which MacShane brings out comparisons and contrasts.
3 What transitional devices does he use at the beginnings of sentence 1, paragraphs 3 and 6?
4 Note how he manages dependent clauses. At what points in the sentences do they occur? Are there too many *who*-clauses?
5 Does MacShane get good variety of sentence length and structure in each paragraph? Do too many of his sentences begin with the subject?

Diction

1 Look up *ratiocination* (paragraph 1), *sophisticates* (3), *diffident* (4), *goon, cynicism* (5), *overt* (6), *amoral* (7).
2 What are the meanings of the roots of *circumspect, omniscient* (1), *pornography* (4), and *hierarchy* (5)?
3 Explain "Robin Hood tradition" in paragraph 2.
4 Do you find that Chandler's adjectives in the quotations of paragraphs 1 and 7 have good descriptive power? Which ones are most effective?

Assignment

1 Analyze the characters who appear in a continuing television show of the crime-police-detective type or of the "soap opera" type.
2 Looking upon a baseball or football game as a drama or pageant, analyze the characters and groups of characters who constitute the huge display.
3 Looking upon your town as a continuing drama, analyze the characters who play parts in it on the basis of political power, wealth, family, culture, and so on.

Reasons for Blacks' Lack of Success

WHITNEY M. YOUNG, JR.

1   Few white Americans understand the depth of the hostility black people face, or the sheer effort blacks have had to make simply to survive. Other groups have met with discrimination but no other minority, with the exception of the American Indian, has been so totally relegated to the farthest corners of American life.

2   One of the questions most often asked is "We made it, why can't they?" Nearly every nationality group in the American melting pot cherishes a newly won middle-class status, erecting myths of the perseverance of immigrant ancestors who, unaided, wrested wealth and respectability from an America willing to reward hard work. "Negroes must be lazy," many whites conclude; "black people want it handed to them on a platter, while we had to work for what we got."

3   No, Negroes aren't lazy. Black men worked and died building America. They worked from sunup to sundown in the fields of the South while their white masters sipped mint juleps in the shade. They built the railroads of the South, and everywhere did the dirty work in the hardest jobs—jobs that white people considered beneath them. Even today, black people perform the grueling stoop labor on the farm, the pick-axe laboring work in the cities. They do the housework and the laundry, and fill a host of other insecure, ill-paid jobs white people won't touch. When Ford and the other auto-makers announced that they would hire 6,500 unemployed workers for factory jobs, 14,000 blacks lined up in front of the unemployment offices before they opened. No, blacks aren't lazy; and if they have learned anything from their experience in America, it is that no one will hand them anything on a platter.

4   But blacks haven't "made it," while other groups have, and the reasons are no less real for being complex.

5   The great waves of immigrants reached these shores at a time when America was underpopulated and the virgin lands of the West were still open to settlement. Land agents plastered Europe with recruiting posters to attract settlers. When the immigrants arrived here, the government turned over to them tracts of fertile land, provided them with low-cost loans to buy equipment, and then taught them how to cultivate their land.

6   Those who stayed in the cities found laboring jobs plentiful. All that was

needed here were a strong back and a willing mind. Men could go into business: there was room for a host of small enterprises servicing the ethnic community. Of course, they met with discrimination, but they could still get jobs at decent pay, and as their numbers increased prejudice gave way to grudging tolerance, and finally to acceptance.

Immigrant groups found ethnic communities already established, which **7** had institutions that helped them to adjust. Jewish immigrants from Eastern Europe found a well-established Jewish community, which included many rich individuals and a tradition of philanthropy. Irish and Italian immigrants were helped by the Catholic church and Catholic relief agencies.

Those who settled in the cities quickly became a political force, catered to **8** and serviced by the big-city political machines. The traditional Christmas basket was just one of a whole range of services that included jobs, recreational facilities for children, and help in dealing with landlords and city agencies. Eventually some of these groups, such as the Irish in Boston, took over the city government from the hostile Yankee patricians.

And it didn't happen overnight. The immigrant father didn't throw away **9** his shovel to work in his son's law office. It took several generations of slow but steady advancement. Children left ethnic enclaves, and their children went on to college. Some changed their names, but all found that they had the choice of remaining hyphenated Americans or of melting into the landscape of white America, virtually indistinguishable from their neighbors. The war and the postwar economic boom catapulted most ethnic groups into middle-class prosperity and full acceptance.

But the black American, who was here before the *Mayflower,* was left behind. **10**

When boatloads of European immigrants were being settled on fertile **11** lands in the expanding West, the black man was tied to the Southern soil in a state of peonage. Legally free, he was in fact as enslaved as ever. Those in the cities saw the few jobs open to them disappear as white employers preferred whites. Even before the Civil War, Frederick Douglass was moved to write of free Negroes in the North: "Every hour sees us elbowed out of some employment, to make room perhaps for some newly arrived immigrants, whose hunger and color are thought to give them a title to especial favor."

Slavery left black people without the strong family structure immigrants **12** found so vital. Black men saw their wives sold, and black mothers lost their children on the auction block. While tightly knit European families were working together, black people were just beginning to build the institution of the family.

By the time black people became immigrants themselves, moving north- **13** ward to settle in the cities, they found a totally different economic environment. Strong backs were no longer needed—machines did the heavy work. Job requirements changed: education was the key to economic success and the schools of the South had been geared to providing farm laborers, not engineers or scientists.

14   The black man was caught in a technological revolution. The unskilled labor, which gave other groups an economic foothold, was no longer needed, and the highly paid skilled trades were locked up tight behind a WHITES ONLY sign. The small businesses, the economic lifeline of other groups, became outmoded in an age of chain stores and shopping centers. The political machines, which helped sustain other groups with jobs and favors, were largely rendered powerless by reform government and civil service. Poor education and prejudice kept blacks out of the white-collar office jobs which were the new stronghold of the emerging middle classes.

15   But the black migrant differed from his predecessors in the city in yet another, more crucial way. He was black. The black man could not change the color of his skin and melt into the white background. He couldn't simply correct an accent or change a name to avoid discrimination. He found himself at the mercy of an economic and social system that excluded all blacks, and there was nothing, absolutely nothing, he could do himself to win an equal chance.

16   Whatever grudging concessions the system was willing to make for European immigrants, it absolutely refused to grant them to the black man. The earlier immigrants may have realized that their ten-hour day of ditch-digging or sweatshop labor would not result in riches for themselves, but they had ample evidence that their efforts would pay off for their children. They knew that the system was open-ended and that whatever they scraped together for a son's education would pay off in his freedom, if not their own. The black worker labored as hard, but he knew that he could only hope to bequeath his shovel to his son; he knew the system was closed, and that a black man dared not hope.

17   In the face of this, the real question that should be asked is not "Why haven't Negroes made it?" but "Why have so many Negroes made it?" It is a testimony to the perseverance of black citizens, and to their abiding faith in an America that systematically persecuted them, that so many black people have wrenched a measure of success from their hostile surroundings.

STUDY QUESTIONS

Organization and Content

1   What is the purpose of paragraphs 1 and 2?
2   What is the topic sentence of paragraph 3? What details are given to support the topic idea? What relation does sentence 8 have to paragraph 2?
3   What special function does one-sentence paragraph 4 have? Young says in paragraph 4 that "the reasons" are complex. What method has he chosen for presenting the reasons?

4   List in brief form the conditions under which "other groups" prospered in America. Relate them to the "myth" of the unaided ancestors (paragraph 2).
5   Why is paragraph 10 left undeveloped with only one sentence?
6   How is Young's analysis of conditions in paragraphs 11–16 related to the earlier analysis in paragraphs 5–9? What principle mainly governs the organization of the whole discussion?
7   What makes paragraph 15 seem especially emphatic?
8   Explain the function of paragraph 17. What key word connects it with paragraph 1?
9   As in many discussions that plead for a particular cause, there is an element of propaganda in this selection. In sentences 2–6, paragraph 3, ideas are expressed as if universally true. What exceptions might be made to them? In paragraph 10, how is "here before the *Mayflower*" to be interpreted? What representatives of "the black American" were in America before 1620? How many of them were there, and where were they living?

Sentence Structure

1   Note the variety of sentence structure and rhythm that Young uses. Contrast sentence 2, paragraph 2—a long, loose sentence with varied modifiers after *status*—with sentences 1 and 2, paragraph 3. What pattern is used in sentence 3, paragraph 3?
2   What transitional device connects the sentences of paragraph 3?
3   Contrast sentence 3, paragraph 5, with sentence 2, paragraph 1. How does it compare with sentence 1, paragraph 11, and sentence 1, paragraph 13?
4   What different sentence pattern do you find in sentences 3 and 4, paragraph 6?
5   In what way is the structure of sentence 4, paragraph 16, parallel to that of sentence 2, paragraph 16?

Diction

1   If you need to, look up *hostility, relegated* (paragraph 1), *wrested* (2), *patricians* (8), *indistinguishable* (9), *peonage* (11), *crucial* (15).
2   What is meant by *middle-class status* (paragraph 2), *ethnic community* (6), *ethnic enclaves* (9)?
3   What connotations are produced by "catered to and serviced by the big-city political machines"? Give an example of such a machine.

Assignment

1   Analyze the situation of some other specific group in America, and show, as Young did, the reasons for their comparative success or lack of success.

2   Analyze the condition of a church in a specific community, demonstrating the reasons for its condition.
3   Analyze the situation of fraternities or sororities on your campus. Is it favorable or unfavorable? What causes have created this situation?
4   Analyze your own (or your family's) success or lack of success.
5   Analyze the success or lack of success of the South or of the Northeast; of the small farmer or small business man; of criminals (*vs.* police); or of children in a typical school.

Levels of Taste in Art

FRANK SEIBERLING

1   We may designate three broad levels of taste in art—the popular taste, the cultivated taste, and the uncultivated taste.

2   In the sweep of history, popular art is known as folk art. It has roots in the dance, in song, and in the crafts, with occasional ventures into painting and sculpture. It is characterized by a vivid sense of form which may be quite simple or quite intricate though not intellectually complex. In music, its content ranges from the melancholy ballad to the gay harvest song, and although fundamental in the sense of touching feelings which are common to mankind, folk art is emotionally uncomplicated. Small wonder that in a sophisticated age like ours, with its many insecurities and tensions, people with cultivated taste are turning back to the simple but strongly felt emotions and the appealingly clear and simple forms of folk art. It is a very interesting sign of our times that two important folk art museums should recently have opened in this country. For folk art as such is directly functional only to those for whom it was intended, and to put it in a museum is immediately to recognize the immense gap in the ways of life of its creators and those who collect it. The number of collectors must be small indeed who can wear a folk costume unself-consciously, or even sing a ballad without feeling its remoteness. Yet the simplicity and emotional directness of these folk expressions have a powerful appeal.

3   It is one of the phenomena of our country today that we have no traditional folk art to speak of. Not that there is no craft work or that there are not "primitive" artists—like John Kane and Horace Pippin—but folk art is certainly not the vital expression of the contemporary small American town that it still is of the small town in India, or that it was in our frontier days of the limner and the traveling cabinetmaker.

From *Looking into Art*. New York: Holt, Rinehart and Winston, copyright © 1959.

What do we have instead as popular art? Jazz music and dancing come **4** the closest today to a folk expression that is widely participated in, although there are some other popular arts which we shall take up later. But in jazz, for example, Louis Armstrong has approximately the qualities in his music that one expects of folk music: basic simplicity of structure, vital energy, and a felt but uncomplicated emotion. Louis's records are already and properly collector's items, along with those of his great predecessors, like Bix Beiderbecke and Jelly Roll Morton. Furthermore, he brings to his performance, and it shows in his playing, the appeal of a hearty, open, and warm personality.

But along with the brightness, directness, and fire of Louis Armstrong we **5** have the treacle of Wayne King and the sheer rhythmic noise of many others. If jazz is our folk music, it reaches heights both of sentimentality and of frenetic, explosive energy hitherto unscaled by the folk artist.

In *form* jazz is a remarkable enough achievement, but it is what it reveals **6** to us about our age that is disturbing. If we compare it with the folk music of the past, we may find nothing comparable in creative zeal; on the other hand the earlier forms express a poise, a melancholy realism, or a heartfelt joy that is alarmingly absent from the nervous tempos or the sentimental banalities of most of today's jazz. With this the chrome-plated automobile, the dazzling neon lights of our city streets, the hop of the jitterbug, the violence of our pulp stories of crime and sex play their various complementary roles.

The vast, sprawling, energetic field of popular taste is accompanied by the **7** equally heterogeneous range of the cultivated taste. The borderlines between the two groups are indistinct or, better, blend together. The best of the popular jazz, for example, is very widely appreciated outside popular levels.

But the instant we reach Beethoven, Shakespeare, and Rembrandt, or **8** even Gershwin, Shaw, and Renoir, we are in the area of cultivated taste, which counts among its following, today, a large and growing group. These people are concerned with the kind of art, by and large, that we have been discussing in these pages, and the reason these art forms represent cultivated taste is exactly that they require a certain effort to be appreciated. Whereas the developer of a cultivated taste is aroused by a challenge in cultural matters, the follower of popular taste takes things as they come.

Some psychologists attribute a conscious desire for art to insecurity and **9** the drive for status—to the snob appeal of culture. This may be a motivating factor, but it cannot be productive of a genuine love of the arts. And in the eighteenth century we have the example of many noblemen who enjoyed both social and economic security but who also became excellent amateur artists or musicians. No, I believe the explanation for the cultivated taste lies in a superior capacity to integrate, fostered in a life situation making for a degree of detachment, and the ability to perceive more easily the uniqueness and character of other people and other expressions. It requires, paradoxically, *detachment, accompanied by perceptive warmth.*

10   These are the qualities, I contend, that we must develop, if we are to make such art works as we have investigated here a meaningful part of our experience in life. If the temperament is ready, then the awakening is a continuous process of growth.

11   We must also account for the fact that not all people of imagination and creativity are interested in the arts, which brings us to the third level of taste, the uncultivated. Andrew Carnegie, a man of enormous creative gifts, although respecting the arts, provides an example of such a taste. So does John D. Rockefeller, Sr. So today do numberless politicians, lawyers, businessmen, and scientists. People of uncultivated taste generally have little awareness of the element of form and so feel that their intelligence is being insulted by nonimitative art, particularly the non-objective. It is they who have openly attacked contemporary art and who have placed the creative artist, in whatever epoch, on the defensive. These able people include among them large numbers of potential enthusiasts for the arts. Unlike the lover of popular art, who within his limits, is an ardent fan, these people have very little positive identification with art of any level; yet if once reached by the simple realization that art is a form of personal unification and therefore must be more than imitative, an esthetic chain reaction might be set in motion which could turn many foes of art into growing friends.

12   Taste, then, does not relate so much to the art object as to the way of life and the experience of the individual; the approach to the art object is its sympathetic projection. This is why equally sensitive people may prefer different art forms and also why explanation of art may fall on "deaf"—that is, unready—ears.

STUDY QUESTIONS
Organization and Content

1   In effect, paragraph 1 serves as a topic sentence for a whole section of analytical exposition. After you have read paragraph 1, specifically what do you expect to follow?

2   In paragraphs 2–6, what does Seiberling discuss? in paragraphs 7–10? in paragraph 11? What purpose does paragraph 12 serve?

3   Make a two-level outline of the selection (use only Roman numerals and capital letters: I. A. B., and so on; this is generally the most useful kind of outline).

4   Sentence 2, paragraph 2, says that folk art has roots in dance, song, and crafts. Can you name examples of folk dance, folk song, and a folk craft?

5   Why do people of cultivated taste enjoy examples of simple folk art?

6   For whom is folk art directly functional? What is the difference between using a locally made quilt on a bed in the Ozark Mountains and seeing a quilt of the same design hung on a wall in a museum in New York?

7   Why is there little traditional folk art in the United States? Why is there not a Grandma Moses who paints in every village and a good candlestick maker or cabinetmaker in every town?

8   What favorable things and what unfavorable things does Seiberling say about the popular music called jazz?

9   What contrast does he make in paragraph 6 between earlier folk music and life in America today?

10 Identify the six men named in sentence 1, paragraph 8, and mention one work by each. In terms of effort needed for appreciation, compare a symphonic piece by Beethoven or Gershwin with a piece of "country" music, a play by Shakespeare or Shaw with a typical TV drama, and a painting by Rembrandt or Renoir with a calendar picture.

11 What is the chief difference between a person with a cultivated taste and one with popular taste?

12 What special capacities does a person have to possess or develop in order to have a cultivated taste?

13 What do people with uncultivated taste practically always value most when they look at a work of art?

14 Seiberling says that great numbers of businessmen, lawyers, scientists, and politicians have uncultivated taste. Since such men are generally educated nowadays, why is it that they have left their tastes uncultivated?

15 Find out something about the artistic taste and preferences of the following prominent Americans: Jimmy Carter, Nelson Rockefeller, Richard Nixon, Lyndon Johnson, Edward F. Kennedy. Did any of them achieve cultivated taste?

16 Taking into account the last part of this selection and your own experience, do you think that heredity, general environment, education, or profession has the most to do with the level of a person's taste in the arts?

Sentence Structure

1   At times Seiberling begins a sentence with a conjunction to gain smooth transition. Point out sentences beginning with conjunctions in paragraphs 2, 4, 5, 8, and 9.

2   In what way is sentence 3, paragraph 4, like sentence 1, paragraph 1?

3   Sometimes Seiberling groups several units in parallel structure. Point out parallel phrase units in sentence 2, paragraph 2; nouns plus modifiers in sentences 2 and 3, paragraph 6; nouns in sentence 1, paragraph 8, and sentence 4, paragraph 11.

4   Point out in paragraph 2 the variety of sentence openings, types of sentences, and ways of ending sentences.

Diction

1   Look up the roots of *popular* and *cultivated*. How is *popular* connected with *people* and *cultivated* with *cult* and *culture?*

2   You may need to look up *designate* (paragraph 1), *intricate, sophisticated, functional* (2), *phenomena, limner* (3), *predecessors* (4), *treacle, sentimentality, frenetic* (5), *zeal, poise, banalities, pulp, complementary* (6), *heterogeneous* (7), *status, snob, integrate, uniqueness, paradoxically* (9), *temperament* (10), *nonobjective, epoch, potential, ardent, esthetic* (11).

Assignment

1   Analyze TV programs according to their levels of complexity.

2   Analyze preferences of people you know—in your dormitory, fraternity, or sorority, for example—in music, art, or reading.

3   Similarly analyze tastes among members of your family.

Check Point

2

At this point you should have made progress in the clear and orderly presentation of materials, and should have maintained the practice of using specific details to supply interest and also support for generalizations. You should be familiar with the techniques of introducing lists of items, have had the opportunity to do a little outlining, and have practiced the extremely important intellectual operation of analysis. You should have achieved some success in analyzing—by both partition analysis and classification analysis—things, processes, problems, and abstract ideas.

Comparison and Contrast

The human mind turns naturally and with ease to the locating of likenesses and differences. It is often convenient to try to explain something unfamiliar by showing how it resembles, or differs from, something familiar. Thomas Hariot, for example, a member of Sir Walter Ralegh's Roanoke colony, describing newly observed American things, wrote: "There are two kinds of Walnuts. . . . The one kinde is of the same taste and forme, or little differing from ours in England, but that they are harder and thicker shelled: the other is greater, and hath a very ragged and hard shell: but the kernel great, very oily and sweet." The ways of resemblance and difference are brought out by producing evidence in the form of specific details, like the hardness, roughness, and thickness of walnut shells that Hariot mentioned. These details are illustrations of the main idea—that is, that likeness and/or difference exists. Thus, comparison and contrast gain their effectiveness and power from their force as examples. The examples, that is, the particular details, are brought into view by observation, analysis, and description.

The mind is probably impressed even more by differences than by similarities. If people travel abroad, they will often be thinking: "This is *not* the way we do it at home." Or when they inspect their personalities, they discover: "This is *not* the way we felt last year, or when we were freshmen, or when we were children." Constantly, too, they are watching to see whether things turn out as had been forecast. "No," they tell the politician, "this is *not* what you promised; the state of affairs is different from what it should be." Since they have noticed a difference, they complain because one condition is less good than another that they hoped for. Contrast is often the basis of criticism and complaint; yet both contrast and comparison may be also the basis of praise. Whenever anything is judged, a standard is used; that is, the thing in question is compared with the standard. Therefore, one is very likely to turn to comparison and contrast when discussing anything in terms of standards of excellence. The selections ahead on the Mississippi, on cultural traditions, and on education and training all involve judgments of worth or value. Comparison and contrast have a special usefulness, then, for the bringing out of values.

Techniques of Presenting Comparison and Contrast

The technique of presenting material according to these methods of exposition offers certain possibilities. Here is a simple example.

There are two species of Sooty Albatrosses (Brown and Antarctic), both of which are quite similar in appearance. They both have dark plumage, a long, wedge-shaped tail, and long wings which are very narrow. On the underside of its body, however, the Antarctic Sooty Albatross has paler plumage than the Brown Albatross, and it flies less gracefully. On their bills both species have a groove called a sulcus, which divides the lower segment of the bill; but the sulcus of the Brown Albatross is yellow or orange, whereas the narrower sulcus of the Antarctic species is blue. For nests, both species build up a low cone of earth hollowed out on top.

This comparison has been made on the basis of the criteria of color, shape, size, and habits. The species of birds are the subjects that have been compared. Some differences have also been pointed out—but when we use the term comparison, we usually intend to include the process of contrast as well. If we were dealing with more species, however, or if these two species had more variations of color and the like, it would be advisable to take up each kind of likeness and difference in turn: so we would discuss the colors of all the species of birds we were comparing, then all the different shapes of their tails, and so forth.

Let us look at another example, in which differences are emphasized.

Even from their birth, girls and boys show many differences. Male babies are born heavier and taller than females. After two months males eat more and they develop hearts and lungs larger in proportion than those of females. But girl babies have more fat at birth than boys have, and during adolescence girls become sleeker and fatter than boys, who are thinner and bonier. Boys become stronger and more muscular than girls, and they take in and digest more protein. Girls, however, develop earlier than boys do: they generally sit up, crawl, and are able to talk before boys can. They also attain physiological and psychological maturity earlier than boys.

All these contrasts have been presented in one paragraph, which is intended to inform us that various differences do exist. But if these same contrasts were brought out in more detail, with statistics for weight, height, strength, age, and so forth, it would be natural to write one whole paragraph on boys and another contrasting paragraph on girls. It might also be easier for the reader to understand the details of the matter if two such paragraphs were used.

But we can also use other ways of handling comparison and contrast. Suppose that two things, A and B, are being compared. The author may write one whole paragraph on A and a second paragraph on B. He or she might, using shorter paragraphs perhaps, do this and then continue with a third paragraph on A, a fourth on B, and so on alternately to the end. On the other hand, the writer might switch from A to B when halfway through the first paragraph and follow that half-paragraph pattern until the comparison is finished. Clearly, one might also write first one sentence about A, the next about B, and so forth, following a pattern of more rapid alternation. As you will see by studying the models, each of these techniques offers advantages and creates certain effects.

Ukrainians and Texans

JOHN FISCHER

1   The Ukrainians are the Texans of Russia. They believe they can fight, drink, ride, sing, and make love better than anybody else in the world, and if pressed will admit it. Their country, too, was a borderland—that's what "Ukraine" means—and like Texas it was originally settled by outlaws, horse thieves, land-hungry farmers, and people who hadn't made a go of it somewhere else. Some of these hard cases banded together, long ago, to raise hell and livestock. They called themselves Cossacks, and they would have felt right at home in any Western movie. Even today the Ukrainians cherish a wistful tradition of horsemanship, although most of them would feel as uncomfortable in a saddle as any Dallas banker. They still like to wear knee-high boots and big, furry hats, made of gray or black Persian lamb, which are the local equivalent of the Stetson.

2   Even the country looks a good deal like Texas—flat, dry prairie, shading off in the south to semidesert. Through the middle runs a strip of dark, rich soil, the Chernozom Belt, which is almost identical with the black waxy soil of central Texas. It grows the best wheat in the Soviet Union. The Ukraine is also famous for its cattle, sheep, and cotton, and—again like Texas—it has been in the throes of an industrial boom for the last twenty years. On all other people the Ukrainians look with a sort of kindly pity. They might have thought up for their own use the old Western rule of etiquette: "Never ask a man where he comes from. If he's a Texan, he'll tell you; if he's not, don't embarrass him."

STUDY QUESTIONS

Organization and Content

1   Can any sentences of the two paragraphs be taken as topic sentences?
2   A comparison might be presented paragraph by paragraph, half-paragraph by half-paragraph, sentence by sentence, and so forth. What is the pattern in which the comparison is presented here?
3   Similarities presented in a comparison might be geographical, historical, traditional, commercial, agricultural, educational, recreational, artistic, psychological, and so forth. What similarities has Fischer stressed?
4   Are both parts of the comparison consistently represented?

5   To what extent is suggestion utilized?
6   In which sentences has Fischer referred to specific things or activities in order to make his comparison vivid?

Sentence Structure

1   What transitional links make it easy for the reader to go from sentence to sentence?
2   Just how is the comparison of Ukrainians with Texans brought out in sentences 3–7, paragraph 1?
3   Fischer's sentences are fairly short. How many are simple, compound, complex?
4   Is the sentence style prevailingly formal or colloquial?

Diction

1   Look up *wistful, throes.*
2   What is the effect on the reader of using contractions?
3   Is this an example of dignified or undignified writing? Consider phrases such as "people who hadn't made a go of it," "hard cases," "to raise hell," "felt right at home."
4   Is it the diction that is responsible for the humorous tone of the selection, or is it something else?

Assignment

Most of the selections in this section show differences and develop contrasts; this selection emphasizes likenesses. Imitate it by writing one or two paragraphs showing how two things are alike. Some suggestions:

1   Scientists are like explorers.
2   Successful college life is like disciplined military life.
3   Twentieth-century American painting or architecture or music is like that of other contemporary Western countries.
4   A great man of the present day is like great men of the past.
5   The American of the present is like Americans of the past.
6   Those who live on the sea or in the mountains are like those of the same environment though in different countries.
7   An athlete is like a soldier.
8   Pigs are like people.

The Mississippi from Two Points of View

MARK TWAIN

1   Now when I had mastered the language of this water [as a pilot], and had come to know every trifling feature that bordered the great river as familiarly as I knew the letters of the alphabet, I had made a valuable acquisition. But I had lost something, too. I had lost something which could never be restored to me while I lived. All the grace, the beauty, the poetry, had gone out of the majestic river! I still kept in mind a certain wonderful sunset which I witnessed when steamboating was new to me. A broad expanse of the river was turned to blood; in the middle distance the red hue brightened into gold, through which a solitary log came floating, black and conspicuous; in one place a long, slanting mark lay sparkling upon the water; in another the surface was broken by boiling, tumbling rings, that were as many-tinted as an opal; where the ruddy flush was faintest, was a smooth spot that was covered with graceful circles and radiating lines, ever so delicately traced; the shore on our left was densely wooded, and the somber shadow that fell from this forest was broken in one place by a long, ruffled trail that shone like silver; and high above the forest wall a clean-stemmed dead tree waved a single leafy bough that glowed like a flame in the unobstructed splendor that was flowing from the sun. There were graceful curves, reflected images, woody heights, soft distances; and over the whole scene, far and near, the dissolving lights drifted steadily, enriching it every passing moment with new marvels of coloring.

2   I stood like one bewitched. I drank it in, in a speechless rapture. The world was new to me, and I had never seen anything like this at home. But as I have said, a day came when I began to cease from noting the glories and the charms which the moon and the sun and the twilight wrought upon the river's face; another day came when I ceased altogether to note them. Then, if that sunset scene had been repeated, I should have looked upon it without rapture, and should have commented upon it, inwardly, after this fashion: "This sun means that we are going to have wind to-morrow; that floating log means that the river is rising, small thanks to it; that slanting mark on the water refers to a bluff reef which is going to kill somebody's steamboat one of these nights, if it keeps on stretching out like that; those tumbling 'boils' show a dissolving bar and a changing channel there; the lines and circles in the slick water over yonder are a warning that that troublesome place is shoaling up dangerously; that silver streak in the shadow of

From *Old Times on the Mississippi* (1875, 1883).

the forest is the 'break' from a new snag, and he has located himself in the very best place he could have found to fish for steamboats; that tall dead tree, with a single living branch, is not going to last long, and then how is a body ever going to get through this blind place at night without the friendly old landmark?"

No, the romance and beauty were all gone from the river. All the value 3
any feature of it had for me now was the amount of usefulness it could furnish toward compassing the safe piloting of a steamboat. . . .

STUDY QUESTIONS
Organization and Content

1   Sentence 1 refers to the preceding paragraph, in which Twain explained that to a river pilot the Mississippi "became a wonderful book." How does sentence 2 contrast with sentence 1? What was the "something" that Twain had lost? What does he describe as an example of the beauty he once enjoyed?

2   What different items does Twain describe in sentence 6? How does he let the reader know the position in space of some of the items?

3   Which words in the description provide the most vivid details of color and movement? Point out similes and metaphors in paragraph 1.

4   Which terms have connotations of grace and beauty? What was Twain's response to the experience?

5   Where does Twain make a transition to his changed attitude toward the river? What word best describes his new attitude?

6   Which of the items of sentence 6, paragraph 1, does Twain mention again in sentence 5, paragraph 2? How do the connotations of the latter sentence contrast with those of the former one? Which terms suggest danger or trouble?

7   Did Twain do well to make his contrast in two paragraphs, or would the contrast have been better if done sentence by sentence?

8   What function does paragraph 3 serve?

Sentence Structure

1   Suppose that after sentence 1 Twain had omitted sentences 2 and 3 and had continued "But for me, all the grace, the beauty, . . ." Would the effect be just as good? What do you learn about the purpose and the effectiveness of repetition in successive sentences by studying sentences 2–4?

2   Sentence 6 is very long and has seven main parts. Is each part of equal grammatical value with the others? How are the parts separated?

3   In the second part of sentence 6, which words receive greatest emphasis? What has Twain done to increase emphasis at the end of that part?

4   In sentence 7 how is the effect of the semicolon different from the one that a comma would have? Show how the part after the semicolon is pleasingly arranged with introductory modifiers, main clause, and later modifiers. Contrast the rhythms of the two main parts of sentence 7.

5   How does sentence 4, paragraph 2, resemble sentence 6, paragraph 1?

Diction

1   In what sense does Twain use *poetry* in sentence 4, paragraph 1?
2   Which adjectives are most effective in paragraph 1?
3   What are the primary meanings of *splendor, rapture,* and *glories*?
4   Is there any difference between *shoaling* and *shoaling up*?

Assignment

1   Write a "before-and-after" contrast similar to Twain's. Possibilities: (1) the world as I saw it before and after taking a course in science; (2) an ocean or lake as I regarded it before and after making a voyage; (3) life as I saw it before being in the armed forces and afterward; (4) married life as I regarded it before being married and after marriage; (5) art or music as I considered it before and after taking courses in art or music; (6) "foreigners" as I thought of them before knowing them and as I think of them after knowing them; (7) my view of some sport before and after I participated in it; (8) how I regarded college before entering and after; (9) my reactions to camping or hitchhiking before and after doing it.

2   Following the Twain model, write on Christmas from two points of view; ice storms from two points of view; or ownership of a car, sailboat, or home from two points of view.

Winter and Summer

LAURIE LEE

1   The seasons of my childhood seemed (of course) so violent, so intense and true to their nature, that they have become for me ever since a reference of perfection whenever such names are mentioned. They possessed us so completely they seemed to change our nationality; and when I look back to the valley it cannot be one place I see, but village-winter or village-summer, both separate. It becomes increasingly easy in urban life to ignore their extreme humours, but in those days winter and summer dominated our every action, broke into our houses, conscripted our thoughts, ruled our games, and ordered our lives.

Abridged by permission of the author, and The Hogarth Press. Copyright © 1959 by Laurie Lee.

Winter was no more typical of our valley than summer, it was not even **2** summer's opposite; it was merely that other place. And somehow one never remembered the journey towards it; one arrived, and winter was here. The day came suddenly when all details were different and the village had to be rediscovered. One's nose went dead so that it hurt to breathe, and there were jigsaws of frost on the window. The light filled the house with a green polar glow; while outside—in the invisible world—there was a strange hard silence, or a metallic creaking, a faint throbbing of twigs and wires.

The kitchen that morning would be full of steam, billowing from kettles **3** and pots. The outside pump was frozen again, making a sound like broken crockery, so that the girls tore icicles from the eaves for water and we drank boiled ice in our tea.

"It's wicked," said Mother. "The poor, poor birds." And she flapped her **4** arms with vigour. . . .

Now the winter's day was set in motion and we rode through its crystal **5** kingdom. We examined the village for its freaks of frost, for anything we might use. We saw the frozen spring by the side of the road, huge like a swollen flower. Water wagtails hovered over it, nonplussed at its silent hardness, and again and again they dropped down to drink only to go sprawling in a tumble of feathers. We saw the stream in the valley, black and halted, a tarred path threading through the willows. We saw trees lopped off by their burdens of ice, cow tracks like potholes in rock, quiet lumps of sheep licking the spiky grass with their black and rotting tongues. The church clock had stopped and the weathercock was frozen, so that both time and the winds were stilled; and nothing, we thought, could be more exciting than this: interference by a hand unknown, the winter's No! to routine and laws—sinister, awesome, welcome. . . .

Summer, June summer, with the green back on earth and the whole **6** world unlocked and seething—like winter, it came suddenly and one knew it in bed, almost before waking up; with cuckoos and pigeons hollowing the woods since daylight and the chipping of tits in the pear blossom. . . .

Summer was also the time of these: of sudden plenty, of slow hours and **7** actions, of diamond haze and dust on the eyes, of the valley in postvernal slumber; of burying birds saved from seething corruption; of Mother sleeping heavily at noon; of jazzing wasps and dragonflies, hay stooks and thistle seeds, snows of white butterflies, skylarks' eggs, bee orchids and frantic ants; of wolf-cub parades and boy-scout's bugles; of sweat running down the legs; of boiling potatoes on bramble fires, of flames glass-blue in the sun, of lying naked in the hill-cold stream; begging pennies for bottles of pop; of girls' bare arms; of unripe cherries, green apples and liquid walnuts; of fights and falls and new-scabbed knees, sobbing pursuits and flights; of picnics high up in the crumbling quarries, of butter running like oil, of sunstroke, fever, and cucumber peel stuck cool to one's burning brow. All this, and the feeling that it would never end, that such days had come for ever, with the pump drying up and the water-butt crawling, and the chalk ground hard as the moon. All sights twice-brilliant and smells twice-sharp, all game-days twice as long. Double charged as we were, like the meadow ants, with the frenzy of the sun, we used up the light to its last violet drop, and even then couldn't go to bed.

STUDY QUESTIONS
Organization and Content

1   In this description of the contrasting seasons of winter and summer in England, what feelings did both of them arouse? Where is this matter discussed?

2   Explain the *place*-idea expressed in sentence 2, paragraph 1, and sentence 1, paragraph 2.

3   What tactual, visual, and auditory details does Lee make the reader aware of?

4   What situation is implied by paragraph 4?

5   All the sentences of paragraph 5, after sentence 1, deal with what particular kind of details?

6   In sentence 7, paragraph 5, Lee asserts that "both time and the winds were stilled"—an occurrence literally impossible. How should this fanciful statement be interpreted? How is it related to "the winter's No!"?

7   What contrast is implied in paragraph 6 by "the whole world unlocked"? Yet what similarity of summer and winter is brought out in this paragraph?

8   What is the long catalogue of details about summer in paragraph 7 intended to make us feel about the season?

9   What does Lee accomplish with the three sentences that follow the catalogue?

Sentence Structure

1   What is the effect of the striking parallel verbs in sentence 3, paragraph 1?

2   In paragraph 5 after *we rode,* note the similarity of sentence pattern. What is the effect of so many sentences with subject-verb-complement pattern?

3   Paragraph 6 consists of one unusual sentence, with subject, appositive, modifiers, then a dash, an interrupter, and the pronoun *it* appearing as a subject. Consider the difference if the appositive *June summer* and the interrupter *like winter* were omitted.

4   Point out the parallelism in sentence 1, paragraph 7. What is its purpose?

5   Sentences 2 and 3, paragraph 7, lack independent clauses. What words do we "understand" to have been left out? Why is it appropriate to have these "fragments" here?

Diction

1   Comment on the choice of diction to express the ideas of paragraph 1. Consider particularly the adjectives of sentence 1 and the verbs in sentences 2 and 3.

2   Look up *humours, conscripted, freaks, nonplussed, potholes, seething, hollowing, vernal, stooks, charged.*

3   Lee writes in vivid, poetic fashion. Analyze and explain the following metaphors: *jigsaws* of frost (paragraph 2); *rode* through its crystal *kingdom,* a *tarred path threading* through the willows (paragraph 5); *snows* of white butterflies, light to its last violet *drop* (paragraph 7).

4   What do Lee's similes contribute to the description? Which of the following does most to stimulate the imagination: "sound like broken crockery"; "huge like a swollen flower"; "like potholes in rock"; "hard as the moon"; "like the meadow ants"?

5   Consider their connotations, and comment on the choice of such terms as *seething* (paragraph 6); *diamond haze, flames glass-blue, hill-cold stream* (sentence 1, paragraph 7). What gives the hyphenated adjectives their power?

6   To appreciate fully the quality of paragraph 7, you ought to read it aloud. (Note the alliteration of "begging pennies for bottles of pop" and the alliteration and economy of "fights and falls and new-scabbed knees, sobbing pursuits and flights.")

Assignment

Write two paragraphs expressing the contrast of spring and fall as you have known them; of school life and vacation life; of civilian life and military life; of daytime activities and nighttime activities; or of summers as a child and summers as a college student.

Similarly contrast days of rain and sunshine on your campus or the campus on a home-game weekend and on a weekend with no game.

Cultural Traditions, East and West

WILLIE MORRIS

1   What strikes me most in reading books like Alfred Kazin's haunting poetic reminiscences of boyhood in an immigrant Jewish neighborhood in the East, is the vast gulf which separates that kind of growing up and the childhood and adolescence of those of us who came out of the towns of the American South and Southwest a generation later. With the Eastern Jewish intellectuals who play such a substantial part in American cultural life, perhaps in the late 1960s a dominant part, the struggle as they grew up in the 1930s was for one set of ideas over others, for a fierce acceptance or rejection of one man's theories or another man's poetry—and with all this a driving determination to master the language which had not been their parents' and to find a place in a culture not quite theirs. For other Eastern intellectuals and writers whom I later was to know, going to the Ivy League schools involved, if not a finishing, then a deepening of perceptions, or of learning, or culture.

2   But for so many of us who converged on Austin, Texas, in the early 1950s, from places like Karnes City or Big Spring or Abilene or Rockdale or Yazoo City, the awakening we were to experience, or to have jolted into us, or to undergo by some more subtle chemistry, did not mean a mere finishing or deepening, and most emphatically did not imply the victory of one set of ideologies over another, one way of viewing literature or politics over another, but something more basic and simple. This was the acceptance of ideas themselves as something worth living by. It was a matter, at the age of eighteen or nineteen, not of discovering *certain* books, but the simple *presence* of books, not the nuances of idea and feeling, but idea and feeling on their own terms. It is this late coming to this kind of awareness that still gives the intellectuals from the small towns of our region a hungry, naïve quality, as opposed to the sharp-elbowed over-intellectuality of some Easterners, as if those from down there who made it were lucky, or chosen, out of all the disastrous alternatives of their isolated lower- or middle-class upbringings, to enjoy and benefit from the fruits of simply being educated and liberal-minded.

3   What we brought to the University of Texas in the 1950s, to an enormous, only partially formed state university, was a great awe before the splendid quotations on its buildings and the walls of its libraries, along with

Willie Morris, *North toward Home,* Houghton Mifflin Co., copyright © Boston, 1962 by Willie Morris, pp. 149–151.

an absolutely prodigious insensitivity as to what they implied beyond decoration. Minds awakened slowly, painfully, and with pretentious and damaging inner searches. Where an Alfred Kazin at the age of nineteen might become aroused in the subway by reading a review by John Chamberlain in the *New York Times* and rush to his office to complain, we at eighteen or nineteen were only barely beginning to learn that there *were* ideas, much less ideas to arouse one from one's self. If places like City College or Columbia galvanized the young New York intellectuals already drenched in literature and polemics, the University of Texas had, in its halting, unsure, and often frivolous way, to teach those of us with good minds and small-town high school diplomas that we were intelligent human beings, with minds and hearts of our own that we might learn to call our own, that there were some things, many things—ideas, values, choices of action—worth committing one's self to and fighting for, that a man in some instances might become morally committed to honoring every manifestation of individual conscience and courage. Yet the hardest task at the University of Texas, as many of us were to learn, was to separate all the extraneous and empty things that can drown a young person there, as all big universities can drown its young people, from the few simple things that are worth living a life by. Without wishing to sound histrionic, I believe I am thinking of something approaching the Western cultural tradition; yet if someone had suggested that to me that September night in 1952, as I stepped off the bus in Austin to be greeted by three fraternity men anxious to look me over, I would have thought him either a fool or a con man.

I emerged from that bus frightened and tired, after having come 500 **4** miles non-stop over the red hills of Louisiana and the pine forests of East Texas. The three men who met me—appalled, I was told later, by my green trousers and the National Honor Society medal on my gold-plated watch chain—were the kind that I briefly liked and admired, for their facility at small talk, their clothes, their manner, but whom I soon grew to deplore and finally to be bored by. They were the kind who made fraternities tick, the favorites of the Dean of Men at the time, respectable B or C-plus students, tolerable athletes, good with the Thetas or the Pi Phis; but one would find later, lurking there inside of them despite—or maybe because of—their good fun and jollity, the ideals of the insurance salesman and an aggressive distrust of anything approaching thought. One of them later told me, with the seriousness of an early disciple, that my table manners had become a source of acute embarrassment to all of them. That night they drove me around the campus, and they were impressed that I knew from my map-reading where the University library was, for two of them were not sure.

STUDY QUESTIONS
Organization and Content

1   Is sentence 1 the thesis sentence?
2   In sentence 1 how does Morris emphasize the contrast that he is going to discuss? Where and how does he signal the beginning of the contrast?
3   Which details of paragraph 1 does Morris negate in paragraph 2, sentence 1?
4   Why is paragraph 2, sentence 2, very important?
5   What more specific contrast does Morris bring out in paragraph 2, sentence 3?
6   What conclusion does he state in paragraph 2, sentence 4, and what implied contrast does sentence 4 convey?
7   What things does Morris contrast within sentences 1, 3, 4, and 5, paragraph 3?
8   Indicate further (mainly implied) contrasts in paragraph 4 between Morris and the three fraternity men. Why could the fraternity men not have become, as Morris became, a Rhodes scholar, journalist, Editor of *Harper's Magazine*, and novelist?
9   What connection does paragraph 4 have with Morris's thesis?
10   Why do you think that young people in such states as Mississippi, Louisiana, and Texas have so little awareness of the importance of learning, of literature, of books, of ideas, of culture? Are there states in other regions where the situation is similar?

Sentence Structure

1   Many of Morris's sentences are from 60 to more than 100 words long. Notice that several sentences have early modifiers, sometimes containing dependent clauses, so that the main verb, and sometimes its subject as well, appear quite late. Analyze the first four sentences, showing the early modifiers, the main verbs, and their subjects.
2   What different kind of structure does Morris use in sentence 5?
3   What third pattern of structure appears in sentences 6 and 7?
4   Explain how, in paragraph 3, sentence 4, Morris develops the thought in this long sentence by adding three parallel clauses, each with internal modifiers.

Diction

1   If you need to, look up *ideologies, nuances* (paragraph 2), *galvanized, polemics, extraneous,* and *histrionic* (3).
2   Some of Morris's adjectives may seem unusually connotative. What contrasting characterizations are implied by *"hungry, naïve* quality" and *"sharp-elbowed* over-intellectuality"? Was it their *"isolated . . .* upbringings" that left Southerners and Southwest-

erners with *"disastrous* alternatives"? What is suggested by *"prodigious* insensitivity"? by *"pretentious* and damaging inner searches"? What sort of action is implied by *"aggressive* distrust"?

Assignment

1   Imitate Morris by contrasting: men students and women students; cultured people and "tired businessmen"; young people of good character and juvenile delinquents; or typical students in two different curricula.
2   Or contrast the advantages of one sort of person with the disadvantages of another sort: a lover of reading with one who does not read; a college graduate with one who is not a college graduate; a person who has traveled with one who has not traveled; a person who loves nature with one who does not love it; or a person reared in a city with one reared elsewhere.

Identity Crisis in the Barrios

MANUEL RAMÍREZ

Social scientists have long been concerned with the plight of the bicul- 1 tural person in our society, the person caught between the merciless demands of two cultures. Because of his inability to comply with the requirements of both groups, the bicultural individual often fails to identify with either. The two different demands of his loyalty keep him under constant stress. His conflicting values give him an uncomfortable sense of insecurity, instability, and disorientation. He usually attempts to resolve the conflict by choosing one group and rejecting the other. Neither choice is entirely satisfactory.

The Mexican-American is one of the many ethnic groups in the United 2 States that is caught in this cultural dilemma. The Anglos pressure him to abandon the mother culture and emulate Anglo behavior. The members of his group who do not admire the Anglo ways encourage him to ignore them and retain the traditional folk culture. Most Mexican-Americans faced with these conflicts find it necessary to become either Identifiers (remaining loyal to their ethnic group and rejecting Anglo ways) or Anglicized (accepting Anglo ways and rejecting their identification with their ethnic group).

3   I recently conducted a study of Mexican-American junior and senior high school students in Sacramento, California, to try to pinpoint the problems of both the Identifier and Anglicized groups. To separate those students who retain the values of the Mexican-American culture from those who do not, I administered a Mexican Family Attitude Scale to two hundred Mexican-American students. The scale used values that usually differentiate between Mexican-Americans and non-Mexican-Americans: (a) loyalty to the family group, (b) a feeling that relatives, no matter how distant, are more important than friends, (c) respect for adults, (d) belief in strict childrearing practices, (e) consideration of the mother as the most loved person in existence, (f) a present time-orientation, and (g) a need to defend one's honor at all costs whenever threatened.

4   From the original group of two hundred subjects, twenty were selected for further study. Ten were adolescents who rejected these values (Anglicized); ten identified strongly with them (Identifiers). These twenty people then completed the Bell Adjustment Inventory Student Form, a personality inventory identifying the areas of life in which the adolescent is experiencing problems of adjustment. It covers six areas: (a) family, (b) health, (c) sex-role, (d) adequacy of relationship with people outside the home, (e) feelings about oneself, and (f) hostility and suspiciousness of others.

5   The results showed striking differences in the problems being experienced by members of the two groups. The Anglicized adolescents reported having experienced many disagreements with their parents. They had a tendency to answer "yes" to the following items on the adjustment inventory: (a) My parents fail to recognize I am a mature person and treat me as if I were still a child. (b) My parents do not understand me. (c) Frequently, I have had to keep quiet or leave the home in order to keep the peace. These same adolescents, however, reported having very pleasant relationships with people outside the home. They were outgoing, friendly, and trusting of others.

6   The adolescents of the Identifier group reported having pleasant relationships with their parents. Their relationships to others outside the group, however, were quite different. They had a tendency to answer "yes" to the following items: (a) There are many people in the world I can't afford to trust. (b) People do not understand me. (c) You must watch your step around people, or they will take advantage of you. (d) I feel self-conscious when I recite in class. (e) I hesitate to volunteer in class recitation. The members of the Identifier group were well adjusted at home, but felt alienated from other people. Both groups of adolescents seemed to be paying a steep price for their one-sided identities. They were confronted with opposing sets of values, and they had to decide whether to retain the values of their parents or to reject them for the values of authority figures outside the

home (teachers, employers, policemen, and so on). Excerpts from interviews with representatives from the two groups further reveal the unhappiness accompanying both of these patterns of adjustment.

Paul is a member of the Anglicized group. This is what he had to say: "I   7
don't want to be known as a Mexican-American, but only as an American. I was born in this country and raised among Americans. I think like an Anglo, I talk like one, and I dress like one. It's true I don't look like an Anglo and sometimes I am rejected by them, but it would be worse if I spoke Spanish or said that I was of Mexican descent. I am sorry I do not get along well with my parents, but their views are old-fashioned. They still see themselves as Mexican, and they do not understand me. Often we have arguments, but I ignore them. In fact, I had to move away from my home because of our disagreements. I wish those people who are always making noise about being Mexican-Americans would be quiet. We would all be better off if they would accept things as they are. I just want a good education. I don't want to be poor. I don't want to be discriminated against."

Roberto, who is an Identifier, has a different opinion: "I am proud of   8
being a Mexican-American. We have a rich heritage. Mexico is a great country that is progressing fast. It has a wonderful history and culture. My family is the most important thing in the world for me. I owe my parents everything and I will never complain when they need me. I don't want to be like the 'Paddys' because they don't care about their families; they just care about themselves and making money. They don't like anybody who is different. At school, the teachers ignored you if they knew you weren't going to college, and most of us Mexicans couldn't afford to go. The things I learned at school were against what my parents had taught me. I had to choose my parents, because they are old and they need my help and understanding. Most people, even some Mexican-Americans, look down on us because we are Mexicans, and I hate them. It is unhealthy and unnatural to want to be something you are not."

So much for the two divergent groups. Let's examine the interview of a   9
Mexican-American adolescent, Rosa, who was fortunate to form an identity within both cultures. She states, "I am happy to be an American of Mexican descent. Because I am a Mexican, I learned to be close to my family and they have been a source of strength and support for me. If things ever get too bad on the outside I could always come to them for comfort and understanding. My Spanish also helped me a lot in my education and will also open a lot of doors for me when I look for a job. As an American I am happy to live in a great progressive country where we have the freedom to achieve anything we want. I feel all that I have achieved I owe to the help of my parents, the encouragement of my teachers, and the chance to live in this country. I feel very rich and fortunate because I have two cultures rather than just one."

Rosa views both the Anglo and Mexican-American cultures favorably,   10 and she has in fact combined the best from each to form a richer more beautiful culture. How can we insure that more bicultural adolescents will achieve such a desirable identity?

11   More efficient lines of communication between parents and school personnel must be established. Otherwise, we will continue to have both groups working against each other, with the adolescent caught between the demands of both. Schools with large Mexican-American populations should hire Mexican-American personnel who speak Spanish and are aware of conflicts that can arise. Anglo teachers and administrators must learn about Mexican-American culture and values. Unless both parents and school personnel understand and respect each other's values, conflicts will continue, with the Mexican-American student suffering the consequences.

12   Counseling programs for the bicultural student geared to help him anticipate the inevitable value conflicts should be instituted in our schools. The more understanding a student achieves about his problems, the better he will be able to cope with the conflict and stress.

13   An accepting, helpful environment that will aid the bicultural student in achieving an identification within two cultures must be established. Only then will he be able to select the best of both without having to reject either.

STUDY QUESTIONS

Organization and Content

1   *Plight* is a key word in sentence 1. When you reach the end of paragraph 1, what do you discover is the plight of "the bicultural person in our society"?

2   What specific dilemma does Ramírez bring up in paragraph 2?

3   For what purpose did he administer the Mexican Family Attitude Scale?

4   On what basis did he select only 20 out of 200 students for further study?

5   What "striking differences" in the problems of the two groups did further study reveal?

6   Why does Ramírez use enumerations in paragraphs 3–6?

7   What parallel pattern of organization do you find in paragraphs 5 and 6?

8   What is the relation of paragraph 7 to paragraph 5? of paragraph 8 to paragraph 6?

9   What further contrast is brought out in paragraph 9?

10   What conclusion does Ramírez draw in paragraph 10? What is the transitional purpose of paragraph 10, sentence 2?

11   Where does the actual contrast of students begin? What are the main sections of this article?

12   What other ethnic groups in the United States may feel similar bi-

cultural conflicts? Do these groups have the same problems with family and outsiders that Ramírez reports, or do they have different problems?

Sentence Structure

1   What is the prevailing sentence pattern throughout this article? Is it suitable to this material? (Remember that Ramírez is mainly making a report.)
2   In paragraphs 5, 6, and 8, in which sentences and with what words does Ramírez indicate contrasts?
3   In paragraph 7 what is the chief method of transition?

Diction

1   If you need to, look up *disorientation* (paragraph 1), *dilemma, emulate* (2), *alienated* (6), and *divergent* (9).
2   Ramírez frequently uses two very abstract terms: *values* and *culture*. What are some concrete actions or situations that might illustrate them?
3   In his last two paragraphs Ramírez uses verb forms different from those in the other paragraphs. Why does he do so?

Assignment

1   Make a survey of opinions of classmates and friends on some matter of politics, religion, or education, and, like Ramírez, contrast the chief differences among them. Illustrate these differences by directly quoting persons with opposing views. (You ought to interview at least 12–20 people.)
2   From your own knowledge, write a short paper contrasting the qualities of people from different cultures, such as Oriental and European; African and British; American Indian and Western white American; Jewish and Irish; Southern black and Southern white, and so forth.
3   In the same way write a paper contrasting the values held by people of such contrasting cultures.
4   To what extent do children of divorced parents have special problems or attitudes that are different from those of other children? Contrast such differences.
5   Contrast two groups of students who have different qualities; these might be athletes and scholars, conformists and non-conformists, liberals a.rd conservatives, religious and non-religious persons.

Education and Training

HARRY KEMELMAN

1 To understand the nature of the liberal arts college and its function in our society, it is important to understand the difference between *education* and *training*.

2 Training is intended primarily for the service of society; education is primarily for the individual. Society needs doctors, lawyers, engineers, teachers to perform specific tasks necessary to its operation, just as it needs carpenters and plumbers and stenographers. Training supplies the immediate and specific needs of society so that the work of the world may continue. And these needs, our training centers—the professional and trade schools—fill. But although education is for the improvement of the individual, it also serves society by providing a leavening of men of understanding, of perception, and wisdom. They are our intellectual leaders, the critics of our culture, the defenders of our free traditions, the instigators of our progress. They serve society by examining its function, appraising its needs, and criticizing its direction. They may be earning their livings by practicing one of the professions, or in pursuing a trade, or by engaging in business enterprise. They may be rich or poor. They may occupy positions of power and prestige, or they may be engaged in some humble employment. Without them, however, society either disintegrates or else becomes an anthill.

3 The difference between the two types of study is like the difference between the discipline and exercise in a professional baseball training camp and that of a Y gym. In the one, the recruit is training to become a professional baseball player who will make a living and serve society by playing baseball; in the other, he is training only to improve his own body and musculature. The training at the baseball camp is all relevant. The recruit may spend hours practicing how to slide into second base, not because it is a particularly useful form of calisthenics but because it is relevant to the game. The exercise would stop if the rules were changed so that sliding to a base was made illegal. Similarly, the candidate for the pitching staff spends a lot of time throwing a baseball, not because it will improve his physique—it may have quite the opposite effect—but because pitching is to be his principal function on the team. At the Y gym, exercises have no such relevance. The intention is to strengthen the body in general, and when the members sit down on the floor with their legs outstretched and practice touching their fingers to their toes, it is not because they hope to become galley slaves, perhaps the only occupation where that particular exercise would be relevant.

In general, relevancy is a facet of training rather than of education. What 4 is taught at law school is the present law of the land, not the Napoleonic Code or even the archaic laws that have been scratched from the statute books. And at medical school, too, it is modern medical practice that is taught, that which is relevant to conditions today. And the plumber and the carpenter and the electrician and the mason learn only what is relevant to the practice of their respective trades in this day with the tools and materials that are presently available and that conform to the building code.

In the liberal arts college, on the other hand, the student is encouraged to 5 explore new fields and old fields, to wander down the bypaths of knowledge. There the teaching is concerned with major principles, and its purpose is to change the student, to make him something different from what he was before, just as the purpose of the Y gym is to make a fat man into a thin one, or a strong one out of a weak one.

Clearly the two types of learning overlap. Just as the baseball recruit gets 6 rid of excess weight and tightens his muscles at the baseball camp and thereby profits even if he does not make the team, so the law student sharpens his mind and broadens his understanding, even if he subsequently fails the bar exam and goes on to make his living in an entirely different kind of work. His study of law gives him an understanding of the rules under which our society functions and his practice in solving legal problems gives him an understanding of fine distinctions.

On the other hand, the Y member, whose original reason for joining may 7 have been solely to get himself in shape, may get caught up in the institution's baseball program and find that his skill has developed to the point where he can play the game professionally. Similarly, the student who undertakes a course of study merely because it interests him and he wants to know more about it may find that it has commercial value. He has studied a foreign language and literature in order to understand the society that produced it, and then he may find that his special knowledge enables him to get a job as a translator. Or he may find that while his knowledge of chemistry is not of professional caliber, it is still sufficient to give him preference in a particular job over someone who lacks even that modicum of knowledge of the subject. But these are accidental and incidental. In general, certain courses of study are for the service of society and other courses are for self-improvement. In the hierarchy of our educational system, the former are the function of our professional schools and the latter are the function of the college of liberal arts.

STUDY QUESTIONS
Organization and Content

1. What special purpose does the one-sentence paragraph serve? Why is Kemelman explaining the difference between education and training?
2. What basic distinction between education and training does Kemelman make? What different services to society are explained in sentences 2–3 and sentences 5–7 and 11, paragraph 2?
3. Explain how the alternatives mentioned in sentence 11, paragraph 2, could come about.
4. How does the analogy used in paragraph 3 enlighten us about education and training? What is the key term in paragraphs 3 and 4?
5. How does Kemelman give a signal for a contrast in paragraphs 5 and 7? What is the function of the liberal arts college?
6. For what purpose does Kemelman speak of the law student in paragraph 6?
7. In paragraph 7 what contrasting example is used?
8. How does the last sentence relate to the early part of the discussion?

Sentence Structure

1. Explain three different reasons for using parallel structure in paragraph 2: in sentence 1, sentences 5–7, and sentences 8–11.
2. How is sentence 2, paragraph 3, constructed so as to show contrast?
3. Show how the same type of comparison is brought out, but in different sentence patterns, in sentence 2, paragraph 5, and in sentence 2, paragraph 6.

Diction

1. You may need to look up *leavening, instigators* (paragraph 2); *fine* (6); and *modicum* (7).
2. What other English words are made on the same roots as *relevant* and *archaic*?
3. What is the difference between *accidental* and *incidental*?

Assignment

Contrast things that have some similarity: for example, (1) the two houses of Congress; (2) religious instruction and public education; (3) a family and an organized community; (4) a city and a village; (5) a college newspaper and a city newspaper; (6) Christianity and the Muslim religion; (7) wit and humor; (8) love and infatuation; (9) fire and heat.

Grant and Lee:
A Study in Contrasts

BRUCE CATTON

When Ulysses S. Grant and Robert E. Lee met in the parlor of a modest 1 house at Appomattox Court House, Virginia, on April 9, 1865, to work out the terms for the surrender of Lee's Army of Northern Virginia, a great chapter in American life came to a close, and a great new chapter began.

These men were bringing the Civil War to its virtual finish. To be sure, 2 other armies had yet to surrender, and for a few days the fugitive Confederate government would struggle desperately and vainly, trying to find some way to go on living now that its chief support was gone. But in effect it was all over when Grant and Lee signed the papers. And the little room where they wrote out the terms was the scene of one of the poignant, dramatic contrasts in American history.

They were two strong men, these oddly different generals, and they repre- 3 sented the strengths of two conflicting currents that, through them, had come into final collision.

Back of Robert E. Lee was the notion that the old aristocratic concept 4 might somehow survive and be dominant in American life.

Lee was tidewater Virginia, and in his background were family, culture, 5 and tradition ... the age of chivalry transplanted to a New World which was making its own legends and its own myths. He embodied a way of life that had come down through the age of knighthood and the English country squire. America was a land that was beginning all over again, dedicated to nothing much more complicated than the rather hazy belief that all men had equal rights, and should have an equal chance in the world. In such a land Lee stood for the feeling that it was somehow of advantage to human society to have a pronounced inequality in the social structure. There should be a leisure class, backed by ownership of land; in turn, society itself should be keyed to the land as the chief source of wealth and influence. It would bring forth (according to this ideal) a class of men with a strong sense of obligation to the community; men who lived, not to gain advantage for themselves, but to meet the solemn obligations which had been laid on them by the very fact that they were privileged. From them the country would get its leadership; to them it could look for the higher values—of thought, of conduct, of personal deportment—to give it strength and virtue.

6   Lee embodied the noblest elements of this aristocratic ideal. Through him, the landed nobility justified itself. For four years, the Southern states had fought a desperate war to uphold the ideals for which Lee stood. In the end, it almost seemed as if the Confederacy fought for Lee; as if he himself was the Confederacy ... the best thing that the way of life for which the Confederacy stood could ever have to offer. He had passed into legend before Appomattox. Thousands of tired, underfed, poorly clothed Confederate soldiers, long-since past the simple enthusiasm of the early days of the struggle, somehow considered Lee the symbol of everything for which they had been willing to die. But they could not quite put this feeling into words. If the Lost Cause, sanctified by so much heroism and so many deaths, had a living justification, its justification was General Lee.

7   Grant, the son of a tanner on the Western frontier, was everything Lee was not. He had come up the hard way, and embodied nothing in particular except the eternal toughness and sinewy fiber of the men who grew up beyond the mountains. He was one of a body of men who owed reverence and obeisance to no one, who were self-reliant to a fault, who cared hardly anything for the past but who had a sharp eye for the future.

8   These frontier men were the precise opposites of the tidewater aristocrats. Back of them, in the great surge that had taken people over the Alleghenies and into the opening Western country, there was a deep, implicit dissatisfaction with a past that had settled into grooves. They stood for democracy, not from any reasoned conclusion about the proper ordering of human society, but simply because they had grown up in the middle of democracy and knew how it worked. Their society might have privileges, but they would be privileges each man had won for himself. Forms and patterns meant nothing. No man was born to anything, except perhaps to a chance to show how far he could rise. Life was competition.

9   Yet along with this feeling had come a deep sense of belonging to a national community. The Westerner who developed a farm, opened a shop or set up in business as a trader, could hope to prosper only as his own community prospered—and his community ran from the Atlantic to the Pacific and from Canada down to Mexico. If the land was settled, with towns and highways and accessible markets, he could better himself. He saw his fate in terms of the nation's own destiny. As its horizons expanded, so did his. He had, in other words, an acute dollars-and-cents stake in the continued growth and development of his country.

10   And that, perhaps, is where the contrast between Grant and Lee becomes most striking. The Virginia aristocrat, inevitably, saw himself in relation to his own region. He lived in a static society which could endure almost anything except change. Instinctively, his first loyalty would go to the locality in which that society existed. He would fight to the limit of endurance to defend it, because in defending it he was defending everything that gave his own life its deepest meaning.

The Westerner, on the other hand, would fight with an equal tenacity for **11** the broader concept of society. He fought so because everything he lived by was tied to growth, expansion, and a constantly widening horizon. What he lived by would survive or fall with the nation itself. He could not possibly stand by unmoved in the face of an attempt to detroy the Union. He would combat it with everything he had, because he could only see it as an effort to cut the ground out from under his feet.

So Grant and Lee were in complete contrast, representing two diametri- **12** cally opposed elements in American life. Grant was the modern man emerging; beyond him, ready to come on the stage, was the great age of steel and machinery, of crowded cities and a restless, burgeoning vitality. Lee might have ridden down from the old age of chivalry, lance in hand, silken banner fluttering over his head. Each man was the perfect champion of his cause, drawing both his strengths and his weaknesses from the people he led.

Yet it was not all contrast, after all. Different as they were—in back- **13** ground and personality, in underlying aspiration—these two great soldiers had much in common. Under everything else, they were marvelous fighters. Furthermore, their fighting qualities were really very much alike.

Each man had, to begin with, the great virtue of utter tenacity and fidel- **14** ity. Grant fought his way down the Mississippi Valley in spite of acute personal discouragement and profound military handicaps. Lee hung on in the trenches at Petersburg after hope itself had died. In each man there was an indomitable quality ... the born fighter's refusal to give up as long as he can still remain on his feet and lift his two fists.

Daring and resourcefulness they had, too; the ability to think faster and **15** move faster than the enemy. These were the qualities which gave Lee the dazzling campaigns of Second Manassas and Chancellorsville and won Vicksburg for Grant.

Lastly, and perhaps greatest of all, there was the ability, at the end, to turn **16** quickly from war to peace once the fighting was over. Out of the way these two men behaved at Appomattox came the possibility of a peace of reconcil- iation. It was a possibility not wholly realized, in the years to come, but which did, in the end, help the two sections to become one nation again ... after a war whose bitterness might have seemed to make such a reunion wholly impossible. No part of either man's life became him more than the part he played in their brief meeting in the McLean house at Appomattox. Their behavior there put all succeeding generations of Americans in their debt. Two great Americans, Grant and Lee—very different, yet under every- thing very much alike. Their encounter at Appomattox was one of the great moments of American history.

STUDY QUESTIONS
Organization and Content

1   It is instructive to see how a noted historian compares and contrasts two great generals. What is the purpose of paragraphs 1–3? What, in particular, does paragraph 3 do?

2   Which general does Catton discuss first? In which paragraph does he turn to the other general? What happens in paragraphs 10 and 11? in paragraph 12?

3   What does Catton do in paragraphs 13–16?

4   How many paragraphs does he give to each general?

5   Outline the selection. Use a two-level outline.

6   What key words represent the kind of man that Lee was? What different terms are applied to Grant to show what kind of American he was?

7   What is the most important way in which Grant and Lee differed? To what extent, however, were they alike?

8   In paragraphs 14 and 15, how and where are the topic ideas supported?

Sentence Structure

1   Both paragraph 1 and paragraph 3 have only one sentence. Contrast the sentence pattern of each paragraph. In each sentence, which words receive the greatest emphasis?

2   Note the contrasts in sentence length that Catton uses. In the first six paragraphs, which sentences stand out as short?

3   Which short sentence in paragraph 8 sums up the philosophy of the people from whom Grant came?

4   Point out how in sentence 1, paragraph 10, Catton makes a transition to a new aspect of the contrast. In sentence 1, paragraph 11, what phrase provides transition?

5   Show how, in paragraph 12, each sentence is constructed to bring out clearly and forcefully the basic contrast of the two generals.

6   In the sentences of paragraphs 13–16, which words make the transitions?

7   How are the two final sentences of paragraph 16 constructed so as to echo the ideas with which Catton opened his discussion?

Diction

1   Look up *virtual, fugitive, poignant* (paragraph 2); *aristocratic, concept, dominant* (4); *culture, tradition, chivalry, legends, country squire, pronounced, inequality, solemn, privileged, values, deportment, virtue* (5); *landed, nobility, sanctifed, justification* (6); *tanner, frontier, sinewy, reverence, obeisance, self-reliant* (7); *implicit* (8); *accessible, destiny* (9); *inevitably, static, endurance* (10); *tenacity, combat* (11); *burgeoning, vitality, champion* (12); *fidelity, profound,*

indomitable (14); *resourcefulness* (15); *reconciliation, succeeding, generations* (16).
2 Learn the meanings of the roots of *fugitive, aristocratic, chivalry, justification, implicit, endurance, combat, indomitable.*
3 Having learned the roots of *justify,* you ought to know the meaning of *sanctify* (6).
4 Is the diction of this selection mainly concrete or mainly abstract? Point out sentences of each kind.

Assignment

1 Compare and contrast two people you know who, like Lee and Grant, have different backgrounds.
2 Compare and contrast two public figures who offer possibilities for comparison and contrast similar to those of Lee and Grant.
3 In two substantial paragraphs, compare and contrast two persons, such as your father and your grandfather, mother and grandmother, or yourself and a brother, sister, cousin, or friend. Use plenty of supporting details.

Two Colonial Attitudes toward Marriage

GEORGE R. STEWART

First, and more commonly, there was what we may call the "unromantic" 1
marriage, most often "arranged" for the girl by her parents. In such a marriage sexuality was secondarily conceived. The assumption was, we may believe, that as a sex partner any woman or any man was likely to be satisfactory enough. As important individually, and much more important in the aggregate, were the other factors of such a marriage—the adjustment of property through dowries and marriage settlements, the setting up of the conventional living arrangement called a home, the perpetuation of the family.

With such a conception of marriage, infidelity raised no serious problem. 2
Since there had been no great love to begin with, there was less likely to be any great jealousy later. In fact, though adultery was established by English law as a cause for divorce, such a charge could be made to stand against the husband only if his adulteries had become public and notorious. Even adul-

tery by the wife, especially after legitimate heirs had been obtained, might be leniently regarded by society, though less leniently by the law.

3   On the other hand, the Elizabethan times had some idea of the "romantic" marriage. Such a marriage was conceived as resulting from the mutual attraction of an individual man and woman, sexuality as primary, and property arrangements, living conditions, and the perpetuation of the family as secondary.

4   From the point of view of the man, we can sum up the two conceptions of marriage briefly. The unromantic marriage is based upon the assumption: "Any normal woman is suitable to share the marriage bed. What is needful, or at least equally important, is a wife to be a good housekeeper and mother, and the possessor of a dowry." The romantic marriage, however, proceeds upon the assumption: "Any woman can be a good housekeeper and so forth. Or, if she is not, that is not most important. What is needed in marriage is a wife who can bring the transcendent bliss of love."

STUDY QUESTIONS
Organization and Content

1   Stewart begins with "first." Where is the contrast to this "first"? What does Stewart call the two opposing attitudes?
2   On what criteria does Stewart base his contrast?
3   What special problem does Stewart discuss in paragraph 3? What question, or objection, did he anticipate that probably made him write paragraph 3?
4   What is the function of sentence 1, paragraph 4? of paragraph 4?

Sentence Structure

1   If sentence 3, paragraph 1, were rearranged, and it began with "The other factors," what would be the difference in emphasis? What construction allows Stewart to achieve the emphasis that he has?
2   Note that all four sentences of paragraph 2 begin with subordinate elements. What is the effect of *in fact* and *even*?
3   In the sentences after sentence 1 in paragraph 4, how much repetition and how much parallelism or close similarity of structure does Stewart use?

Diction

1   What are the roots of *aggregate* (paragraph 1) (how is it related to *gregarious?*), *infidelity* (2) (how related to *confidence?*), *dowry*, and *transcendent* (4)?

2   Why does Stewart place quotation marks around three single terms?

Assignment

1   Contrast two opposing views about marriage at the present time. Follow the principles of organization and parallelism that Stewart used.
2   Similarly contrast opposing views on divorce, abortion, or childrearing.
3   Or contrast opposing views on the value of higher education.

Two Attitudes toward Success

NORMAN PODHORETZ

My second purpose in telling the story of my own career is to provide a concrete setting for a diagnosis of the curiously contradictory feelings our culture instills in us toward the ambition for success, and toward each of its various goals: money, power, fame, and social position. On the one hand, we are commanded to become successful—that is, to acquire more of these worldly goods than we began with, and to do so by our own exertions; on the other hand, it is impressed upon us by means both direct and devious that if we obey the commandment, we shall find ourselves falling victim to the radical corruption of spirit which, given the nature of what is nowadays called the "system," the pursuit of success requires and which its attainment always bespeaks. On the one hand, "the exclusive worship of the bitch-goddess SUCCESS," as William James put it in a famous remark, "is our national disease"; on the other hand, a contempt for success is the consensus of the national literature for the past hundred years and more. On the one hand, our culture teaches us to shape our lives in accordance with the hunger for worldly things; on the other hand, it spitefully contrives to make us ashamed of the presence of those hungers in ourselves and to deprive us as far as possible of any pleasure in their satisfaction.

STUDY QUESTIONS
Organization and Content

1 Podhoretz is discussing "contradictory attitudes" toward what two things?
2 What goals of success does Podhoretz enumerate?
3 In sentence 2, what contradictory attitudes are contrasted?
4 What judgments concerning success in America are contrasted in sentence 3?
5 In sentence 4, what contrasting effects that "our culture" has upon us are emphasized?
6 Podhoretz says in sentence 2 that if we gain success, we are victims of "radical corruption of spirit"—which is a very abstract term. In what specific ways might a successful person become corrupted in spirit?
7 In sentence 2 Podhoretz refers to "these worldly goods" and in sentence 4 to "worldly things." What, presumably, would such worldly goods or things include?

Sentence Structure

1 In sentences 2–4, how has Podhoretz given us a clear signal before the two contrasting parts of each sentence?
2 In these sentences, what mark of punctuation clearly separates the two contrasting parts of each sentence?
3 Notice how Podhoretz extends sentence 2 in the second half with a *that*-clause and two *which*-clauses. What interrupters does he include in sentence 2 and in the first part of sentence 3?
4 In sentence 4, what elements has Podhoretz arranged in a parallel structure?

Diction

1 Look up and learn the roots of *diagnosis, contradictory, radical, consensus.*
2 You may need to find out the meanings of these words also: *curiously, instills, exertions, devious, corruption, attainment, bespeaks, contrives.*

Assignment

Write a paragraph explaining what opposite feelings a person may have toward: working for high grades, marriage, sex, the opposite sex, social life, following the family business or profession, one's own family.

Western Farmers: Myth and Reality

HENRY NASH SMITH

The yawning gap between agrarian theory and the actual circumstances of 1
the West after the Civil War must have contributed greatly to the disillusionment which comes out in the farmers' crusades of the last quarter of the
century. The Western farmer had been told that he was not a peasant but a
peer of the realm; that his contribution to society was basic, all others deriv-
ative and even parasitic in comparison; that cities were sores on the body
politic, and the merchants and bankers and factory owners who lived in
them, together with their unfortunate employees, wicked and decadent. He
had been told that he was compensated for any austerity in his mode of life
by being sheltered against the temptations of luxury and vice, and against
the ups and downs of the market. His outstanding characteristic, according
to the conventional notion, was his independence, which was understood to
be at once economic self-sufficiency and integrity of character. For all these
reasons, the farmer had been assured, correct political theory required the
government to make a particular effort to guard his interests.

But after the Civil War Republican policy obviously favored the city 2
against the country, the banker and the merchant against the farmer, the
speculator against the settler. Whatever may have been the theoretical advantages of the simplicity of rural existence, the ostentatious luxury of the
newly rich in the growing cities was paraded in the press with a kind of prurient fascination as evidence of what a free society might achieve by way of
the good life. And the Western farmer found that instead of being independent, he was at the mercy not only of the Chicago and New York and
Liverpool grain pits, but also of the railways and elevator companies and
steamship lines upon which he must rely to get his crop to market. Even the
nature that had formerly hovered over the garden of the world as a benign
presence, a goddess of fertility and a dispensatrix of inexhaustible bounty,
seemed on the high plains to become periodically an avenging deity who
sent scourges of drouth, sandstorms, and grasshoppers upon suffering humanity. The scope of this contrast between image and fact, the ideal and the
actual, the hope and the consummation, defines the bitterness of the agrarian revolt that made itself felt with increasing force from the 1870's onward.
Hamlin Garland declared in 1892 that the high-sounding clichés had done

serious mischief by masking the plight of the poverty-stricken Western farmer. Speaking through the character Radbourn in his powerful story "Lucretia Burns," he wrote: "Writers and orators have lied so long about 'the idyllic' in farm life, and said so much about the 'independent American farmer,' that he himself has remained blind to the fact that he's one of the hardest working and poorest-paid men in America."

STUDY QUESTIONS

Organization and Content

1 What contrasting ideas does Smith pair up in sentence 1? What is his key word in the latter part of the sentence?
2 Which of the concepts concerning the Western farmer were most flattering to him? Which were the most comforting?
3 How does sentence 1, paragraph 2, show contrast and provide transition?
4 What specific terms in paragraph 1 are contrasted by the statements in paragraph 2, sentences 1–3?
5 What further contrast is expressed in paragraph 2, sentence 4? How does Smith make this sentence seem climactic?
6 What are the key words of sentence 5?
7 Why was the Western farmer so slow to perceive his real situation?

Sentence Structure

1 Point out parallelism of ideas and structure in paragraph 1, sentences 2–4.
2 Point out the three parallel direct objects in paragraph 2, sentence 1. What is the advantage of using these three terms? What would be lost if any two of them were omitted?
3 In paragraph 2, sentence 2, which terms are thrown into contrast? Do you think the alliterative *p*'s are effective?
4 What is the effect of opening sentence 3 with *and*?
5 In sentence 5, do the three double objects of *between* produce an emphatic effect or merely seem wordy?

Diction

1 If you need to, look up *agrarian, disillusionment, decadent, austerity, ostentatious, prurient, clichés,* and *idyllic.*
2 What difference in meaning is there between *peer* as used here and as used by Padilla?
3 What different connotations do *speculator* and *settler* have in paragraph 2, sentence 1? What are the connotations of the terms applied to *nature* in paragraph 2, sentence 4?

Assignment

1   Write a paper contrasting expectation and reality. For example, some women students might write about men, and some men students about women. Other possibilities: a trip to a big city, a vacation at the beach or in the mountains, a bullfight, a carnival, a fishing or hunting trip, spending the holidays at home.
2   Many people have dreams of success or of a perfect kind of life. Using one of the following suggestions, write a paper in which you contrast dream and reality: being self-sufficient on a small farm; going to a big city to "make it" on the stage, in business, or in art; going off to college; going to live in a special region such as the Sunbelt, the slow, gracious South, the romantic West, the dynamic North; retirement; or retirement in one of the regions just mentioned.

Urban Society and Folk Society

PHILIP M. HAUSER

"Urbanism as a way of life" has been contrasted with life in a "folk society." Folk society is made up of relatively small homogeneous population groupings which are comparatively isolated from interrelations with other groupings. It is characterized by simple technology and simple division of labor, and tends to be economically autonomous. The social order in the folk society is integrated by the force of tradition and convention. Such a society has no systematic knowledge of the type available through the funded knowledge of science in books and in libraries.

Urbanism as a way of life, in contrast, is characterized by large clumpings of populations in densely settled patterns. The concomitants of such living, it is held, include weakening of the bonds of kinship, declining role of the family, and substitution of secondary, utilitarian and rational contacts for primary contacts based on personal contact, emotion, and sentiment. In the urban setting traditional institutions such as the family are greatly modified, and new and specialized types of institutions emerge to deal with the new problems of urban existence. Such new institutions include police departments, public health agencies, insurance, workmen's compensation laws, unemployment compensation, labor unions, and civilian defense organizations. That is, the urban environment forces modification of the inherited

From *Population Perspectives* by Philip M. Hauser. Copyright © 1960 by Rutgers, The State University. Reprinted by permission of Rutgers University Press.

social structure and institutions and is responsible for the formation and development of new institutions to deal with the new and unprecedented problems of urban living.

3   One of the most important differences between the urban and folk environments in the effect upon the conduct of the individual is the extent to which urbanism as a condition of living necessitates the exercise of choice. It forces the substitution of rational for traditional ways of doing things. In the folk setting there is generally a prescribed way of dealing with most situations, certainly with the most important and recurring situations in life. In the city there are almost always alternatives, and therefore enforced rationalism.

4   The freeing of the individual from the constraints of tradition and convention has had quite differing consequences. On the one hand, it has opened up new channels for self expression, new opportunities for shaping both man's environment and his destiny. In freeing man's mind from the restraints of the past, urbanism as a way of life has promoted the exercise of ingenuity and creativity. It is not a coincidence that the great centers of learning, invention, art, and culture have historically been located in urban areas. The "city mentality" has been characterized by objectivity, sophistication, utilitarianism, and rationalism. It is both the product of the urban environment and a force in producing and influencing the continuing changes in urban living.

5   But the same factors in the urban environment that are responsible for the great achievements of modern civilization also produce social and personal disorganization. The modification and disruption of inherited social institutions have their counterpart in personal disorganization. The juvenile delinquent and the criminal, for example, are manifestations of the breakdown of traditional social controls. They are symptoms of the diminishing influence in the urban environment of such social institutions as the family, the church, the community, and the school. Similarly, unemployment and old age dependency are results of frictions in the changing social and economic order created by urban living. The corrupt political boss, the "big fix," the unscrupulous lobbyist are likewise evidence of frictions in a political order undergoing modification in the urban setting. In brief, many of the problems of contemporary urban living may be viewed as conflicts brought about by man's effort to adapt himself to the urban environment which he himself has created.

STUDY QUESTIONS

Organization and Content

1   The main interest of Hauser, a sociologist, is ''mutation'' of various kinds, as he states in sentence 1. In the rest of his discussion he

develops a contrast in order to make us understand how the way of life must change for people who move from a farm or village to a big, densely populated city. What are the technical names of the types of social life that Hauser is contrasting?

2   What several qualities of non-urban life does Hauser list in paragraph 1?

3   In paragraph 2 what obvious specific difference is first mentioned? Then what untraditional and unconventional changes and developments are enumerated? How is paragraph 2, sentence 4, related to paragraph 1, sentence 1?

4   What further contrast does Hauser explain in paragraph 3? What reason does he give for city dwellers' having more alternatives to choose among?

5   Paragraph 3 is abstract; Hauser provides no specific illustrations. Can you think of some possible illustrations? (For an example, you might look back at Toffler's work, p. 97.)

6   Do you think that the "funded knowledge of science" that Hauser mentions in paragraph 1 is largely responsible for the existence of the great urban centers of creativity (paragraph 4), or are other factors more significant?

Sentence Structure

1   Point out transitional links among the six sentences of paragraph 1.

2   How much variety of sentence length do these six sentences have? How much variety of sentence structure?

3   How does Hauser use parallel elements in the sentences of paragraphs 2–5?

Diction

1   Hauser's vocabulary is quite abstract, and many of our abstract terms came into English from Latin or Greek. You will profit from learning the meanings of the roots of *homogeneous, autonomous* (paragraph 1), *concomitants* (2), *rationalism* (3), *sophistication* (4), *disruption* (5).

2   In paragraph 1, sentence 4, Hauser speaks of "the *funded* knowledge of science in books and libraries." What are the denotation and connotation of *funded*?

3   What would be the "folk" opposites of the city qualities listed in paragraph 4, sentence 4?

Assignment

Write a paper that is more specific than Hauser's piece on one of the following topics:

1   Contrast the opportunities for learning and self-expression, or

for different kinds of activities, in a large city and in a small town or on a farm or ranch.

2   Similarly contrast the relations with family, church, and community of a person of about your age in such a city and town.

3   Do you think that there is a "professional mentality" which is different from a farmer's, laborer's, or factory worker's mentality? If so, write a paper bringing out the contrasts between them.

Movie Gangsters and Westerners

ROBERT WARSHOW

1   The two most successful creations of American movies are the gangster and the Westerner: men with guns. Guns as physical objects, and the postures associated with their use, form the visual and emotional center of both types of films. I suppose this reflects the importance of guns in the fantasy life of Americans; but that is a less illuminating point than it appears to be.

2   The gangster movie, which no longer exists in its "classical" form, is a story of enterprise and success ending in precipitate failure. Success is conceived as an increasing power to work injury, it belongs to the city, and it is of course a form of evil (though the gangster's death, presented usually as "punishment," is perceived simply as defeat). The peculiarity of the gangster is his unceasing, nervous activity. The exact nature of his enterprises may remain vague, but his commitment to enterprise is always clear, and all the more clear because he operates outside the field of utility. He is without culture, without manners, without leisure, or at any rate his leisure is likely to be spent in debauchery so compulsively aggressive as to seem only another aspect of his "work." But he is graceful, moving like a dancer among the crowded dangers of the city.

3   Like other tycoons, the gangster is crude in conceiving his ends but by no means inarticulate; on the contrary, he is usually expansive and noisy (the introspective gangster is a fairly recent development), and can state definitely what he wants: to take over the North Side, to own a hundred suits, to be Number One. But new "frontiers" will present themselves infinitely, and by a rigid convention it is understood that as soon as he wishes to rest on his gains, he is on the way to destruction.

4   The gangster is lonely and melancholy, and can give the impression of a profound worldly wisdom. He appeals most to adolescents with their impa-

Reprinted by permission of Paul Warshow. From *The Immediate Experience* by Robert Warshow. (Garden City, N.Y.: Doubleday, 1962).

tience and their feeling of being outsiders, but more generally he appeals to that side of all of us which refuses to belive in the "normal" possibilities of happiness and achievement; the gangster is the "no" to the great American "yes" which is stamped so big over our official culture and yet has so little to do with the way we really feel about our lives. But the gangster's loneliness and melancholy are not "authentic"; like everything else that belongs to him, they are not honestly come by: he is lonely and melancholy not because life ultimately demands such feelings but because he has put himself in a position where everybody wants to kill him and eventually somebody will. He is wide open and defenseless, incomplete because unable to accept any limits or come to terms with his own nature, fearful, loveless. And the story of his career is a nightmare inversion of the values of ambition and opportunity. From the window of Scarface's bulletproof apartment can be seen an electric sign proclaiming: "The World Is Yours," and, if I remember, this sign is the last thing we see after Scarface lies dead in the street. In the end it is the gangster's weakness as much as his power and freedom that appeals to us; the world is not ours, but it is not his either, and in his death he "pays" for our fantasies, releasing us momentarily both from the concept of success, which he denies by caricaturing it, and from the need to succeed, which he shows to be dangerous.

The Western hero, by contrast, is a figure of repose. He resembles the **5** gangster in being lonely and to some degree melancholy. But his melancholy comes from the "simple" recognition that life is unavoidably serious, not from the disproportions of his own temperament. And his loneliness is organic, not imposed on him by his situation but belonging to him intimately and testifying to his completeness. The gangster must reject others violently or draw them violently to him. The Westerner is not thus compelled to seek love; he is prepared to accept it, perhaps, but he never asks of it more than it can give, and we see him constantly in situations where love is at best an irrelevance. If there is a woman he loves, she is usually unable to understand his motives; she is against killing and being killed, and he finds it impossible to explain to her that there is no point in being "against" these things: they belong to his world.

Very often this woman is from the East and her failure to understand rep- **6** resents a clash of cultures. In the American mind, refinement, virtue, civilization, Christianity itself, are seen as feminine, and therefore women are often portrayed as possessing some kind of deeper wisdom, while the men, for all their apparent self-assurance, are fundamentally childish. But the West, lacking the graces of civilization, is the place "where men are men"; in Western movies, men have the deeper wisdom and the women are children. Those women in the Western movies who share the hero's understanding of life are prostitutes (or, as they are usually presented, barroom entertainers)—women, that is, who have come to understand in the most practical way how love can be an irrelevance, and therefore "fallen" women.

The gangster, too, associates with prostitutes, but for him the important things about a prostitute are her passive availability and her costliness: she is part of his winnings. In Western movies, the important thing about a prostitute is her quasi-masculine independence: nobody owns her, nothing has to be explained to her, and she is not, like a virtuous woman, a "value" that demands to be protected. When the Westerner leaves the prostitute for a virtuous woman—for love—he is in fact forsaking a way of life, though the point of the choice is often obscured by having the prostitute killed by getting into the line of fire.

STUDY QUESTIONS
Organization and Content

1   In what respects are the movie gangster and Western hero shown in paragraph 1 to be similar?
2   Which character does Warshow discuss first?
3   At what point does he turn to the second character? In what sentences after that does he bring in contrasts with the first character?
4   How does Warshow define the gangster movie?
5   What special characteristics does the movie gangster have? Where does he live and "work"?
6   Why does he go down in defeat?
7   According to Warshow, why is he lonely and melancholy?
8   What feeling does Warshow communicate by terms such as "nightmare inversion of the values of ambition" and "caricaturing" of "the concept of success"?
9   How is the Western hero said to resemble the gangster hero? Even so, how are they different?
10   What contrast does Warshow make between the Westerner and the woman he loves?
11   Do you agree with the statement about "the American mind" in sentence 2, paragraph 6?
12   Explain how, in view of sentence 6, paragraph 5, Warshow states in the final sentence of paragraph 6 that by marrying for love the Westerner is "forsaking a way of life."

Sentence Structure

1   What key word appears in each sentence of paragraph 1? Explain how this word is placed in each sentence. Where does it get the most emphasis?
2   In sentence 1, paragraph 2, point out the interrupting clause between subject and verb. What modifiers of the complement come at the end? (The sentence follows a much-used pattern of structure.)

3 Sentence 2, paragraph 2, has a different—but also much used—pattern. Show the balancing of parallel elements in it. Note the use of parentheses for a high degree of separation of the last element in the sentence.

4 In sentence 1, paragraph 3, note how the semicolon is used before the contrast brought out in the second half of the sentence. What transitional phrase signals the contrast?

5 Indicate what links relate "what he wants" in sentence 1, paragraph 3, to the "way to destruction" that ends the paragraph.

6 Point out the noun-and-pronoun repetition that supplies transition all through paragraph 4.

7 What transitional phrase does Warshow use in sentence 1, paragraph 5?

8 What transitional words begin sentences 3 and 4, paragraph 5? How does each one function?

9 What are the subjects of sentences 5 and 6, paragraph 5? Do they make an effective contrast?

10 In sentence 5, paragraph 6, how does Warshow smoothly introduce a reference to the gangster? and how does he sum up his idea in that sentence?

11 Explain how sentence 6, paragraph 6, is balanced by the colon. How is the part after the colon set up in idea and in structure?

Diction

1 Look up *precipitate, utility, culture, debauchery* (paragraph 2); *tycoons, inarticulate, introspective, convention* (3); *melancholy, profound, worldly, adolescents, authentic, ultimately, inversion, fantasies, caricaturing* (4); *repose, disproportions, organic, irrelevance, motives* (5); *fundamentally, availability, quasi* (6).

2 Learn the roots of *precipitate, utility, introspective, adolescents.* What other words are formed from the same roots?

3 What is the difference in meaning between *culture* (2) and *cultures* (6)?

Assignment

Compare and contrast, in moving pictures and TV programs, the detective and the patrolman; the reporter-interviewer and people interviewed. Or contrast people in TV advertisements and real people.

Classic and Romantic

ROBERT M. PIRSIG

1   The terms *classic* and *romantic*, as Phaedrus used them, mean the following:

2   A classical understanding sees the world primarily as underlying form itself. A romantic understanding sees it primarily in terms of immediate appearance. If you were to show an engine or a mechanical drawing or electronic schematic to a romantic it is unlikely he would see much of interest in it. It has no appeal because the reality he sees is its surface. Dull, complex lists of names, lines and numbers. Nothing interesting. But if you were to show the same blueprint or schematic or give the same description to a classical person he might look at it and then become fascinated by it because he sees that within the lines and shapes and symbols is a tremendous richness of underlying form.

3   The romantic mode is primarily inspirational, imaginative, creative, intuitive. Feelings rather than facts predominate. "Art" when it is opposed to "Science" is often romantic. It does not proceed by reason or by laws. It proceeds by feeling, intuition and esthetic conscience. In the northern European cultures the romantic mode is usually associated with femininity, but this is certainly not a necessary association.

4   The classic mode, by contrast, proceeds by reason and by laws—which are themselves underlying forms of thought and behavior. In the European cultures it is primarily a masculine mode and the fields of science, law and medicine are unattractive to women largely for this reason. Although motorcycle riding is romantic, motorcycle maintenance is purely classic. The dirt, the grease, the mastery of underlying form required all give it such a negative romantic appeal that women never go near it.

5   Although surface ugliness is often found in the classic mode of understanding it is not inherent in it. There is a classic esthetic which romantics often miss because of its subtlety. The classic style is straightforward, unadorned, unemotional, economical and carefully proportioned. Its purpose is not to inspire emotionally, but to bring order out of chaos and make the unknown known. It is not an esthetically free and natural style. It is esthetically restrained. Everything is under control. Its value is measured in terms of the skill with which this control is maintained.

6   To a romantic this classic mode often appears dull, awkward and ugly, like mechanical maintenance itself. Everything is in terms of pieces and parts and components and relationships. Nothing is figured out until it's

run through the computer a dozen times. Everything's got to be measured and proved. Oppressive. Heavy. Endlessly grey. The death force.

Within the classic mode, however, the romantic has some appearances of 7 his own. Frivolous, irrational, erratic, untrustworthy, interested primarily in pleasure-seeking. Shallow. Of no substance. Often a parasite who cannot or will not carry his own weight. A real drag on society. By now these battle lines should sound a little familiar.

This is the source of the trouble. Persons tend to think and feel exclu- 8 sively in one mode or the other and in doing so tend to misunderstand and underestimate what the other mode is all about. But no one is willing to give up the truth as he sees it, and as far as I know, no one now living has any real reconciliation of these truths or modes. There is no point at which these visions of reality are unified.

And so in recent times we have seen a huge split develop between a classic 9 culture and a romantic counterculture—two worlds growingly alienated and hateful toward each other with everyone wondering if it will always be this way, a house divided against itself. No one wants it really—despite what his antagonists in the other dimension might think.

STUDY QUESTIONS
Organization and Content

1 Many people have written on the perennial contrast of classic and romantic. Robert Pirsig discusses the topic in an unusual context—that of motorcycle maintenance. (Phaedrus, incidentally, is Pirsig's name for himself at an earlier stage.) How does he manage the contrast in paragraph 2? What are his key terms?

2 What are his units of contrast in paragraphs 3 and 4? Identify the key terms in these paragraphs?

3 What different aspect of the contrast is brought out in paragraphs 6 and 7? What repeated term helps to bind paragraphs 3–7 together?

4 In paragraph 8, sentence 1, what does *this* comprise? How does Pirsig more specifically interpret the situation in sentence 2? What criticism of both classic and romantic groups does he make in paragraph 8?

5 What purpose is served by paragraphs 8 and 9? In the final paragraph what terms does Pirsig apply to people with a classic understanding and to those with a romantic understanding?

6 According to Pirsig what professional areas of our culture are predominantly classic in outlook? predominantly romantic?

7 Do you agree that there are few women in science, law, and medicine for the reasons that Pirsig gives?

8 Are people in technological areas such as engineering and agriculture primarily classic or primarily romantic in their "visions of real-

ity''? How about those in journalism, home economics, history, theater, architecture, and education?

9   In paragraph 3 Pirsig says that ''the romantic mode is primarily . . . imaginative, creative. . . .'' Do lawyers, scientists, and physicians, then, tend to be unimaginative and uncreative?

Sentence Structure

1   In paragraphs 2, 6, and 7 Pirsig uses several incomplete sentences. What do these adjectives, nouns, and so on, without predicates, represent?

2   Contrast the sentences of paragraph 3 and those of paragraph 4 in terms of length and variety of structural pattern.

3   How does Pirsig convey all the information about classic style in paragraph 5, sentence 3? How does he secure transition in the sentences of paragraph 5 that follow?

4   Comment on the pattern of those sentences (4–8) in relation to their purposes.

5   In paragraph 9, sentence 1, what is the effect of beginning with *and so?* In both sentences of paragraph 9 what kind of material does Pirsig set off by dashes? What is the effect of setting it off in that way?

Diction

1   You may need to look up *schematic* (paragraph 2), *intuitive, esthetic* (3), *inherent, subtlety* (4), *frivolous, erratic* (7), *reconciliation* (8), *alienated* (9).

2   Learn the roots of *inspirational, predominate* (3), *oppressive* (6).

3   Is Pirsig's style too colloquial at times? Consider *it's* and *everything's got to be* (6) and *real drag* (7).

4   What do you understand by *culture* and *counterculture* (9)?

Assignment

Like Pirsig, contrast persons of different temperaments and/or interests such as: 1. early risers and late sleepers; 2. theoretical people and practical people; 3. thinkers and doers; 4. city lovers and country lovers; 5. artistically inclined people and mechanically inclined people; 6. athletic people and sedentary people; 7. game-loving people and game-hating people.

English Translations of the Bible

STANLEY N. GUNDRY

Many Christians are confused, some dismayed, by the numerous Bible 1
translations available. It is not unusual for a Sunday school teacher to use
one version, with at least five or six other versions in use by class members.

Since World War II, English readers have had more than twenty new 2
translations, in addition to reprints of at least eighteen earlier versions.
With this variety, many wonder which one is really best.

One article cannot clear this confusion. Nor can anyone achieve unifor- 3
mity by decreeing that from this time on we will all use. . . .

Evangelical Christians, however, will see no progress toward agreement 4
until they understand some basic considerations long understood by scholars.

Why can't we continue to use the King James Version (KJV)? Many 5
people believe that everyone should use the KJV. Many have an enduring
affection for the version they have used all their lives.

This version was a monumental achievement, and it has had a useful his- 6
tory. Based on the best scholarship of the early 1600's, it communicated in
the common English language to the people of the seventeenth century. Although it was initially opposed by the Puritans (they would not even allow
a copy of it on the Mayflower, preferring instead the Geneva Bible of 1560),
after a few years the KJV won its place in the hearts of English-speaking
people.

But this is the problem. The KJV was an achievement for the seven- 7
teenth century. Yet many changes have occurred. Most biblical students
agree that better Hebrew and Greek manuscripts are available today. Tremendous strides have also been made in our understanding of the original
languages. While the KJV is a good translation, the tools of scholarship
have created the possibility of better translations.

The English language itself has changed significantly since 1611. There 8
have been changes in grammar, idiom, and meaning of words. Though
most people still understand thee's and thou's, howbeit's and wherefore's,
we no longer speak this way.

Some words in the KJV can't be accurately understood without explana- 9
tion because their meaning is different than in 1611. For example, "to al-
lege" meant to produce as evidence or to prove (Acts 17:3 KJV); now it

From "Which Version Is Best?" by Stanley N. Gundry, originally appearing in
Moody Monthly, January, 1979. Used by permission.

means to claim or assert without proof. "To let" meant to hinder (2 Thess. 2:7 KJV); now it means to permit. "To prevent" meant to precede (Matt. 17:25 KJV); now it means to stop or hinder. "Conversation" meant manner of living or way of life (Gal. 1:13 KJV); now it means informal discussion.

10   The KJV has more than three hundred such words. It is unreasonable to expect that any translation could be permanent because our language is in a slow process of change.

11   Why are there so many different versions? There will always be an individual or group ready to produce what they think will be a better translation. No agency exists that could produce one uniform translation that we would all accept.

12   Another problem is that translations inevitably seem to reflect the theological convictions of their translators. People are dissatisfied with translations which reflect theological views contrary to their own.

13   Two significant examples are the Revised Standard Version (RSV) and the New English Bible (NEB). Both were the work of translators who generally held liberal theological and higher critical views. They did not believe the Bible was verbally inspired; to them it was a basically human book. Many believe this view of the Bible affected the translations at certain points. They have not been generally accepted in evangelical circles.

14   Another set of circumstances also contributes to the number of translations. Every translator faces a set of problems. How does one transfer equivalents of money, measurement, clothing, and custom from one language and culture into another? Should we use names of Roman units of money (denarius, etc.), or should we translate Roman money into dollars and cents? If we do, how do we establish equivalent values? If we solve that, how do we allow for the constantly decreasing value of the dollar? Do we use ancient names for units of measurement, or modern equivalents? Do we go metric?

15   Do we literally translate ancient customs (such as the disciples reclining to eat) that would puzzle many today? Or do we translate that they sat down to eat, which is our cultural equivalent? Or does that convey a mistaken impression?

16   What should the translator do with idiomatic expressions—expressions with a meaning different from a strictly literal understanding of the words? A literal translation might fail to communicate the original meaning. Paul uses a phrase which translated literally reads, "May it never be!" Even with an exclamation mark, it still comes across comparatively weak and insipid in English. But Paul's phrase expresses the strongest sense of repudiation. Consequently, many have translated it, "God forbid!" Yet Paul did not use the Greek equivalent of either "God" or "forbid."

17   Few words of one language have an exact equivalent in another language. Words have areas of meaning. For instance, our word "horse" refers to an

animal, but can also be used of horse flies, horse radish, horsepower, horse play, and a game played with a basketball. But we cannot expect the nearest equivalent word in any other language to have this same variety of usage.

Another problem is how closely the translator should follow the word **18** order, word for word equivalency, and sentence construction of the original language. The more closely these are followed, the less likely the translation will sound like a natural English sentence. It produces what is called "translation English." The reader has the feeling that it is not quite the right way to say it. But the more latitude the translator takes in rephrasing the statement in natural English, the farther he gets from the actual words of the original.

The Bible also contains a significant number of terms that have acquired **19** rather technical theological meanings which may not be understood by the uninformed—justification, reconciliation, grace, atonement, propitiation, sanctification, and even blood. People without specific teaching or study of these terms wouldn't comprehend their biblical significance. If we decide not to use these theological terms, how do we translate them? If we use a simpler term, we will lose some of the rich meaning. If we explain the term every time, we create an interpretation rather than a translation.

There is no simple answer to these problems. But until we understand the **20** problems, we are unable to understand the strengths and weaknesses of individual versions.

What types of versions are there? There are many ways to classify types of **21** versions—literal, thought for thought, colloquial or idiomatic, simplified, expanded, and paraphrase. But linguists today generally speak of translations as having either literal or dynamic equivalence.

These two types describe two different approaches to most of the transla- **22** tion problems discussed above. Rather than being concerned about word-for-word translation, dynamic equivalence is more concerned about the natural structure and expression of the English sentence. It aims for cultural equivalence rather than mere verbal equivalence.

Dynamic equivalence strives to communicate the over-all message and re- **23** produce the original impact on the reader. The concern is to communicate in the common language of the people, just as Scripture in the Greek and Hebrew did for its original readers. It is less concerned with translating the details of the original text if these detract from the translation's dynamic equivalence.

When skillfully done, this approach produces very readable translations. **24** Dynamic equivalence versions are *New International Version, Modern Language Bible, New English Bible, Today's English Version,* Phillips' paraphrase, and *Living Bible.* They are listed in order from more to less literal.

This approach also has disadvantages. These versions tend to become in- **25** terpretations rather than translations. Some of the nuances of the original text are lost by creating an easily understood English reading. People tend to read implications into the wording of dynamic translations, especially paraphrases.

26   For example, the Living Bible (LB) renders Phil. 1:6, "And I am sure that God who began the good work within you will keep right on helping you grow in His grace until His task within you is finally finished when Jesus Christ returns."

27   Notice the phrase "helping you grow in His grace." Paul did not refer directly to either helping, growing, or grace—"He who began a good work within you will perfect it. . . ."

28   Galatians 6:16 in the LB is a typical example of the interpretative nature of paraphrases. This verse literally translated refers to the "Israel of God." Grammatically, this could refer to the remnant of Jewish believers within the church or to the church as a new spiritual Israel displacing literal Israel. This is a critical text for one's view of Israel and the church. But you would never know there was a debate from reading the Living Bible. It refers to "those everywhere who are really God's own."

29   When reading a paraphrase, one cannot distinguish between translation and interpretation without also reading a more literal translation or consulting the text in the original language.

30   The more translations follow the principle of dynamic equivalence, the less appropriate they are for use as a study Bible or as a Bible for public teaching and preaching. They may be quite suitable for reading by the unconverted, new believers, the person who has been mystified by Scripture, or by one who simply has found the Bible hard to read because it seems to be written in a strange style. These versions should also be consulted when literal translations are stilted or obscure in meaning.

31   Literal translations aim for word for word equivalence. The more literal a translation is, the less it will sound like commonly spoken English. Some are rigidly literal, others give more attention to English style. Although they tend to read less easily, skillful translators can still produce an acceptable English translation.

32   The American Standard Version, New American Standard Bible, and Revised Standard Version are best included in this class, with the first being rigidly literal and the other two more attuned to acceptable English usage. The obvious advantage of literal translations is that they allow less freedom to the translator to interpret. Consequently, a good literal translation makes the best Bible for personal study and public exposition.

33   Which version is best?

34   No single version could fulfill all possible needs. So one should also ask, "Best for what purposes and for whom?"

35   I prefer translations produced by persons whose theology reflects a respect for the Bible as God's written Word. Within that guideline for general use in preaching, teaching and study, I prefer a version that is literal enough to

be concerned about word for word equivalency where reasonably possible, but flexible enough to read as good English. Two recent versions stand at the top of my list: the New American Standard Bible and the New International Version. Leaning toward the more literal, I prefer the NASB. But the credentials of the NIV merit its careful consideration.

STUDY QUESTIONS
Organization and Content

1 This article, like that of Ramírez, shows comparison and contrast used as part of a broader discussion, which also makes use of analysis. Note that the author, a professor of theology at Moody Bible Institute, is concerned that a biblical translation be appropriate especially for "Evangelical Christians." In his first four paragraphs what reason does Gundry give for people's confusion and uncertainty about translations of the Bible?

2 What are the purposes of paragraphs 3 and 4?

3 For what reasons does Gundry praise the noted and beloved King James Version? What reasons does he present for not simply adopting it as the most thoroughly acceptable translation?

4 What are the chief problems that translators of the Bible must deal with?

5 Into what two main groups does Gundry divide translations? How does he organize his comparison of these groups?

6 What are the advantages and disadvantages of each type of translation?

7 Where does Gundry most effectively use concrete examples?

8 Make a two-level outline of the article.

Sentence Structure

1 Several of Gundry's sentences in different paragraphs are questions. For what purpose does Gundry use them?

2 Analyze the three sentences in paragraph 21 and the three in paragraph 30 to show how their patterns fit their purposes.

3 What is the advantage of parallel structures in paragraphs 14–15 and 19?

4 Point out the means of transition that Gundry uses in paragraphs 22–26 and 30–31.

Diction

1 What are the best synonyms for *evangelical*, *literal*, and *dynamic* as Gundry uses them?

2 How is *credentials* (paragraph 35) related to *creed* and *credit*?

3   If you need to, look up *monumental* (6), *idiom* (8), *theological* (12), *higher criticism* (for *critical*) (13), *insipid, repudiation* (16), *nuances* (25).

Assignment

1   Get hold of some of the translations that Gundry mentions, and compare their versions of some well-known passage in the Bible: for example, the temptation of Adam and Eve (*Genesis* 3), the story of Noah and the ark (*Genesis* 6–8), the calamities of Job (*Job* 1–2), or the sermon on the mount (*Matthew* 5–7). Then judge them for their excellence in terms of ease of understanding, dignity of expression, and beauty of rhythm.
2   Compare accounts of some battle (Bunker Hill, say) in different American history books. Think about level of language, skill of sentence management, use of concrete material, and clearness of presentation.
3   Similarly compare accounts in newsmagazines of some striking event of the last several years in such an area as sports, science, crime, exploration, or weather.
4   If you are in a position to do so, compare British English with American English; English as spoken in the Middle West with that spoken in New York City or in the South; standard English with the English of freshman students; student English with professorial English.
5   Or similarly compare such magazines as *True Confessions* or *The Ladies' Home Journal* with *Harper's, The Atlantic,* or *Commentary;* educational television (PBS) network programs with popular television programs; art films with popular moving pictures.

Check Point

3

By now you should have developed skill in writing solid, unified paragraphs well linked by transitions—paragraphs that are developed with plenty of examples. You should have experimented with more than one technique of comparison and contrast and should be especially aware of the usefulness of sentences with parallel grammatical elements for this kind of exposition as well as for clear and economical communication of ideas generally. You should be expected to be able on occasion to compose sentences that are not only varied in form but also skillfully constructed for emphasis.

Definition

If someone is asked to "define" a word, one knows that one is expected to explain the meaning of that word, and one may be able to give a satisfactory explanation of the meaning—that is, a *definition*. On the other hand, one may flounder; one's attempt at a definition may be inefficient. There is an efficient way to make a definition, and one should always have it in mind when setting forth meanings of terms.

In the first place, the word *define* has as its root the Latin word *finis*, which means *limit*. If a limit is placed on something, a line is drawn, either physical or mental, beyond which no one can go. To put a limit to a term is to draw a line around it, to mark a line between the meaning of that term and the meanings of all other terms. By doing so, one is saying, "This is the territory that properly belongs to this term; over there beyond the line is the territory which properly belongs to that other term."

Two Necessary Steps

When any word is defined in an efficient way, it is necessary to take two steps. One must (1) put the word in the right class; (2) explain what different qualities the word has from every other word that also belongs in that class. This is rather like making a map. The people of the United States are spoken of as Americans; yet there is a line between New York and Pennsylvania and another line between Pennsylvania and Ohio. The Americans of New York do not vote, pay taxes, or buy licenses in Pennsylvania, and though in some communities two Americans live only a block apart, one will vote for a governor of New York and the other for a governor of Pennsylvania because there is a map line drawn between these two persons' houses.

If someone asks for a definition of *marble,* one would tell that person first that it is a kind of rock. Thus the first step would be taken; the term would be put in the right *class.* It has now been established that marble is not a bird or a plant or a liquid; it is a rock. Of course, there are many other kinds of rocks. How is one to know marble from granite, for example? The person will know by understanding the differences between marble and granite. If the class called *rock* is compared to the map of the United States, then the territory within that class called *marble* is like the state territory called New York, and the territory within that class called *granite* is like the state territory called Pennsylvania. What the definer has done is draw mental lines on the class-map between marble and granite.

Every correct definition has as its basis the two-step operation: placing in class—showing differences.

The class in which a term is placed should not be too large. If one is asked to define a *cabin* and one states, "A cabin is a thing," one has made a poor start. One might also say, "A fork is a thing." As a class, *thing* is much too general. Somewhere between the most *particular* term and the most *general* term there will be a term that will most efficiently classify the word being defined. A cabin is something like a hut, shack, mansion, or house. All of these are *dwellings. Dwelling* is a more general term than *cabin.* A dwelling could be classified as a *building.* A building would be placed in the class of *structures.* A *structure* is "something constructed." Thus, a structure is a *thing.*

So from the most general term to the least general term one goes through the series—thing-structure-building-dwelling-cabin. A more efficient definition of *cabin* will be made if *cabin* is included in the class of *dwelling* rather than in some more general class.

In the same way one might go through another series of gradually narrowing classes, from thing to living thing to animal to mammal to human being to man to hero. If an attempt is being made to define *hero,* it will clearly be better to place the term in the class of *man* rather than in *animal* or even in *mammal.* Thus, having classified a hero as a man, one must show how he is different from all other men. A hero is a man acting in a certain way; the second step is explaining how the ways in which a hero acts are different from the ways of other men.

Concrete Terms and Abstract Terms

A word that is a name for a particular object can sometimes be explained most easily by simply pointing to the object—thus if one points at a tree or shovel or table, a quick definition without words is given. Such words stand for concrete things; they are called *concrete* terms. But what if it is necessary to define a term that does not stand for a concrete thing? How can *honesty* or *generosity* be defined? These are *abstract* words, which express a quality or characteristic. It is possible to say, "The man gave back to its owner a purse containing 100 dollars." The sentence tells of a concrete action. It would be an example to support such a statement as "He has often shown his honesty." "The owner of the purse showed his generosity by rewarding the man for his honesty." This sentence contains two abstract words, or *abstractions*—words representing qualities, words without a material basis such as *tree* or *shovel* has. But both of these abstractions, *generosity* and *honesty,* can be illustrated. "The owner showed his generosity by giving him a 10-dollar bill." When defining abstractions, one is constantly impelled to illustrate their meanings by using concrete examples. In general, whenever one uses abstract words, one will "come down" from the mental area of ideas (honesty, sweetness, condition) to the physical area of concrete objects and actions. Suppose that a storekeeper says, "Economic conditions are bad." Just what does he mean? Furthermore, is he right? What evidence does he have about those abstract "conditions"? Suppose he gives evidence: "Ten of my customers, young married men who work for the steel company, have been laid off." From such concrete evidence the idea at once becomes clearer. The concrete and the specific are of much value in the process of definition.

Extended Definitions

Very often people know fairly well what the meaning of a word is. However, they have not considered it carefully; they do not know its meaning as well as does an expert or a careful thinker who has taken the trouble to consider it. Therefore, the type of exposition known as definition encountered in books and articles is somewhat more extensive than the definitions found in dictionaries. Such "extended definitions" are likely to be written to answer one or more of the following questions: In precisely what sense is the word being used? Just how much does this term take in? What new sense does the word now include? Regardless of other uses, or the general use, of the word, just what is its basic meaning?

Some writers may write pages or whole chapters that can be called definition. But even though their work is far more extensive than the definitions of a dictionary maker, these writers will always take the two essential steps of classification and differentiation. Then they may discuss the problem of classification—why one class is better than some other one that people have previously used—or they may discuss differences at length. They may go to some trouble to show what the word does *not* include—what is outside of the limit that should mark the meaning; they may give illustrations and make comparisons that are helpful; they may analyze the term, showing what its different parts are and explaining each part and its relation to the other parts; they may tell the reader something of the history of the word and why certain meanings developed as they did. Whatever methods they use, they are always using their minds to try to communicate a sharper and clearer idea or a broader and more stimulating idea of the meaning of the word.

Both analysis and definition are much used and highly important types of writing. Apprentice writers need to practice them until they are efficient, for in life today writers will never be able to avoid them.

A Cove

MAURICE BROOKS

It is appropriate, I suppose, to define the term "cove." In hilly or mountainous country, rainfall and melted snow pour down the slopes in torrents, these carrying soil, gravel, and other products of erosion. As slopes become more gentle and water is slowed in its course, some of this debris is deposited, the larger elements first and then finally smaller soil particles. The result of such deposition is a fan delta, a common land form in the Southwest at the mouths of arroyos. In older mountain areas these fan deltas become

From Maurice Brooks, *The Appalachians,* Houghton Mifflin Company. Copyright © 1965 by Maurice Brooks. Reprinted by permission of Houghton Mifflin Company.

stabilized by vegetation, and time softens their outlines. Each year there is an accretion of eroded material from above, and each year growing plants and animals contribute to soil formation. After enough millennia have passed the result is a cove, a naturally terraced valley near the foot of a mountain slope. Such areas are likely to be well watered, and to have deep and fertile soils. They are protected by heights to the rear and by flanking ridges on either side. They are good places for human habitation.

STUDY QUESTIONS

Organization and Content

1 Professor Brooks, an ecologist, decided that his discussion in a book about the Appalachians would be more meaningful if he defined the word *cove*. Is his first sentence a topic sentence?
2 What principle of organization has Brooks followed in sentences 2–7? Why do sentences 2–4 have the order they appear in? sentences 5–7?
3 Is it correct to say that sentences 2–4 constitute one unit and sentences 5–7 another unit?
4 At what point does Brooks tell us what class *cove* belongs in?
5 What are the chief differences that set a cove apart from other members of the same class?
6 What do sentences 8–10 contribute to the paragraph?

Sentence Structure

1 Sentences 2 and 3 have three parts each. Explain how the parts operate in the sentences.
2 What similarity of structure do sentences 4 and 7 have?
3 In sentences 2–7, how is transition achieved by terms referring to place, time, or result?
4 What sort of transitional links connect sentences 7–10?
5 Point out how repetition and parallel structures help toward clarity in sentences 6, 8, and 9.

Diction

1 Look up *torrents, erosion, debris, arroyos, secretion, millennia.*
2 Explain the etymological connections among *torrents, toast, thirst,* and *torrid.* How is *erosion* related to *rodent*?
3 From what languages were *debris, delta,* and *arroyos* borrowed?
4 What other words are based on the same roots as *deposition* and *accretion*?
5 What is the singular of *millennia?* What are the meanings of its roots?
6 What other meanings does *cove* have?

Assignment

Following Professor Brooks's method of definition, define (1) *river, mountain,* or *mesa;* (2) a man-made object such as *book, library,* or *automobile;* or (3) *dam* or *pond.*

The Quipu

VICTOR WOLFGANG VON HAGEN

1   The *quipu* (pronounced "kee-poo"), which means simply "knot," and which the couriers passed from hand to hand, was as close to writing as man got in South America; still no matter how much writers have strained their imagination, the *quipu is not writing,* and, moreover, the device is not even an Inca invention. It is simply a mnemonic device to aid the memory and its knotted strings are based on a decimal count. Too, all *quipus* had to be *accompanied by a verbal comment,* without which the meaning would have been unintelligible.

2   The *quipus* have been thoroughly studied and described. The *quipu* was a simple and ingenious device; it consisted of a main cord (ranging from a foot to many feet in length) and from this cord dangled smaller colored strings which had at intervals knots (*quipus*) tied into them. It has been shown most conclusively by those who have studied them that the strings were used to record numbers in a decimal system, and that there was a symbol for zero, that is, a string with an "empty space"; this allowed them to count over ten thousand. Knots were tied into the string to represent numbers; if a governor was visiting a newly conquered tribe and the Inca wanted to know how many able-bodied Indians there were, these were counted and the number tied into the *quipu.* It may be that there was a certain symbol or heraldic device for "men," but if there was one it is not known. There was attached to the governor an official knot-string-record interpreter known as a *quipu-camayoc,* whose duty it was to tie in the records. He then had to remember which *quipu* recorded what; numbers of men, women, llamas, etc., in the newly conquered lands. When a governor had an audience with the Inca he could, with this knot-string record plus the "rememberer," recite the facts as gathered. It was a surprisingly efficacious method of counting and one that their Spanish conquerors much admired.

Brief excerpt from *The Ancient Sun Kingdoms of the Americas* by Victor Von Hagen (World Pub. Co.). Copyright © 1957, 1958, 1960, 1961 by Victor W. Von Hagen. Reprinted by permission of Harper & Row, Publishers, Inc.

STUDY QUESTIONS

Organization and Content

1   What misuse or misunderstanding of the term *quipu* does Von Hagen wish to guard against? How far has he proceeded in his definition in paragraph 1?
2   In what class does the term *quipu* belong?
3   Where does Von Hagen explain what made a *quipu* different from all other members of the same class?
4   Explain why a *quipu* ''had to be accompanied by a verbal comment.''
5   How does the material of sentences 4–7, paragraph 2, differ in function from that of sentences 1–3?
6   What is the purpose of sentence 8, paragraph 2?

Sentence Structure

1   Explain how the structure of sentence 1 provides a pattern of contrast.
2   How is the function of the material after the semicolon in sentences 3 and 4, paragraph 2, different from that after the semicolon in sentence 2, paragraph 2?

Diction

1   Look up *couriers, mnemonic, heraldic, efficacious.*
2   What words are used for transition and emphasis in paragraph 1?

Assignment

Write a definition of an object with which people in our society are perfectly familiar, so that its components and its mode of operation will be clear to a person in another society who has never seen that object—for example, an egg beater, corkscrew, can opener, clothespin, mousetrap, double boiler, pair of shears, crochet hook, dress pattern, vacuum cleaner, safety razor, typewriter, cash register, calendar, or newspaper.

The Confidence Game

LESLIE CHARTERIS

In the simplest basic version of the "confidence" game, the sucker or mark sees a stranger drop a wallet, and naturally picks it up and restores it to its owner. The owner thanks him, and keeps on talking to reveal that he is burdened with the job of distributing a huge charitable fund, or some similar sinecure involving the handling of large sums of money: his problem is to find an absolutely trustworthy assistant, and by a happy coincidence the boob who returned the wallet has just given unsolicited proof of unusual honesty. However, the operator has associates who will demand more substantial evidence that the dupe is a man of means who can be trusted with the virtually blank checks they will be handing him; so it is suggested that he bring to a meeting the largest amount of cash he can raise, to exhibit to them to win their confidence—from which theme the racket derives its name. The fool does so, his money is examined and returned to him, his candidacy is unanimously approved with handshakes, and the session rapidly adjourns on promises that formal agreements will be signed with him in a few days. It is not until after the crooks have departed that the victim discovers that the wad of currency which he got back contains only one bill of large denomination, on the outside, while the bulk of it has been dextrously transformed into single dollars or even rectangles of blank paper of the same size.

STUDY QUESTIONS

Organization and Content

1 Evidently the author is placing "confidence" game in a class of "game"; but in what sense is *game* being used? We might think of *game* as a kind of process. If so, what kind?
2 What are the steps by which the confidence game is worked out to a successful conclusion?
3 What principle of organization has Charteris used in this paragraph?

Sentence Structure

1 What happens in the two parts of sentence 2—before the colon and after the colon?

From "The Bunco Artists" by Leslie Charteris, in *The Saint Detective Magazine*, Vol. 6, No. 6 (December 1956), pp. 4–5. Copyright © 1956 by Leslie Charteris.

2   What repeated word provides transition from sentence 1 to sentence 2? By what means of transition is sentence 3 connected with sentence 2?

3   What is the relation of the second part of sentence 3 to the first part? Why is the semicolon used in the middle?

4   Sentence 4 has a balanced structure of parallel clauses. Point out the parallel clauses. Why are such clauses suitable in this part of the definition?

5   Sentence 5 is of the periodic type: we have to go on a long time in suspense before we reach a word that makes the statement complete. At what point in the sentence do you first find the meaning completed? (The "it is not . . . that" construction is helpful in postponing the completion of meaning.)

Diction

1   Look up *sinecure, coincidence, unsolicited, virtually, theme, candidacy, session, denomination, dextrously, transformed.* Which of these words have Latin roots?

2   What are the meanings of the roots of *virtual, candidacy, session, dextrously?*

3   What five other names are given to the "mark" who returns the wallet? What connotations do these words have? Are these words slang?

4   Are *racket, crooks,* and *wad* slang terms, colloquial terms, or formal English terms?

Assignment

Write a definition of a process such as blackmail, the shell game, fortune-telling or "mind-reading" for profit, or racketeering. Be as specific as you can.

Folklore

ROBERT E. HEMENWAY

1   Folklore is exceedingly difficult to define, and folklorists themselves quarrel over precisely what it is. Some claim simply to know it when they see it; all agree that folklore is not error, as in the phrase "That's only folklore." Two common definitions are "verbal art" and "literature transmitted orally." The well-known folklorist Francis Lee Utley once tried to define it by description, indicating that American folklore included the arts and crafts, the beliefs and customs of our lumber camps, city evangelical storefront churches, back-alley dives, farmers' festivals and fairs, hill frolics, carnivals, firemen's lofts, sailors' cabins, chain gangs, and penitentiaries. In other words, folklore touches everyone's life, whether it is a belief that a broken mirror brings seven years' bad luck, a tale of Brer Rabbit, or a song about a frog who goes a-courting. In an age of media, so much folklore is popularized for mass consumption that its origins are easily forgotten, and it is sometimes difficult to distinguish between authentic lore and creative art, between traditional heroes and popular imitations. "The Saint Louis Blues," published by W. C. Handy in 1914, is not a folksong, but a famous composition by a composer of genius; a spiritual such as "Swing Low, Sweet Chariot" *is* folklore, created by "black and unknown bards," then preserved as one slave generation taught the words and melody to the next. The northwoods demigod, Paul Bunyan, may or may not have originated in a folktale told by lumberjacks, but by the time he had been popularized in the advertising of the Red River Lumber Company of Minnesota and described by countless authors of children's stories, he had become a fictional rather than a folk hero.

2   Separating genuinely traditional materials from those of contemporary authorship is only one of many factors making the study of folklore a challenging task. The collector may enter a community, often as a stranger, attempt to establish rapport, and then write down (or, now, tape-record) as many of the communal traditions as the people choose to share. *Tradition* is the key word, for the folklorist seeks especially those forms of communicative behavior—usually verbal, although they may also be evident in crafts or kinetic movements—that have survived through time by oral transmission. The hex signs on the barns of the Pennsylvania Dutch, the square dances of Texas ranchers, and the legend of John Henry, "the steel drivin' man," are all folklore. Put another way, folklore consists of unwritten traditions which cause people to perform in familiar ways, the performance of each generation and each individual contributing to the tradition from within

From *Zora Neale Hurston,* with a foreword by Alice Walker. Urbana: University of Illinois Press, 1977.

the security of its familiarity. It is behavior replicated through history, and it reflects the common life of the mind existing at a level other than that of high or formal culture. Formal culture grows primarily from the presumption of the written heritage; traditional culture arises primarily out of the communicative expectations of a given group.

STUDY QUESTIONS
Organization and Content

1 Why should a term such as folklore be difficult to define? What is Hemenway's purpose in making such a statement?
2 In which sentence does he first provide formal definition? In what class does each definition place folklore? Can you justify the different classes?
3 What is the purpose of paraphrasing Utley? Does this cataloguing contribute considerably to your understanding of the term? Why or why not?
4 What problem of definition does Hemenway introduce in sentence 6?
5 Why is Paul Bunyan considered "a fictional rather than a folk hero"?
6 How do the examples in paragraph 1, sentence 4, differ from those in sentence 5? From what areas of folklore do those in sentence 5 come?
7 Would another composition and another spiritual instead of "The St. Louis Blues" and "Swing Low" be equally good examples?
8 How does the illustration in paragraph 2, sentence 2, differ from other examples in this selection?
9 Does Hemenway need the additional examples in paragraph 2, sentence 4? How do they relate to the preceding sentence?
10 How great a use of concrete examples does Hemenway make?
11 Where does Hemenway introduce his own formal definition into the discussion? What class or classes does he place *folklore* in? What are the differences (*differentiae*) in each case?

Sentence Structure

1 To what extent does Hemenway make use of parallel construction? Point out the sentences that are particularly effective because of parallel construction.
2 What transitional expression does Hemenway use in paragraph 1, sentence 5? Why has he chosen this particular one? Compare it to the means of transition used in paragraph 2, sentence 3.
3 What relationship does paragraph 1, sentence 7 have to sentence 6? Would sentence 7 be better if it were made into two sen-

tences? Why or why not? Does Hemenway need a transitional expression after the semicolon? To what extent is sentence 7 a balanced sentence?

4 How does Hemenway provide good transition from paragraph 1 to paragraph 2?

5 Why are the dashes used in paragraph 2, sentence 3? What other marks of punctuation might conceivably be used?

6 What structural similarity is there between paragraph 1, sentence 7, and paragraph 2, sentence 7?

7 What other pattern of exposition do you find in the two final sentences? Is it effective?

8 How many sentences begin with the subject? Point out those that begin with other sentence elements. Do the sentences have a monotonous pattern of construction, or is there sufficient sentence variety?

Diction

1 When was the term *folklore* invented? What term did it replace? Which term is more precise? Which is better?

2 *Media* is plural. What is its singular? Compare it with *bacteria, data, esoterica,* and *phenomena.*

3 Be sure you know the meaning of *popularized.* What is its root?

4 Look up the etymology of *rapport.* What was its literal, original meaning? How does this meaning relate to the contemporary meaning?

5 What are *kinetic* movements? How can these be folklore? What is the origin of the word *hex?*

6 Does *replicated* have a different meaning from *repeated?* How is it related to *complicated, implicit,* and *reply?*

7 Does Hemenway use more concrete or more abstract words? Does he conclude his definition in more concrete or less concrete terms than he used previously? Why?

Assignment

1 Write a definition of some form of music, such as jazz, Dixieland jazz, bluegrass, or country music.

2 Define news media—like folklore the term embraces a variety of things.

3 After doing some reading in the library, define popular culture; or similarly define the elitist culture or the American dream.

Biography

JOHN CALVIN METCALF

It is not easy to construct a definition of biography that fully covers the 1
various kinds of life-writing through the ages. If biography should be defined as the truthful record of a human life, it would be objected, first, that
most early and many later biographies are not truthful; and, second, that a
mere record is just a dry chronicle. It might be more satisfying to the modern mind to describe biography as that type of writing which reveals, in
narrative form, the outer and inner experiences of one personality through
another. A biography is permanently interesting when, through the insight,
sympathy, and art of the writer, it has become an expression of personality
rather than simply the history of a life. In a sense biography is personalized
history, and all successful life-writing is in essence the refinement of fact
into spirit.

Biography is related to history on the one side and to literature on the 2
other, and in more recent times it might claim kinship with philosophy and
even with science. Earlier life-writing was regarded as a branch of history.
The story of a man's life, or of an important section of it, was frequently
included, for diversion or instruction, in a long stretch of historical narration. The familiar story of Joseph and his Brethren, which has been called
the first biography, is a memorable part of the Book of Genesis; the life of
David is recorded in other books of the Bible; and many little biographies
are embedded in the histories of Herodotus. Centuries later, in England,
Bede's *Ecclesiastical History* and Geoffrey of Monmouth's *History of Britain*
mingle biography with history. Even Plutarch, in the first century, the most
famous of ancient biographers, made large use of history in treating comparatively the lives of illustrious men. It is hardly possible, of course, to isolate
the career of a notable man from the life of his time, the stuff of which history is made, unless emphasis should be shifted from external events to
those inward workings of the mind which essentially reveal a man's self.
The older biographers were more outward in their processes, not much
given to the analytical probing of souls which delights their modern succes-
sors. As long as biography was merely a handmaiden of history, it had no
general recognition as an art. When, later on, life-writing was undertaken
by literary men, it naturally became more artistic and at last won a distinctive place and a name.

The word "biography" was first used by Dryden, poet and essayist, in 3
1683, and "biographer" was first employed by Addison, essayist and poet, in
1715. By this time, as will be shown later, biography was allying itself with

From *The Stream of English Biography* by John Calvin Metcalf. Appleton-Century-
Crofts.

literature. Biographical writing had, of course, been long practised in England before it became a literary art. The same is true of prose fiction. Long stories and short stories are plentiful in English literature before Daniel Defoe and Samuel Richardson, but not until their time, the early eighteenth century, did the type we call the novel come of age, after a somewhat errant and dissolute youth. It is worth noting, moreover, that the early English novel, like biography, was, or at least professed to be, related to history. Defoe and Fielding called their novels "histories"; other novelists then and since have also used the biographical method, while still others have regarded the life of their hero as the history of a soul. The close connection between the novel and biography, both in form and spirit, has often been remarked. The older fashion of biographizing fiction has yielded to the later vogue of novelizing biography. This reciprocal relation between biography and the novel, growing out of the traditional affinity of the two types, shows that the biographer has contributed something of ballast to the airy bark of fiction, while the captains of that ancient vessel have invested the biographer with a shining garment of fancy. As the art of biography has grown more literary, its practitioners have tended to become interpreters by touching their material with imagination and humanity.

STUDY QUESTIONS
Organization and Content

1   What two difficulties in defining *biography* does Metcalf point out? He suggests an oversimple definition. Then what two objections does he make to it?
2   What are the six elements of the basic definition that he proposes?
3   What qualities does a biographer need to make a biography permanently interesting? What key word indicates the essential element of a permanently interesting biography?
4   To what two main kinds of writing is biography related? In paragraph 2 which relationship is Metcalf discussing? What idea is supported by the numerous specific examples of paragraph 2?
5   What eventually made biography recognized as an art? Indicate the transitional function of the last two sentences of paragraph 2.
6   In this extended definition what is the usefulness of the historical references in sentence 1, paragraph 3?
7   Why did history, biography, and prose fiction become interrelated in the eighteenth century? Does a relationship between biography and the novel still exist?
8   Explain the metaphor that Metcalf uses in sentence 10, paragraph 3. What is the key word in sentence 11? How is sentence 11 related to the ideas of paragraph 1?

Sentence Structure

1 Though Metcalf uses a varied sentence style, he constructs a good many complex sentences. The subordinate clauses, however, sometimes appear at the beginning, and sometimes at the end, of the sentence. Show how the arrangement of material is varied in sentences 1–4, paragraph 1.

2 How does sentence 5 differ in form from sentences 1–4?

3 By what means is sentence 3, paragraph 2, made longer and more informative than sentence 2, paragraph 2?

4 Note that Metcalf does not try to place all of his examples in a single sentence. How does he link three of them in sentence 4, paragraph 2? Contrast the arrangement of material in sentences 5 and 6 (which also contain examples) with that of sentence 4.

5 Sentences 9 and 10, paragraph 2, are similar in arrangement. In these sentences, in which a contrast of eras of time is significant, how has Metcalf handled the terms referring to time?

6 Both sentence 5 and sentence 10, paragraph 3, are rather long, elegant arrangements of clauses and phrases. Which one has an appositive? Which one has a participial phrase? Which one has two independent clauses? Which one closes with a dependent clause?

Diction

1 You may need to look up *illustrious* (paragraph 2), *reciprocal, affinity,* and *bark* (3).

2 What are the meanings of the roots of *isolate* (paragraph 2), *errant,* and *dissolute* (3)? Give another English word based on each root.

3 What do *biographizing* and *novelizing* (sentence 9, paragraph 3) mean? By what method were these words created?

Assignment

After a little research, imitate Metcalf by writing a definition of epic, sonnet, short story, novel, news story, or feature story. Go through the steps of basic definition, briefly give some historical background, and mention a few examples.

A Fairy Story

W. H. AUDEN

1   A fairy story, as distinct from a merry tale, or an animal story, is a serious tale with a human hero and a happy ending. The progression of its hero is the reverse of the tragic hero's: at the beginning he is either socially obscure or despised as being stupid or untalented, lacking in the heroic virtues, but at the end, he has surprised everyone by demonstrating his heroism and winning fame, riches, and love. Though ultimately he succeeds, he does not do so without a struggle in which his success is in doubt, for opposed to him are not only natural difficulties like glass mountains, or barriers of flame, but also hostile wicked powers, stepmothers, jealous brothers, and witches. In many cases indeed, he would fail were he not assisted by friendly powers who give him instructions or perform tasks for him which he cannot do himself; that is, in addition to his own powers, he needs luck, but this luck is not fortuitous but dependent upon his character and his actions. The tale ends with the establishment of justice; not only are the good rewarded but also the evil are punished.

2   Take, for example, "The Water of Life." Three brothers set out in turn on a difficult quest, to find the water of life to restore the King, their sick father, to health. Each one meets a dwarf who asks him where is he going. The two elder give rude answers and are punished by being imprisoned in ravines. The third brother gives a courteous answer and is rewarded by being told where the water of life is and how to appease the lions who guard it, but is warned to leave before the clock strikes twelve. He reaches the enchanted castle, where he finds a Princess who tells him to return in a year and marry her. At this point he almost fails because he falls asleep and only just manages to escape as the clock strikes twelve and the iron door shuts, carrying away a piece of his heel. On the way home he again meets the dwarf and begs him to release his brothers, which he does with a warning that they have bad hearts. The brothers steal the water of life from him and substitute salt water so that his father condemns him to be secretly shot. The huntsman entrusted with the task has not the heart to do it, and lets the young Prince go away into the forest. Now begins a second quest for the Princess. She has built a golden road to test her suitors. Whoever rides straight up it is to be admitted, whoever rides to the side is not. When the two elder brothers come to it they think "It would be a sin and a shame to ride over that" and so fail the test. At the end of the year, the exiled brother rides thither but is so preoccupied with thinking of the Princess that he never notices the golden road and rides straight up. They are mar-

ried, the King learns how the elder brothers had betrayed the Prince, and they, to escape punishment, put to sea and never come back.

The hero is in the third or inferior position. (The youngest son inherits 3 least.) There are two quests, each involving a test which the hero passes and his brothers fail.

The first test is the encounter with the dwarf. The elder brothers disre- 4 gard him (a) because he looks like the last person on earth who could help them, (b) they are impatient and thinking only of their success, and (c) what is wrong with their concentration on their task is, firstly, overconfidence in their own powers and, secondly, the selfishness of their motive. They do not really love their father but want him to reward them.

The hero, on the other hand, is (a) humble enough, (b) cares enough for 5 his father's recovery, and (c) has a loving disposition toward all men, so that he asks the dwarf for assistance and gets it.

The second test of the golden road is a reversal of the first: the right thing 6 to do this time is to take no notice of it. The brothers who dismissed the dwarf notice the road because of its worldly value, which is more to them than any Princess, while the hero, who paid attention to the dwarf, ignores the road because he is truly in love.

The Water of Life and the Princess are guarded by lions; these, in this 7 tale, are not malevolent but ensure that no one shall succeed who has not learned the true way. The hero almost fails here by forgetting the dwarf's warning and falling asleep; further it is through falling asleep and not watching his brothers that they almost succeed in destroying him. The readiness to fall asleep is a sign of the trustfulness and lack of fear which are the qualities which bring about his success; at the same time it is pointed out that, carried too far, they are a danger to him.

STUDY QUESTIONS
Organization and Content

1 In what class of things does the author place the term *fairy story?*
2 According to sentence 1, what differences exist between a fairy story and other kinds of stories?
3 We can hardly take sentence 1 as a sufficient definition. What other main differences should be added from the rest of paragraph 1? What contrasting situation of a tragic hero is implied in sentence 2?
4 What is the relation of paragraph 2 to paragraph 1?
5 Does ''The Water of Life'' meet all the requirements laid down for the fairy story in paragraph 1?
6 What is the main problem in organizing the material of paragraph 2?
7 To what extent does the interpretation in paragraphs 3–7 help in defining the term?

8   Point out how the author has used analysis in paragraphs 3, 4, 5, and 6.

Sentence Structure

1   What is the function of the colon in sentence 2, paragraph 1? In which other sentence is a colon used? Why? Does paragraph 1 or paragraph 2 have the longer sentences?
2   What is the most likely reason why the average sentence length of the one paragraph is so much less than that of the other?
3   In the sentences of paragraphs 1, 4, 5, and 6 the author uses much parallel structure. Point it out, and explain why it is especially suitable in these paragraphs.
4   In sentence 2 of paragraph 6 which words receive chief emphasis?
5   Explain how sentence structure functions in terms of contrasts, which are important in paragraph 7.

Diction

1   Look up the meanings of the following words and learn what roots they come from: *demonstrate, ultimately, fortuitous, quest, appease, encounter, malevolent.*
2   Is there a difference between *ultimately* and *lastly, fortuitous* and *accidental, malevolent* and *malicious*?
3   Explain how the words *appease* and *pacify* can come from the same root.
4   What are the differences among *quest, question, query, inquest, inquiry, inquisition*?

Assignment

Write a definition in three paragraphs of a fable or a joke. In the first paragraph, classify the term and show how it differs from other things in the same class. In the second paragraph, summarize a fable or tell a good joke to illustrate the basic definition. In the third paragraph, interpret your example in terms of the requirements you laid down in paragraph 1. Or define in the same way a myth, mystery story, parable, or ballad.

Pseudo-Events

DANIEL J. BOORSTIN

The new kind of synthetic novelty which has flooded our experience I 1
will call "pseudo-events." The common prefix "pseudo" comes from the
Greek word meaning false, or intended to deceive. Before I recall the historical forces which have made these pseudo-events possible, have increased the
supply of them and the demand for them, I will give a commonplace example.

The owners of a hotel, in an illustration offered by Edward L. Bernays in 2
his pioneer *Crystallizing Public Opinion* (1923), consult a public relations
counsel. They ask how to increase their hotel's prestige and so improve their
business. In less sophisticated times, the answer might have been to hire a
new chef, to improve the plumbing, to paint the rooms, or to install a crystal chandelier in the lobby. The public relations counsel's technique is more
indirect. He proposes that the management stage a celebration of the hotel's
thirtieth anniversary. A committee is formed, including a prominent
banker, a leading society matron, a well-known lawyer, an influential
preacher, and an "event" is planned (say a banquet) to call attention to the
distinguished service the hotel has been rendering the community. The celebration is held, photographs are taken, the occasion is widely reported, and
the object is accomplished. Now this occasion is a pseudo-event, and will
illustrate all the essential features of pseudo-events. . . .

A pseudo-event, then, is a happening that possesses the following charac- 3
teristics:

It is not spontaneous, but comes about because someone has planned, (1)
planted, or incited it. Typically, it is not a train wreck or an earthquake, but
an interview.

It is planted primarily (not always exclusively) for the immediate purpose (2)
of being reported or reproduced. Therefore, its occurrence is arranged for
the convenience of the reporting or reproducing media. Its success is measured by how widely it is reported. Time relations in it are commonly fictitious or factitious; the announcement is given out in advance "for future
release" and written as if the event had occurred in the past. The question,
"Is it real?" is less important than, "Is it newsworthy?"

Its relation to the underlying reality of the situation is ambiguous. Its inter- (3)
est arises largely from this very ambiguity. Concerning a pseudo-event the
question, "What does it mean?" has a new dimension. While the news interest in a train wreck is in *what* happened and in the real consequences, the

interest in an interview is always, in a sense, in *whether* it really happened and in what might have been the motives. Did the statement really mean what it said? Without some of this ambiguity a pseudo-event cannot be very interesting.

(4) Usually it is intended to be a self-fulfilling prophecy. The hotel's thirtieth-anniversary celebration, by saying that the hotel is a distinguished institution, actually makes it one. . . .

4 Pseudo-events from their very nature tend to be more interesting and more attractive than spontaneous events. Therefore in American public life today pseudo-events tend to drive all other kinds of events out of our consciousness, or at least to overshadow them. Earnest, well-informed citizens seldom notice that their experience of spontaneous events is buried by pseudo-events. Yet nowadays, the more industriously they work at "informing" themselves the more this tends to be true. . . .

5 Here are some characteristics of pseudo-events which make them overshadow spontaneous events:

(1) Pseudo-events are more dramatic. A television debate between candidates can be planned to be more suspenseful (for example, by reserving questions which are then popped suddenly) than a casual encounter or consecutive formal speeches planned by each separately.

(2) Pseudo-events, being planned for dissemination, are easier to disseminate and to make vivid. Participants are selected for their newsworthy and dramatic interest.

(3) Pseudo-events can be repeated at will, and thus their impression can be re-enforced.

(4) Pseudo-events cost money to create; hence somebody has an interest in disseminating, magnifying, advertising, and extolling them as events worth watching or worth believing. They are therefore advertised in advance, and rerun in order to get money's worth.

(5) Pseudo-events, being planned for intelligibility, are more intelligible and hence more reassuring. Even if we cannot discuss intelligently the qualifications of the candidates or the complicated issues, we can at least judge the effectiveness of a television performance. How comforting to have some political matter we can grasp!

(6) Pseudo-events are more sociable, more conversable, and more convenient to witness. Their occurrence is planned for our convenience. The Sunday newspaper appears when we have a lazy morning for it. Television programs appear when we are ready with our glass of beer. In the office the next morning, Jack Paar's (or any other star performer's) regular late-night show at the usual hour will overshadow in conversation a casual event that suddenly came up and had to find its way into the news.

(7) Knowledge of pseudo-events—of what has been reported, or what has been

staged, and how—becomes the test of being "informed." News magazines provide us regularly with quiz questions concerning not what has happened but concerning "names in the news"—what has been reported in the news magazines. Pseudo-events begin to provide that "common discourse" which some of my old-fashioned friends have hoped to find in the Great Books. Finally, pseudo-events spawn other pseudo-events in geometric progression. (8) They dominate our consciousness simply because there are more of them, and ever more.

STUDY QUESTIONS
Organization and Content

1   What does Boorstin accomplish in paragraph 1? What does sentence 3 lead you to expect in paragraph 2?
2   How does sentence 2, paragraph 1, help us to an understanding of the term to be defined?
3   In paragraph 2 Boorstin calls the pseudo-event a celebration, a banquet, and an occasion; in paragraph 3 he calls it a happening. In what class should the term be placed?
4   Where does Boorstin give us the differentiae by which to set pseudo-events off from other members of the same class?
5   How do pseudo-events differ from spontaneous events? What results come about because of the difference?
6   How does paragraph 5 further develop an idea introduced in paragraph 4?

Sentence Structure

1   In the enumeration of paragraph 3, what construction is repeated to secure clearness and good transition?
2   In sentence 12, paragraph 3, show how the parallel structures are ideal for bringing out the contrast between a real event and a pseudo-event.
3   In paragraph 5, point out how the main sentences in the enumeration are varied in structure.

Diction

1   Look up *synthetic* (paragraph 1); *prestige, sophisticated, society matron, essential* (2); *spontaneous, incited, media, ambiguous, prophecy, distinguished* (3); *dramatic, suspenseful, consecutive, dissemination, vivid, participants, extolling, intelligibility, reassuring, effectiveness, conversable, discourse, spawn, dominate, consciousness* (5).
2   Remember that *media* is plural. What is the singular form? (What is the singular form of *bacteria?* of *phenomena?* of *criteria?*)

3   What are the basic meanings of the main roots of *disseminate,
dominate, consciousness?* Give other words with the same root as
consciousness.
4   What is the difference between *fictitious* and *factitious* (paragraph
3)?
5   *Spawn* is an interesting verb. Look up examples of its use in the
Oxford English Dictionary. Does *spawn* have favorable or unfavorable connotations?

Assignment

Define ''the media''; a celebration; dramatic events; or novelties.

Happiness

JOHN COWPER POWYS

1   We all know roughly what the words Happiness and Unhappiness mean,
but like all human names for important reactions to life they seem to indicate states of feeling that quickly tend to blend with, and lose themselves in,
other states of feeling, for which there have been found, by the selective in-
stinct of our particular tribe, quite different names.

2   Joy, ecstasy, rapture, delight, satisfaction, enchantment, peace, content-
ment, enjoyment, blessedness, pleasure—all these indicate conditions of
human feeling that cannot be rigidly separated off from what we call Happiness. Pleasure, I suppose comes on the whole nearest to it in our ordinary
speech and the antithesis Pleasure-Pain corresponds roughly, in most of our
minds, with the antithesis Happiness-Unhappiness.

3   *Pain,* however, though applicable as we all know to mental suffering,
strictly belongs to the physical side of things, while even *Pleasure,* the other
member of this great rival antithesis, though less consistently than *Pain,* has
like it a physical implication.

4   There is always a considerable margin, a sort of obscure twilight-nimbus,
left vague and undetermined around every great human word, as it descends
the stream of the generations, and certain important nuances of meaning are
constantly being added, while others are being taken away, without the possibility of any individual mind in one life-time catching the drift of the
change.

5   Personally I like the sound of the word "pleasure" a good deal better than
the sound of the word "happiness." There seems to me something at once
more fluid and more organic about it; while the word "pain" is certainly
more expressive than the word "unhappiness." The syllables "happy" have

something jaunty about them, something brisk and bouncing. They suggest an element less dignified, less poetical, than the psychic over-tone conveyed in the syllables "pleasure." Take for instance that characteristic line of Wordsworth's, "The pleasure which there is in life itself," and substitute the word "happiness." It would not be only the scansion of the verse that would be broken. There would be a loss of some deep organic quality in the meaning.

Nevertheless, in spite of the annoying jauntiness, and even the bouncing 6 babyishness, of the word "happy," it is hard to see how it can be avoided. What it possesses, that the more poetical word "pleasure" lacks, is an over-tone of mental volition. You can will to be happy—you cannot evoke the mystery of pleasure by any willing.

It seems indeed as though happiness might be considered the subjective 7 counterpart to pleasure. I mean that while it would be natural to say: "Be happy or die!" there would be something strained, something even violent, about the expression: "Get pleasure or die!" The more you concentrate on the difference between these words the most clearly does it appear that while pleasure is something that comes to you from outside, happiness is something that, though it may often be "roused to reciprocity" by pleasure, is intrinsically a mental, or even a moral state. You could also, I think, maintain without contradiction that there is an implication of lastingness about happiness, whereas the idea of pleasure suggests something not only more physical but much more transitory.

STUDY QUESTIONS
Organization and Content

1 By what pattern of exposition other than definition does Powys primarily develop his definition of *happiness*?

2 Does he provide a formal definition in paragraph 1? any part of a formal definition?

3 Why does Powys list so many terms in paragraph 2, sentence 1?

4 What important characteristic of Pleasure-Pain does he point out in paragraph 3? Where in the selection does he refer again to this characteristic?

5 What does paragraph 4 contribute to the discussion?

6 What difference in the words *happy* and *pleasure* does he point out in paragraph 5? What does he use in the last part of paragraph 5 to make his discussion clearer? Does he use this device elsewhere?

7 What characteristic of *happy* does he bring out in paragraph 6? Which previous paragraph concerning *pleasure-pain* does this paragraph correspond to? Why has he delayed in presenting the contrast?

8 What new characteristics of *happiness* appear in paragraph 7?

9 Write a one-sentence formal definition of *happiness* using Powys's main points.

Sentence Structure

1 How has Powys provided transition from paragraph 1 to paragraph 2?

2 Note the use of the dash in paragraph 2, sentence 1. What is its purpose? Does it seem effective? Why?

3 Which of the paragraphs contain only one sentence? What special reasons are likely to make one-sentence paragraphs justifiable?

4 Analyze the patterns of the long sentences in paragraphs 1 and 4.

5 How has Powys managed his sentences so as to get an important word at the end of paragraphs 1 and 3?

6 By what different means does Powys handle contrasting ideas in the last two sentences of paragraph 7?

Diction

1 Look up the following words: *antithesis* (paragraph 2), *nimbus, nuances* (4), *volition* (6), *subjective, counterpart, reciprocity, intrinsically, transitory* (7). Some of these words are very interesting: for example, note the exact meanings of the prefixes *anti-* and *counter-;* check the many synonyms for *transitory* under the definition of *transient* for subtle shades of meaning; find out the common origin of *nimbus* and *nuance*. What is the plural of *nimbus*?

2 Can *ecstasy* and *rapture* (2) be differentiated in meaning?

3 How does Powys depend on connotations of words to further his control of the reader's feelings in paragraph 6? Which words does he connect to words from paragraph 5 that enhance their connotative value?

4 What does he mean when in paragraph 4 he says, "as it [the word] descends the stream of the generations"? Is he using literal or figurative language? What about "a sort of obscure twilight-nimbus"?

Assignment

Using the same method that Powys used, define a word mainly by reference to another term with which it has much in common, such as *opportunity-chance; misery-sorrow; honesty-integrity; success-prosperity; hatred-loathing; love-devotion; courage-daring; resolution-firmness.*

The Spirit
of the City

JOHN FRIEDMANN

One must, to start with, see the city as a whole. There are many different 1
kinds of city, classifiable according to size or density of population, economic base, principal functions, legal institutions, provision for defense, or
place in a hierarchy of cities; indeed there is no end to the number of view-
points that may be adopted. The names given to different types—garden
city, coke-town, *civitas,* metropolis, linear city, temple city, market city, capital, satellite, railroad city—evoke concrete images of their essential character. Yet all are cities. The common denominator among them is principally
a way of life, a frame of mind, and a manner of thinking, speaking, and behaving. It is its spirit that makes a city. What is this spirit? What is the
urban prototype?

The spirit of the city arises from its social heterogeneity. The city may 2
also be culturally, even racially, heterogeneous, a place where different languages are spoken, different customs practised, different gods worshipped.
Always it is a brilliantly exciting contrast to the monotony of a village in
which life is bound to the cycle of the seasons. The city has the heady excitement of politics with its periodic crises and occasional pomp, its whis-
pering campaigns, conspiracies and rumors, its public press and factionalist
parties, with its essential mystery of power. The city has color and variety in
its markets, bazaars and workshops. It has the glittering bubble of entertainment: circuses, games, dancing-girls, music, theatres, restaurants, tav-
erns. Was a wineshop in Alexandria so different from a *Weinstube* in medieval Schwaebisch Hall or a modern tea room in Tokyo? It is to visits in these
and to stimulating talk with friends and colleagues that many a peasant boy
looks forward on moving to the city.

The city thus becomes a place of immense cultural vitality, where the 3
consciousness of self is brought to an acute sensibility. Ideas are formed,
change in fads and fashions is the order of the day. News and the discussion
of news are essential to it. Here the present and the future intersect. The
true urbanite is always *en courant.* There is a place also for scholars who peer
into the past and into cosmic space. Every major creative effort either origi-
nates or comes to full bloom in the city. Here the important decisions are
made.

The city has also a rationality that acts as a sobering influence upon the 4

Reprinted from *Regional Development and Planning: A Reader.* John Friedmann and
William Alonso, eds., by permission of The MIT Press, Cambridge, Massachusetts.

hurly-burly of its life. It is thrown down, indeed, as a rational act in defiance of nature. If on a grid plan, its lines are carefully drawn in a Euclidian pattern that is in contrast with the curving and organic forms of nature. Parks and gardens are carefully delimited, if they are permitted at all, and are parcelled out according to what are believed to be the special requirements of the urban population. The life of the city is *zwecksrational:* means are fitted to ends agreed upon, and efficiency is introduced as a unit of measure relating input to output. With the city comes administration and the law, compiled into a rational code and a legal-administrative apparatus. Money and accountancy govern its trade, and most things become eventually reduced to their value in cash—whether it be labor, a work of art or a parcel of land. Universities pursue science, mathematics and philosophy (all three distinctively urban forms of mental activity) to the limits of reason and into the realm of ultimate doubt. "What can I know?" is a question the urban immigrant from a traditional rural environment learns to ask. . . .

5   It must be recognized that there has been a tendency for the city to disappear as a distinctive way of life in recent decades, as urban culture has successfully invaded the countryside in what is surely the most comprehensive imperialism known to history, and urban populations have vastly increased in number and proportion, overflowing the old boundaries and sprawling in more or less unruly patterns over vast portions of the earth. In a sense, the mass communications industry has placed the city in everybody's living room, from the shores of Alaska to the Belgian Congo. And yet, something of the city remains and probably will always remain, if only as a sense of the city as we approach it: the hum and vibrations of life become louder, the intersection of intelligences becomes more frequent and intense, vitality and movement are raised to a high pitch. *This is the center:* it may be physically distinguishable or not; but it is here.

STUDY QUESTIONS
Organization and Content

1   What is the purpose of suggesting ways of classifying cities in paragraph 1, sentence 2? in sentence 3?
2   Is the very short sentence 4 effective? Why? What purpose does it serve?
3   Where does the author really introduce his subject?
4   Why does he use questions at the end of paragraph 1?
5   Is paragraph 1 a good introduction to his topic?
6   How does the illustrative material in paragraph 2, sentence 7, differ from that in sentences 4, 5, and 6?
7   Contrast the ideas presented in paragraph 2 and in paragraph 3.
8   What evidence does Friedmann present in paragraph 4 to support the idea that "the city has also a rationality"?

9   Why does he say in paragraph 5 that there is "a tendency for the
     city to disappear as a distinctive way of life"? What evidence sup-
     ports this idea?
10   What relationship do sentences 3 and 4 of paragraph 5 have with
     sentence 1? What transitional expression does Friedmann use to
     indicate this relationship?
11   In paragraph 5, sentence 3, what purpose does his listing serve?
12   What forms of expository development other than definition does
     Friedmann use?
13   Do you agree that "the mass communications industry has placed
     the city in everybody's living room"?
14   Why are science, mathematics, and philosophy "*urban* forms of
     mental activity"?

Sentence Structure

1   Point out parallel construction in paragraph 2, sentence 2.
2   What is the relation of paragraph 2, sentences 4–6, to sentence
     3? What similarity of structure binds sentences 4, 5, and 6 to-
     gether, providing good transition?
3   How does paragraph 2, sentence 8, act as a transitional device?
4   Paragraph 3, sentence 2, contains a comma splice or comma
     fault. Why do you think Friedmann used only a comma to separate
     the clauses? Is he justified in doing so?
5   Are most of the sentences in paragraph 3 simple, complex, com-
     pound, or compound-complex? Would it be preferable to combine
     several of them?
6   Paragraph 2 has several lists (enumerations). How does Fried-
     mann keep the sentences from being monotonous in structure?
7   To what word in paragraph 4, sentence 1, does the *it* beginning
     sentence 2 refer?
8   Paragraph 5, sentence 1, is a rather long and involved sentence.
     Analyze its structure. Why is it important that *earth* be placed at
     the end of the sentence?
9   Why does the author use colons in paragraph 4, sentence 5, and
     in paragraph 5, sentence 3?
10   Ordinarily a good writer uses verbs in active voice rather than
     passive voice to make strong, effective sentences. Does Fried-
     mann use passive voice more than other writers you have read in
     this text? If so, is there any justifiable reason for using it?

Diction

1   Why are *civitas* (paragraph 1), *en courant* (3), and *zwecksrational*
     (4) italicized? Look at the etymology of *city* to find *civitas*. What is
     the meaning of *en courant*? What languages do these words
     come from?
2   Look up *prototype* (1) and *heterogeneity* (2). What are other words
     that have the roots *proto-, hetero-,* and *gene*?

3   What is the difference in the meanings of *rationality* (4), *rationale,*
     rationalize, ratiocination?
4   Look up *satellite* (1), *imperialism, comprehensive* (5), *hurly-burly*
     (4). Note the manner in which *hurly-burly* was formed.
5   In paragraph 1, sentence 3, there is a list of descriptive names of
     types of cities. What concrete images do you get from each of
     these? How do the types of cities differ?
6   What is a "Euclidian pattern" (4)?
7   How does the author provide evidence of the city's being "a bril-
     liantly exciting contrast to the monotony of the village"? Which
     words are most effective in doing this—in creating images?
8   Why does Friedmann refer to Alexandria, Schwaebisch Hall, and
     Tokyo? What or how do these references contribute to the idea in
     paragraph 2?
9   Does paragraph 2 or paragraph 3 contain more concrete nouns?
     Why is there a difference in the use of concrete and abstract
     words?

Assignment

1   Following the Friedmann model, write a paper defining the spirit or
     "frame of mind" of the country or a small town.
2   Similarly define the spirit of a university or the spirit of scholarship,
     which is presumably at the heart of a university.
3   People in different parts of a country have different attitudes. You
     might define the spirit or "frame of mind" of New England, the
     West, or the South; or of the people of a particular state, such as
     California, Florida, Massachusetts, Wyoming, or Indiana.
4   Some people believe that there is a special spirit about certain
     franchised eating establishments that serve hamburgers, fried
     chicken, pizza, or tacos. You might define it and contrast it with
     that of a traditional restaurant or of a tavern.

Play and Leisure

MORTIMER J. ADLER

Leisure activities, in sharp distinction from labor or work, consist of those 1
things that men do because they are desirable for their own sake. They are
self-rewarding, not externally compensated, and they are freely engaged in.
They may be morally necessary, but they are not biologically compulsory.
You can see the trouble with this definition as soon as you say it. You may
ask at once, What is play? Is not play self-rewarding? Is not play distinguished from labor by the negative distinction that it is something you do
not have to do? Something that you freely choose to do?

I think we can get some light on how to sharpen the definition of leisure, 2
and keep it distinct from play, by etymological considerations. I must confess to being genuinely fascinated by the background of the word "leisure."
The word which in Greek means "leisure" is *scole*. Notice that our English
word "school" comes from *scole*.

Now the Greek word *scole* has two meanings, just as the English word 3
"pastime" has two meanings. In the dictionary the first meaning of "pastime" refers to the time itself, to *spare* time. The second meaning of "pastime" refers to what is done with such time, namely, *play*. It is this second
meaning that we usually intend by our use of the word. So the first meaning
of *scole* refers to the time; the second, to the content or use of the time. The
first is leisure in the merely negative sense of time *free from* labor, or spare
time; but the second meaning, which appears very early in Greek literature,
refers to what men should *do* with this time, namely, learn and discuss. It is
the second meaning—what one does with time free from labor—which permits *scole* to become the root of the word "school." This, it seems to me,
throws a fascinating light on a phrase that was used frequently in my youth
when boys of sixteen faced, with their parents, the question, "Shall I go to
work or shall I go to *school?*" Making this a choice of opposites is quite right,
because work is one thing and school is another. *It is the difference between
labor and leisure.*

When we look for the Latin equivalent of the Greek word *scole*, more 4
light is thrown on the subject. The first meaning, time free from work or
labor, appears in the Latin word *otium*. *Otium* is the root of the word *negotium,* which means "negotiation" or "business." *Otium* is the very opposite
of *negotium* or "business"; it simply means time *free from* work. What is
wonderful here is that the English word "otiose" is not a very complimen-
tary word—it means "unemployed, idle, sterile, futile, useless." The second

From Mortimer J. Adler, "Labor, Leisure, and Liberal Education," *Journal of General
Education,* 6, 1 (October 1951), pp. 39 and 41. Reprinted by permission of The Pennsylvania State University Press.

meaning of *scole* is translated by the Latin *schola*. This again is a source of "school." Finally, the first meaning of *otium* has a synonym in Latin, *vacatio*, from which we get the word "vacation" and also, interestingly enough, "vacancy."

5   The English word "leisure" comes down a totally different line. It comes from the French *loisir*, and from the Latin *licere*; it has the root meaning of the permissible and the free. The Latin *licere* is also the root of "liberty" and "licence," in addition to "leisure." I think it is extraordinary to see these three words related in that one Latin root.

6   In the light of this etymology, I think we can distinguish leisure from play as two quite different uses of free or spare time, that is, *not-working time*. Play may be one of two things. It may be biologically useful like sleep, just as vacations and recreational activities are biologically useful. Just as sleep is a way of washing away fatigue, so a certain amount of play or vacation or recreation has the same kind of biological utility in the recuperation of the body. Play may be, however, something in excess of this. Obviously, children play to excess; they do not play just to refresh themselves. And I often wonder whether this does not have a bearing on the role of play in adult life, that is, whether or not the role of play in adult life is not always a temporary regression to childhood. I ask this question quite seriously, because after one has passed the point where play is biologically useful, all it can be is otiose, sterile, and useless.

7   One can admit, I think, that life involves two kinds of play: play for the sake of work, when it serves the same purpose as sleep, and play for its own sake. Sensual pleasure is admittedly a part of human life, but only in a limited quantity. Beyond that you have licentiousness; so, too, licentious play is a misuse of leisure.

8   Certainly, no quality attaches to useless play other than pleasure. I, for one, can see no perfection, no improvement, resulting from it. But leisure consists of those intrinsically good activities which are both self-rewarding and meaningful beyond themselves. They need not be confined to themselves. They can be both good things to do and good in their results, as, for example, political activities, the activities of a citizen, are both good in themselves and good in their results. This does not mean that leisure activities are never terminal, never without ends *beyond* themselves; it means only that they must be good *in themselves,* things worth doing even if there were no need for them to be done.

9   The results of leisure activity are two sorts of human excellence or perfection: those private excellences by which a man perfects his own nature and those public excellences which can be translated into the performance of his moral or political duty—the excellence of a man in relation to other men and to society. Hence I would define leisure activities as those activities desirable for their own sake (and so uncompensated and not compulsory) and also for the sake of the excellences, private and public, to which they give

rise. This means, by the way, that *leisure activities are identical with virtue.* . . .

. . . Suppose we draw a line between economically or biologically useful **10** activities and those which are morally or humanly good, what Aristotle calls the "honorable" or "noble" activities. What results from making this separation? We get a threefold division: from the biologically necessary, we get sleep, work, and play (in so far as these serve to recuperate the body or to remove fatigue); from the humanly, morally good, the noble or honorable, we get all leisure activities; and from the superfluous, the otiose, we again get play, but here we mean play as it consists entirely in killing or wasting time, however pleasant that may be.

We see, furthermore, that the very same activities can be either labor or **11** leisure, according to the conditions under which they are performed. Let us take manual work again—for instance, carpentry. Manual work can be leisure if it is work done for the sake of the art that is involved and for the cultivation of an artist. It is labor if it is done for compensation. That example may be too obvious, but we can see the same thing in teaching or painting, composing music, or political action of any sort. Any one of these can be labor as well as leisure, if a person does it in order to earn his subsistence. For if, to begin with, one accepts the proposition that no man shall get food or clothing or shelter, no man shall get the means of subsistence, without earning them, then some activities which would otherwise be leisure must be done by some persons for compensation. This makes them no less intrinsically rewarding but gives them an additional character. This double character causes certain activities to be labor, looked at one way, and leisure, looked at another.

STUDY QUESTIONS
Organization and Content

1. What kinds of activities does Adler begin by contrasting? What are the affirmative and the negative qualities of leisure? To what problem regarding the definition does Adler draw attention?
2. In paragraph 2, between which ideas is Adler drawing a line? What approach is he taking that leads him to discuss the Greek *scole*?
3. What analogy does Adler make between *scole* and *pastime*?
4. What different ideas are represented by the Latin *otium* and *negotium*? What is the basic idea of *school-schola-scole*? What is the meaning of the root behind *leisure*?
5. In paragraph 6, how does Adler distinguish between leisure and play? What are the purposes of the two kinds of play?
6. How, in paragraphs 8 and 9, does Adler further analyze leisure? What addition does he make to the definition of leisure with which he began in paragraph 1?
7. What are the foundations of the threefold division of activities mentioned in paragraph 10?

8 Adler says in paragraph 11 that work and leisure can be the same thing. How is this paradox possible? Is the result of carpentry a private or a public excellence?

9 What is the function in this definition of the early etymological discussion?

Sentence Structure

1 Point out, in sentence 1, paragraph 1, the subject, intervening modifiers, verb, and further modifiers. What are the main rhythmic units of the sentence? Which words receive the most emphasis?

2 How does Adler arrange the affirmative and the negative elements in sentences 2 and 3?

3 In paragraph 3 several sentences refer to a first and a second meaning. Indicate the different ways in which these references are handled in sentences 2, 3, 5, and 6.

4 Note how in paragraph 6 Adler discusses two different aspects of play in separate sentences. What is the function of the short sentence 2? By what words are sentences 3 and 5 connected with sentence 2? What arrangement is made in sentence 1, paragraph 7, to repeat both ideas about play in a single sentence? (All these sentences use normal patterns for discussing contrasting things in pairs.)

5 How does Adler bring out the contrast of leisure and play in sentence 3, paragraph 8?

Diction

1 Look up *distinction, etymological, regression, licentious,* and *intrinsically.* Do all these words come from Latin?

2 Give another English word based on the root of each one.

Assignment

Define two or three terms that have some common elements. Here are several possibilities: hobby, sport, and game; science and technology; science and sympathetic magic; medicine and faith healing; art and esthetics; "welfare" and charity; journalism and literature; politics and statesmanship; farming and forestry; farming and ranching; gymnastics and exercise; gambling, speculation, and investment.

Use Adler's etymological methods if appropriate; be sure to include specific examples.

Values

THOMAS ELLIOTT BERRY

As man, somewhere before the dawn of recorded history, first gave **1** thought to his place and purpose in life, he began the consideration, in his crude way, of a matter that has an all-powerful influence on every normal man's existence—his set of values.

The phrase "set of values" is largely self-explanatory. It denotes the total- **2** ity of the values which a man assigns to every phase of life which circumstances lead him to evaluate. Thus a man acquires his set of values as he decides upon the degree of loyalty to give to his friends; the place, if any, of hobbies in life; the amount of respect or disdain to be accorded social climbing; the conditions under which gambling is to be approved or condemned; and the precise role or significance of every other part of life about which he thinks. In each case, he establishes a conclusion which becomes, in essence, a value within his set of values.

On every hand, sets of values are in evidence. The brilliant research scien- **3** tist points his best efforts toward discovering a cure for a baffling disease; the unskilled laborer economizes fiercely in order to educate his children; the property owner in suburbia strains his financial resources to build the swimming pool that will give him "status" in the eyes of his neighbors; and the college student strives to be tapped by the "right" fraternity. In each instance, a value is clearly reflected in a course of action.

As can be seen readily, a man's set of values reflects his personality by re- **4** vealing the "things" that he considers important, those which he feels are unimportant, and those which he places at various points between these extremes. Therefore, to gain a remarkably clear insight into a personality, one need only ask such questions as: How is "success" to be defined? How important is wealth? What persons make the greatest contribution to society in general? As the answers to these and similar questions are given, a set of values and a personality reveal themselves in sharp outline.

The assigning of values is sometimes the result of extensive and logical **5** thought—as in the case of the graduate student who weighs values with great care before deciding to specialize in educational psychology. Yet on other occasions, the assigning of values follows a course of thought that is so erratic and complex that it defies analysis. For example, most persons move through a strange maze of mental experiences and undetected influences as they establish their values concerning the importance of a college education, the place of ethics in the professional world, and the basis for choosing friends. In fact, when one attempts to trace the formation of his values on such questions, he generally has limited success.

6   In still other instances, however, the assigning of values is done with little or no thought whatever. One simply adopts a value vaguely or broadly in the manner of the man who reaches routinely for a cigar from a box; that is to say, one engages in little or no thought beforehand because he feels little or no compulsion to think. Many persons, for instance, give only superficial thought and hence assign only a loosely defined value to the seriousness of violating minor automobile traffic laws and to cases of "small" dishonesty. Consequently, they really never decide how to label the driver who ignores the stop sign on the rural road or the employee of the large corporation who pads his expense account. Is the driver a "lawbreaker," is he simply a person using common sense, or precisely what is he? Is the employee a "thief," is he a normal man following a normal pattern, or is he something between these extremes? Certainly these situations illustrate values which, at best, are established broadly by most people; and as a result, most people are startled on those rare occasions when circumstances reveal the vagueness of such values.

7   Despite the thought or lack of thought with which values may be acquired, they are the very essence of a man's life. For man must give himself direction; he must point his thoughts and actions toward specific goals. Therefore, his values become the guideposts on the road of his existence. As such, they determine every premeditated move he makes. Because of differing values, one student in a school of medicine may resolve to become a medical missionary while a classmate, interested primarily in financial gain, settles on a career as a carriage trade physician. The honest used car dealer handles only top quality cars while his less-than-honest competitor turns back speedometers, places quieting agents in worn transmissions, and employs other deceptions in order to make sales. Similarly, lawyers, architects, and others in a position to make decisions point their careers as their values dictate.

8   An even more striking illustration of the role of values can be seen in socalled "day-to-day" living. The mother whose principal concern is the happiness and success of her children patterns her day in the light of that goal. The father who is attempting to give his young son the opportunities he himself missed aims his life in that direction. The child who wants to please his parents strives to act accordingly. In each instance, the course of daily living flows as values prescribe.

STUDY QUESTIONS

Organization and Content

1   What is Berry trying to do in the one-sentence paragraph 1?
2   In paragraph 2 Berry relates values to varying degrees of loyalty

and respect. Is one's *set* of values then practically infinite—a kind of rating of each possible experience that a person can have?

3 What does Berry accomplish with paragraph 3? What happens in each sentence of paragraph 3?

4 Paragraph 4 connects values and what?

5 What are the functions of the questions that Berry puts in paragraphs 4 and 6?

6 How are values likely to be formed?

7 In what situations are one's values likely to be vague, or "broad"?

8 How does Berry try to convince us that values are extremely important in life?

9 What idea do the examples of paragraph 8 illustrate?

10 On the basis of Berry's explanation, write a one-sentence definition of values.

Sentence Structure

1 In sentence 3, paragraph 2, Berry presents a list of items separated by semicolons. In what other sentence does he do the same? What purpose do both sentences have?

2 Point out terms used for transition in paragraphs 2–6.

3 In sentence 1, paragraph 7, how does Berry throw emphasis on his main thought?

4 In sentence 2, paragraph 7, what is the relation of the part after the semicolon to the earlier part of the sentence?

5 How are sentences 2–7, paragraph 7, related? Could any of them be placed in a different position in the sequence?

6 Why do sentences 2–4, paragraph 7, start as they do?

7 How do sentences in paragraph 8 resemble, and differ from, those of paragraph 3?

Diction

1 Look up and learn the meanings of the roots of *essence* (paragraph 2), *suburbia* (3), *erratic, ethics* (5), *compulsion* (6).

2 You may also need to look up *totality, assigns, evaluate, disdain* (paragraph 2), *baffling* (3), *insight* (4), *undetected* (5), *superficial, violating* (6), *premeditated, deceptions* (7), *prescribe* (8).

3 Berry places quotation marks around several terms. What are the likely reasons why he does so, for example, with *status, right* (paragraph 3), *things* (4), *small, thief* (6)?

4 What kind of doctor is a "carriage trade" physician (paragraph 7)?

Assignment

Define one of these abstract terms: culture, art, science, judgment, justice, friendship, love. As Berry does in several paragraphs, use concrete examples to make the meaning of the term clear.

Check Point

4

At this point, after studying varied examples of definition and imitating several models, you should understand how to recognize and employ the two steps basic to this method of precise identification. In your writing you should demonstrate both accuracy of thinking and effective use of illustrations to back up your ideas. You ought to punctuate sentences according to the usual conventions and be able to use a fair variety of sentence structures as well as to compose substantial discussion paragraphs.

SECTION THREE

Argument

An argument is not a quarrel. Originally *to argue* meant to make clear, and thus to show, to prove, to give evidence. An argument is a presenting of reasons for or reasons against something; it implies that the person who states an argument has tried to understand the matter in question and is using powers of reason to show why evidence supports his or her position. The setting forth of a conviction or belief and the evidence for it does not need to imply any opposition. Perhaps everyone in the world would agree with the argument.

However, there is always potential disagreement with an argument; and on many matters people disagree. An argument for one side of a question calls forth an opposing argument from a person who disagrees. When two people engage in argument, they disagree. When two people quarrel, they also disagree. But a quarrel implies that they become angry; they may call each other names, make threats, shake their fists, break off friendly relations. When they are so filled with emotion, they are not likely to be very reasonable. It is hard to think of either person *winning* a quarrel.

In an argument, however, one person may win. If one wins, one wins because one's *evidence* is greater in quantity or superior in importance to the evidence of the other person, or because one reasons better, shows more clearly the *logical conclusions* that must be drawn from the material. Even the opponent may be completely convinced by the winning argument—particularly if he or she has not thought very much or very deeply about the subject before. To win an argument properly, then, one should have both knowledge that provides evidence and good powers of reasoning. To become violently emotional, to become quarrelsome, unpleasant, or nasty, is not likely to help one to argue well.

Many people, when they find that someone else disagrees with them, tend to start a quarrel rather than an argument. They may make attacks on the other person's character, accuse that person of selfish motives for his or her beliefs, treat the reasoning and evidence with scoffing and sarcasm. They

gument, so that they will not confuse an argument with a quarrel or mistake sarcasm for evidence.

The next step for the apprentice writer is to learn (it seems to be difficult for many people) that mere assertion has no value in argument. There are any number of assertions which people make and their statements may represent very strong belief, yet such statements, without evidence, will not convince another person that they are true. People disagree on a great many questions, but often they disagree because they have not thought enough about these questions, because they have not gathered evidence or have not analyzed the evidence to discover what it really means.

Below are some examples of assertions that are often made (but with which other people may disagree and therefore argue):

> The team is better this year than last.
> This novel is well written (or dramatic, significant, and so on).
> Everyone should vote for Candidate X.
> Smoke PQR cigars for the best flavor.
> President X was right (or wrong).
> Senator X was wrong (or right).
> Take this course, not that one.
> Mr. ABC is a better teacher (singer, scientist) than Mr. XYZ.

Many assertions will immediately bring exactly opposite statements of belief from some listener or reader. For example:

> We should raise taxes—tax property owners more.
> We should lower taxes—exempt the property owners.

> We ought to have censorship of "comic" books.
> No, we ought to have complete freedom of the press.

> We ought to take Latin (a dead language) out of the curriculum!
> No, we ought to make *everybody* study Latin!

> Children need more discipline!
> No, more freedom!

Importance of Evidence

Such assertions immediately raise questions in the minds of those who hear them. Listeners will say: "You have made a statement; you two have made opposing statements. But what *is* the truth of the matter? What *should* we do? What course *should* we follow?" In order to answer these questions, of course, evidence must be produced. "What is the truth?" is a question of fact. Often it can be satisfactorily answered, sometimes easily answered. If it is asserted that Mrs. A's living room is longer than Mrs. B's, the truth can be found just by taking a tape measure or a yardstick and measuring the two rooms. In such a situation there could properly be no argument. Often questions can be settled (and quarrels avoided) by the simple means of looking up the facts.

However, very frequently the facts are not so easily found; and sometimes, even when found, they do not automatically decide an argument. Suppose that someone says, "Team X is better than Team Y." If arrangements could be made for the two teams to play several games, then very likely the evidence would be clear; people would say that the question of fact had been answered. If such arrangements could not be made, many facts about the teams, all sorts of records, could be listed; yet whether the assertion were true or not may still be a matter of doubt. Of course, the question of fact involved in the assertion "Our team this year is better than our team was last year" cannot be settled by playing. It is impossible for the two teams in question to play any games. It would be necessary to work on the question of fact entirely by statistics. Similarly, two teams of the same year may not have a chance to play against each other enough to show without doubt which is the better team, so that it is then necessary to gather statistical evidence to try to settle the question of fact. This sort of evidence will never be so convincing as the scores of actual games.

Interpretation of Evidence

Without clear evidence of actual scores, the question of whether one team is "better" than the other cannot be measured like two living rooms; it is not a simple question of fact alone. Interpretation of facts is involved, and evaluation may enter in. Many people will be inclined to "weight" or "discount" some of the evidence. Will it not make a difference whether a team is excellent in defensive strength, or speed, or deceptiveness, or plodding power, or its capacity to take advantage of opponents' mistakes?

Let us look at an actual example. In 1863 the noted American preacher Henry Ward Beecher went to England to convince the British that the North would win the Civil War and to win support for the Northern side. In a speech at Manchester he said:

> We do not allow ourselves to doubt the issue of this conflict. It is only a question of time. . . . The population is in the North and West. The wealth is there. The popular intelligence of the country is there. There *only* is there an educated *common people*. The right doctrines of civil government are with the North. It will not be long, before one thing more will be with the North—Victory.

Beecher made several assertions supporting his belief that the North would win the war. But to make these assertions effective, he would have had to back them up with evidence. Thus, for example, he might have told his listeners that the North had about 72 percent of the population of the country against some 28 percent in the South. He might likewise have given comparative figures on wealth and resources. Even so, it would be harder to judge the influence of schools and education, whatever the figures might have been, and all such evidence might well need to be discounted because of possible factors such as the greater skill of Southern generals or a more fiery spirit and enthusiasm for war in Southern armies. Thus, reasonable interpretation of all the factual evidence would properly enter into the argument.

Yet questions of fact and questions of fact-plus-interpretation are usually easier to deal with than questions of policy, questions in which *should* is the key word. "Everybody should study Latin." "Children should have freedom." "The United States should not support dictatorships in Latin America." "Our foreign policy should be based on principles of Human Rights." Such propositions involve judgment as well as fact; they involve the weighing of facts; they involve values; and they may involve experience as well as information. Judgments are based upon standards that people accept; that is, they are based upon certain assumptions regarding what is valuable. And when one is trying to look into the future (which one must always do when a question of policy is being argued), one's argument may depend strongly upon one's reasoning from what has happened in the past—and this is why the light that experience gives may play an important part in deciding arguments on questions of policy.

At any rate, in all arguments the evidence should have a bearing upon the question (it must be *relevant*), it should be presented *logically*, and it should have the power to convince (it should be *cogent*).

Inductive Logic

Here is a recent example of argument in which two sociologists present evidence to prove the idea that persons who have committed murder are likely to have received excessive punishment and frustration when they were children.

> Both popular writers and scientific investigators have focused considerable attention through the years on case-history backgrounds of individual murderers, in the attempt to understand particularly violent or bizarre killings or those in which prominent persons were involved. In addition, psychiatrists, examining defendants for the courts, have accumulated elaborate dossiers on a number of murderers.
>
> Several clues pointing toward the direction in which such investigations might head are provided by a pilot study of six murderers serving life sentences in the Minnesota State Prison at Stillwater. Five collaborators from several academic disciplines conducted the research. Their subjects were chosen because they were normally intelligent members of the white race, not associated with gangs or with groups for whom crimes of violence were part of a way of life. The murder each committed was an isolated act, and the murderer himself showed no prior record of violent crime. All six murderers came from middle-class backgrounds, had no history of drug or alcohol use, and showed no traces of organic disease or epilepsy. The research team felt that offenses such as those studied "are sociologically determined and are more or less predictable, and that prevention is largely a broad social problem."
>
> Both parents of each of the six murderers, as well as the murderers themselves, were interviewed. The researchers were impressed with the readiness with which the murderers discussed both the crime and the events leading up to it. They found that the prisoners

ers themselves, were interviewed. The researchers were impressed with the readiness with which the murderers discussed both the crime and the events leading up to it. They found that the prisoners did not either try to escape responsibility for their crime or to lay the blame on others. Almost without exception, when the stories of the prisoners and their families were at variance, the prisoners were found to be telling the truth.

The study confirmed a finding that has received attention in the field of juvenile delinquency—that the worst offenders do not tend to be those who have been undisciplined, as public opinion often assumes, but those who have been strenuously subjected to constant physical punishment. The Minnesota research team found that for the six murderers "remorseless physical brutality at the hands of the parents had been a constant experience. Brutality far beyond the ordinary excuses of discipline had been perpetrated on them; often, it was so extreme as to compel neighbors to intercede for the boy." The study does not, of course, claim to have unraveled a total etiological pattern, but it is noteworthy in pointing to a common thread in the cases: Conditioned to violence, each of the murderers eventually resorted to the techniques that had been indelibly impressed upon him. . . .

Physical beatings by parents as part of the developmental history of murderers and manslaughter offenders are also reported by Stuart Palmer in his study of fifty-one New England prison inmates. Palmer found a whole complex of frustrating experiences in the backgrounds of the murderers; his research supported the hypothesis that there is a significant, positive, functional relationship between the amount of frustration experienced by individuals in infancy, childhood, and adolescence, and whether or not they later commit murder.

In formal terms the argument of Bloch and Geis, the two sociologists, rests on the proposition that many people who commit homicide have been treated brutally by their parents. This is an example of *inductive logic*. The process of inductive logic is as follows: (1) In Case A a person who had committed homicide had been treated brutally in childhood. (2) In Case B the same thing happened. (3) In Case C the same thing happened. If anyone observes the same result in a sufficiently large number of cases, then he will believe that the probability is very high that in the same circumstances the same result will occur. One cannot regard the occurrence of this result as a complete certainty. One can, however, regard it as having a high probability because, if the series of cases were indefinitely extended, one would expect to learn that in Case N another person who committed homicide had been treated brutally in childhood. Actually the cases cannot be extended indefinitely. But Bloch and Geis cite reports of six cases from Minnesota and fifty-one cases from New England, all of which show the same kind of childhood experience in the background of murderers. Thus, though the authors cautiously do not claim to have solved the whole problem of the causes of homicide, they are impressed by the "common thread" that has been observed. We might say that the cases cited seem to constitute good, even if not conclusive, evidence favoring a proposition of fact.

Technically speaking, what Bloch and Geis have done is to take a sample that is representative of a whole class, and then, according to the conditions found in the sample, they have made an inference, more or less probable, about the make-up of the whole class. If they had examined a larger sample of the class called murderers, they would have had a greater chance of discovering exceptions and variations which might exist within the class. But examining a larger sample might also increase the probability that their inference is correct. As we said, the number of cases cannot be indefinitely extended—for, disregarding practical considerations of time and money, there is no way that anyone can know how large the class of murderers is. But Bloch and Geis assume that if a result occurs under a variety of conditions where there is only one common factor (here, the excessive punishment and frustration endured in childhood by the murderers), then that common factor is the (probable) cause of the result.

Thus, they would be taking the next logical step, which is to make what is called an *inductive leap* to a conclusion. That is, they would leap over all the other cases which may exist but which have not been examined, on to Case N representing the last case in the possible series. And in Case N they would expect that on the basis of the cases already observed, the same thing would hold true. Thus arrived at, the inductive conclusion would be regarded as a general truth or a universal rule: murderers are likely to be people who have been badly frustrated and treated brutally in childhood.

Propositions

In effect, Bloch and Geis enter into a kind of contract with their readers. It is as if they said, "In order to convince you that our *proposition* is true, we are bound to show you that, in case after case, murderers do have the childhood experiences we have described. If we demonstrate the same situation for each murderer, we increase the probability that our proposition is true; therefore we increase your willingness to believe that it is true; and so, eventually, you must logically take the inductive leap with us and must agree to the truth of the proposition."

If there were any exceptions among the cases examined, the probability of the inductive conclusion would, of course, be weakened. This idea is brought out in the old saying that "the exception proves the rule," which does not mean that an exception gives a proof or support of the rule but that an exception tests the rule, that is, the conclusion or generalization. If an example were found in which a murderer had not been brutally treated in childhood, the conclusion would have to be modified. We should have to say something like, "Nearly all murderers were severely disciplined and frustrated in childhood," or, "All murderers except Irish murderers are people who had been severely disciplined and frustrated in childhood."

Deductive Logic

But—this is of utmost importance—once an inductive conclusion has been established, it can be used to cover every individual case. It must have taken a great many observations to establish the rule that at sea level water freezes at 32 degrees Fahrenheit. But as soon as people knew this universal rule, they could use it in every individual case when the temperature was likely to go down to 32 degrees. In any such case they would know that to keep water from freezing they must plan to use antifreeze, make a fire, add hot water, or take some such measure. Such a universal proposition, well based in induction, gives the human mind an enormous amount of practical power.

If we believed that by their inductive logic Bloch and Geis had established the universal truth that murderers have been frustrated and brutally punished when they were children, then we could apply this knowledge by using *deductive logic*. The universal truth would become the major premise of a syllogism. Suppose that evidence indicates that a man has been murdered. Then our syllogism would follow this pattern:

Major Premise: Murderers have been frustrated and brutally punished during childhood.
Minor Premise: Some person in this city is a murderer.
Conclusion: We should look for a person who was frustrated and brutally punished in childhood.

To deal practically with such a situation, assuming that the police had four suspects in the case and they could establish that only one of them had been brutally punished as a child, they would believe that the suspect who had been so punished was most likely to have committed the murder.

Issues

If we believed that the inductive conclusion of Bloch and Geis was true, we could also use it as the basis of propositions of policy. For example: Congress should pass a law protecting children against brutal punishment by their parents. Before Congress passed such a law, however, there would be argument, which would be focused on certain *issues*. Issues are points that must be proved if an argument is to be won. Let us limit ourselves to only two of the possible issues in this argument. (1) First is the humanitarian issue: We need such a law because brutal punishment is inhumane. (Behind such a view is probably the assumption that a civilized country cannot permit any of its citizens to be treated in a cruel or brutal manner.) The opposing view on this issue might be that parents have traditionally always had authority to discipline their children and it is better to put up with occasional excessive punishment than to weaken parents' authority. Besides, punishing children makes them respect authority and obey regulations; therefore it makes them good citizens. (2) This brings us to the second issue, the sociological issue: We need such a law because excessive punishment may incline children to commit murder as adults. Instead of making them good citizens, it makes them frustrated, resentful, callous, and inclined to violence. Then, of course, the evidence cited by Bloch and Geis would be presented in support of this issue.

But whatever syllogisms we may use in argument, for a syllogism to be true, the premises must be true. If we believe that the major premise is true in the syllogism presented above, we must have observed, or know for certain that other people have observed, enough such cases in the past to give the major premise a high probability. Thus inductive logic and deductive logic work together and support each other; in our thinking we are constantly using both the inductive process and the deductive process in an interlinked manner. When properly employed in argument, they must convince any person who can reason, that the conclusions from either induction or deduction are completely reasonable.

Use of Emotion

Yet there are two modifications of the preceding ideas which should be kept in mind. In the first place, though it is wrong to become overemotional to the point that reason, evidence, and logic are tossed aside, an argument does not have to be utterly cold and unemotional. Naturally, personal feeling enters into much argument, both spoken and written. And the presence of such feeling may help very much to make the argument seem convincing. A good example of personal feeling helping the effectiveness of an argument is the famous funeral oration of Marc Antony for Julius Caesar in Shakespeare's *Julius Caesar*. Brutus had spoken briefly and rather coldly: he said that he honored Caesar for many good qualities—"but, as he was ambitious, I slew him." (*Ambitious* here means aggressively determined to seize power.) Marc Antony's speech is, in terms of argument, largely a refutation of the idea that Caesar was "ambitious." He cites several pieces of evidence indicating that Caesar was not, after all, really "ambitious."

> He was my friend, faithful and just to me:
> But Brutus says he was ambitious;
> And Brutus is an honourable man.
> He hath brought many captives home to Rome,
> Whose ransoms did the general coffers fill:
> Did this in Caesar seem ambitious?
> When that the poor have cried, Caesar hath wept:
> Ambition should be made of sterner stuff:
> Yet Brutus says he was ambitious;
> And Brutus is an honourable man.
> You all did see that on the Lupercal
> I thrice presented him a kingly crown,
> Which he did thrice refuse: was this ambition?
> Yet Brutus says he was ambitious;
> And sure he is an honourable man.
> I speak not to disprove what Brutus spoke,
> But here I am to speak what I do know.

Since Antony had been ordered by Brutus to say nothing against the conspirators who had killed Caesar, Antony kept to the letter of the order; but he was trying to persuade the crowd that the conspirators were really murderers—"butchers"—and not saviors of Rome. So Antony mentions four pieces of evidence: faithful friendship, captives, sympathy with the poor, refusal of a crown, all of which contradict the idea of ruthless, aggressive "ambition." Furthermore, he uses two questions—"rhetorical" questions—which provide a personal contact with the audience, and he mentions himself and his own feeling—note the emphasis of "just to *me*" and "here I am to speak what *I do know.*" Such sincerely felt emotion will impress the audience. But Antony does not allow the emotion to get out of control; he systematically cites four examples intended to refute the veracity of the motives Brutus had alleged. We should say, then, that although overemotional arguments are not good, emotion in argument is not ruled out. Some authorities give the name of *persuasion* to arguments that have emotional appeals.

Use of Analogy

In the second place, though arguments should be logical, considerable use is made in argument of analogy, and analogy does not force one to inescapable logical conclusions. Nevertheless, similarities between situations, when such similarities exist, cause people to tend to think that the situation being argued about should be treated in the same manner that a former situation was treated. The effect of analogy may be expressed in such a phrase as "the same treatment for the same disease"; or it may be regarded as a kind of extension of the mathematical axiom that things equal to the same thing are equal to each other.

John Locke, a seventeenth-century philosopher, believed that a young man should not be kept without any knowledge of worldly matters, even though there is evil in the world. Locke argued that it was especially important to have a tutor teach a knowledge of "men and their manners." The pupil should be "warned who are like to oppose, who to mislead, who to undermine him, and who to serve him. He should be instructed how to know and distinguish them."

Locke then uses an analogy in his argument.

> Therefore I think it of most value to be instilled into a young man upon all occasions which offer themselves that when he comes to launch into the deep himself he may not be like one at sea without a line, compass or sea-chart, but may have some notice beforehand of the rocks and shoals, the currents and quicksands, and know a little how to steer that he sink not before he get experience.

In Locke's analogy the world is like the ocean, and the young man is like a captain who has the responsibility of sailing a ship safely through the ocean. The dangers and evils of the world are like rocks, shoals, and quicksand. Knowledge of the world gained from a tutor is like a compass and a chart, which supply information regarding the ocean.

If it seems reasonable that a captain should have experience and knowledge of the ocean, then it should seem reasonable that a young man should have knowledge and experience of the world. Locke was certainly assuming that the likenesses between the two situations were significant ones. Unless they were, his analogy would be worthless. And though likenesses may exist, the analogy does not *prove* the point. Possibly worldly knowledge might damage the character of the young man in a way that knowledge of the sea would not harm the capabilities of a captain for handling a ship. One situation in the analogy concerns a physical matter or problem; but the other situation concerns a moral and psychological problem. Therefore, this analogy, and all analogies, must be viewed with some caution. They may be very effective illustrations, but they are not proofs.

Locke made the assumption that knowledge of evils is a significant requirement for success in managing one's life, just as knowledge of the location of rocks and quicksands is a significant requirement for success in sailing a ship. Yet he did not state clearly that he was making that assumption. Assumptions are often hidden in arguments. They are often taken for granted—that is, the speaker feels that the assumption made is so reasonable, so natural, so unquestionable, that he or she does not even realize that other people may regard it differently. Consequently, it is essential to be on guard for this tendency in all arguments; one ought to test one's own arguments as well as those of opponents to find out what assumptions have actually been made.

In a sense, of course, all exposition is argument; that is, the writer wishes the reader to feel satisfied that what has been written is true. It was stated earlier that each paragraph should contain evidence to support the topic idea. The writer wants the reader to think: "Yes, this paragraph is a solid one; I believe what the writer says"—perhaps that two things are similar, or that the meaning of a term has changed, or that a machine has four main sections, or that a certain person was both brilliant and responsible. . . . But, in the kind of writing properly called argument, the writer is presenting a *justification* of a belief, an opinion, a judgment, a preference; the writer is always trying to convince the reader that he or she is *right* and frequently is trying to persuade the reader that the reader ought to do something: cast a ballot, purchase an article, give money, write a letter, use influence. . . . And this is why arguers are tempted to use tricks—anything to get the reader to do the thing desired.

Fairness in Argument

Honorable people ought not, however, to try to trick other people in argument. To use devices of "one-upmanship" or to use fallacies in argument is improper. *Fallacies* are falsities of argument—tricky, deceptive, *faulty* ways of persuasion. There are many of them. One book[1] on this subject lists fifty-one fallacies classified under "Material Fallacies," such as faulty generalization and faulty analogy; "Psychological Fallacies," such as abusing the emotional power of words, ridicule, appealing to prejudice, or using the *argumentum ad hominem*, that is, making personal attacks and discrediting an opponent's character instead of discussing the issues; and "Logical Fallacies," such as the undistributed middle term in a syllogism, circular definition, and begging the question. If the apprentice writer has the opportunity to take a course in logic or in argumentation, he or she will become more

[1] W. Ward Fearnside and William B. Holther, *Fallacy: The Counterfeit of Argument* (Englewood Cliffs, N.J.: Prentice-Hall, Inc., 1959).

skillful in detecting fallacies. But, in the meantime, he or she as an apprentice writer can consistently try to be fair and logical in all arguments.

In writing arguments, one will, of course, make use of all of the other forms of writing that have been set forth in this text. Definitions appear in arguments—in fact, defining terms is often necessary so that people can agree on exactly what the argument is about—as do analysis, enumeration, comparison, and contrast; all of these types of writing have their function. There may even be examples of description, characterization, and narrative, as writers undertake to make people understand historical backgrounds, physical situations, and the attitudes of people involved in public questions.

The Committee for Cultural Freedom, which was established in 1939, set forth a Code of Ethics to be followed in political controversy. Sidney Hook was the main author of this Code.

> These are the ten points by which we think all political controversy ought to be guided:
>
> 1   Nothing and no one is immune from criticism.
> 2   Everyone involved in a controversy has an intellectual responsibility to inform himself of the available facts.
> 3   Criticism should be directed first to policies and against persons only when they are responsible for policies, and against their motives or purposes only when there is some independent evidence of their character.
> 4   Because certain words are legally permissible, they are not therefore morally permissible.
> 5   Before impugning an opponent's motives, even when they legitimately may be impugned, answer his arguments.
> 6   Do not treat an opponent of a policy as if he were therefore a personal enemy, or an enemy of the country, or a concealed enemy of democracy.
> 7   Since a good cause may be defended by bad arguments, after answering the bad arguments for another's position, present positive evidence for your own.
> 8   Do not hesitate to admit lack of knowledge or to suspend judgment if evidence is not decisive either way.
> 9   Because something is logically possible, it is not therefore probable. "It is not impossible" is a preface to an irrelevant statement about human affairs. The question is always one of the balance of probabilities.
> 10   The cardinal sin, when we are looking for truth of fact or wisdom of policy, is refusal to discuss, or action which blocks discussion.

These are wise rules to observe in all arguments. They apply especially to politics, but whether one is trying to convince scientists that something they had not known before is really true (such as William Harvey presenting the case for the circulation of the blood), whether one is arguing for a particular business policy, or defending a client in a law case, or showing why a college curriculum needs changes, or why art enriches life, or why a Beethoven symphony has higher esthetic value than a popular song—no matter what the area of argument, one does best to argue honestly, with pertinent evidence, good reasoning, and good manners.

The readings that follow can be divided into two general groups. The first group—from Russell through Shahn—could be conveniently classified as examples of Evidence for Proof; the second group—those from Jacobs through Postman—as More Complex Arguments.

Acceptance of Law
or Destruction of Mankind

BERTRAND RUSSELL

1   Modern warfare, so far, has not been more destructive of life than the warfare of less scientific ages, for the increased deadliness of weapons has been offset by the improvement in medicine and hygiene. Until recent times, pestilence almost invariably proved far more fatal than enemy action. When Sennacherib besieged Jerusalem, 185,000 of his army died in one night, "and when they arose early in the morning, behold they were all dead corpses" (II Kings xix. 35). The plague in Athens did much to decide the Peloponnesian War. The many wars between Syracuse and Carthage were usually ended by pestilence. Barbarossa, after he had completely defeated the Lombard League, lost almost his whole army by disease, and had to fly secretly over the Alps. The mortality rate in such campaigns was far greater than in the two great wars of our own century. I do not say that future wars will have as low a casualty rate as the last two; that is a matter to which I will come shortly. I say only, what many people do not realize, that up to the present science has not made war more destructive.

2   There are, however, other respects in which the evils of war have much increased. France was at war, almost continuously, from 1792 to 1815, and in the end suffered complete defeat, but the population of France did not, after 1815, suffer anything comparable to what has been suffered throughout Central Europe since 1945. A modern nation at war is more organized, more disciplined, and more completely concentrated on the effort to secure victory, than was possible in pre-industrial times; the consequence is that defeat is more serious, more disorganizing, more demoralizing to the general population, than it was in the days of Napoleon.

3   But even in this respect it is not possible to make a general rule. Some wars in the past were quite as disorganizing and as destructive of the civili-

zations of devastated areas as was the Second World War. North Africa has never regained the level of prosperity that it enjoyed under the Romans. Persia never recovered from the Mongols nor Syria from the Turks. There have always been two kinds of wars, those in which the vanquished incurred disaster, and those in which they only incurred discomfort. We seem, unfortunately, to be entering upon an era in which wars are of the former sort.

The atom bomb, and still more the hydrogen bomb, have caused new **4** fears, involving new doubts as to the effects of science on human life. Some eminent authorities, including Einstein, have pointed out that there is a danger of the extinction of all life on this planet. I do not myself think that this will happen in the next war, but I think it may well happen in the next but one, if that is allowed to occur. If this expectation is correct, we have to choose, within the next fifty years or so, between two alternatives. Either we must allow the human race to exterminate itself, or we must forgo certain liberties which are very dear to us, more especially the liberty to kill foreigners whenever we feel so disposed. I think it probable that mankind will choose its own extermination as the preferable alternative. The choice will be made, of course, by persuading ourselves that it is not being made, since (so militarists on both sides will say) the victory of the right is certain without risk of universal disaster. We are perhaps living in the last age of man, and, if so, it is to science that he will owe his extinction.

If, however, the human race decides to let itself go on living, it will have **5** to make very drastic changes in its way of thinking, feeling, and behaving. We must learn not to say: "Never! Better death than dishonor." We must learn to submit to law, even when imposed by aliens whom we hate and despise, and whom we believe to be blind to all considerations of righteousness. Consider some concrete examples. Jews and Arabs will have to agree to submit to arbitration; if the award goes against the Jews, the President of the United States will have to insure the victory of the party to which he is opposed, since, if he supports the international authority, he will lose the Jewish vote in New York State. On the other hand, if the award goes in favor of the Jews, the Mohammedan world will be indignant, and will be supported by all other malcontents. Or, to take another instance, Eire will demand the right to oppress the Protestants of Ulster, and on this issue the United States will support Eire while Britain will support Ulster. Could an international authority survive such a dissension? Again: India and Pakistan cannot agree about Kashmir, therefore one of them must support Russia and the other the United States. It will be obvious to anyone who is an interested party of one of these disputes that the issue is far more important than the continuance of life on our planet. The hope that the human race will allow itself to survive is therefore somewhat slender.

But if human life *is* to continue in spite of science, mankind will have to **6** learn a discipline of the passions which, in the past, has not been necessary. Men will have to submit to the law, even when they think the law unjust and iniquitous. Nations which are persuaded that they are only demanding the barest justice will have to acquiesce when this demand is denied them by the neutral authority. I do not say that this is easy; I do not prophesy that it will happen; I say only that if it does not happen the human race will perish, and will perish as a result of science.

STUDY QUESTIONS
Organization and Content

1   Point out the topic sentences of paragraphs 1–3.
2   With what kind of material does Russell support the ideas in the topic sentences?
3   What points in his argument has Russell tried to make in the first three paragraphs?
4   In paragraph 1 mention is made of conditions in the past, the present, and the future. What determined the order in which the author took up these conditions?
5   What new idea is brought out in paragraph 4?
6   Note that in paragraph 4 Russell presents his readers with a dilemma (either . . . or). Explain what logical force this presentation of alternatives is intended to have.
7   What is the relation of paragraph 5 to paragraph 4?
8   Why does Russell mention the Jews, Eire, and Pakistan? Have developments since 1952 in Israel, Ireland, and Pakistan supported Russell's argument or not?
9   Paragraph 5 ends rather pessimistically; to what extent is a contrasting optimism apparent in paragraph 6?
10   Complete the following statement: The proposition that Russell is arguing may be stated as follows:_____.
11   What issues does Russell deal with in his argument?

Sentence Structure

1   Russell uses few sentences in paragraph 1 in which clauses are connected with coordinating conjunctions. What purpose of this paragraph probably caused him to put sentences in the form that he did?
2   Paragraph 2 has three sentences. What considerations determine the pattern and the length of each sentence?
3   Sentences 2 and 3 of paragraph 2 are long. Why are the sentences of paragraph 3 so much shorter?
4   Point out the ways in which transitional links are made between sentences in paragraph 4.
5   In paragraph 5 how does Russell introduce concrete examples?
6   In what different ways does he move from one concrete example to another?

7 How is a contrasting idea introduced at the beginning of paragraph 6?

8 Is sentence 2 of paragraph 6 arranged so as to provide enough emphasis?

9 The last sentence has three parts. Explain how the arrangement of words in the three parts makes this a very emphatic sentence.

Diction

1 Are there differences of meaning between *medicine* and *hygiene; pestilence* and *plague; mortality* and *casualty; extermination* and *extinction; dispute* and *dissension; injustice* and *iniquity?*

2 Look up *vanquished, eminent, arbitration.*

3 Is it because the extermination of the human race seems so horrible that Russell adopts an ironic tone in the second half of his argument? Consider the irony in paragraph 4 from: "... we must forgo certain liberties which are very dear to us, more especially the liberty to kill foreigners whenever we feel so disposed." Explain the effect of the connotations of words here which produces a shock in the last part of the sentence.

4 Similarly, when Russell says, "The choice will be made, of course ...," what is the effect of the "of course"?

5 What is the effect in paragraph 5 of including in one sentence *submit, imposed, aliens, hate, despise, blind?*

6 What is the great significance of *interested party* later in paragraph 5? How does the diction of the last two sentences of paragraph 5 produce an ironic effect?

Assignment

Write two or three paragraphs using Russell's technique of argument—an argument, that is, in terms of alternatives. Some possibilities:

1 Either we must pay college professors higher salaries, or college education will be greatly weakened.

2 Either we must admit to college all who wish to attend, or the public will remain dangerously ignorant.

3 Either we must drastically limit college admissions to the best students, or the quality of college training will be seriously diluted.

4 Either we must lessen the cost of political campaigns, or we shall be governed by rich men only.

5 Either the public must provide increased funds for medical research, or we must accept higher mortality rates for cancer and other diseases.

6 Either engineers and others with highly specialized training must have a broader education, or they will be unable to participate in our public life.

7   Either we must admit more foreign students to our colleges and send more of our native students abroad, or expect that effective international understanding will be dangerously delayed.

8   Either we must revise our police procedures, or expect further increases in crime.
     Be sure to support the issues of your argument with good evidence.

Why the Mountain West Is Conservative

GRACE LICHTENSTEIN

1   Liberals as I knew them in the East—the Bella Abzug kind—do not exist in the mountain West. There's no market for them. The traditional liberal domestic concerns—jobs, fair housing, civil liberties, civil rights, adequate welfare for deserving recipients, more educational opportunities, industrial safety—are concerns of working-class people in large, aging metropolitan areas. In the West people like these are a tiny constituency. Here and there are pockets of Eastern-style industrialism such as Butte, Montana. But the old West is still vastly rural and the new West mostly middle-class suburban.

2   Native Westerners come from families who put the greatest stress on fending for oneself. White people settled the West in gold camps before traditional legal authority (courts, sheriffs, the army) had a chance to establish itself. Thus the early West relied on makeshift law—what is now called frontier justice. The vigilante movement was the ultimate expression of this. The descendants of pioneer families thus have been schooled in the Jeffersonian ideal—that government is best which governs least.

3   To many new Westerners traditional liberal concerns are in some ways anathema. Many of them had fled aging Eastern cities riddled with social problems. They are likely to be unmoved by appeals to their consciences about the less fortunate. They no longer pay taxes in Cleveland, Chicago, Saint Louis, or New York; they have become suburban "moderates" seeking better suburban schools, lower property taxes and smaller welfare payments in their adopted environment.

4   The innate conservatism in the mountain West is very closely tied to the traditional values of land and free enterprise. In the late nineteenth and

early twentieth centuries this region appealed to many outsiders as a place to make a fresh start. It still has this appeal. Ambitious young doctors, lawyers, politicians, and business executives can move up the career ladder faster in young Western cities where their professions are not yet stratified, where there are fewer competitors, where family bloodlines and a Harvard education don't mean as much as they do in the East. But the West has also become a region that seems to preserve its gains, not to innovate.

Another factor working against traditional liberalism in the West is the   5 fact that except for Hispanics there are only small populations of ethnic minorities. The Hispanic people themselves are largely the offspring of Spanish families who had been in the West for a generation or more. The history of the region shows the hostility of the white majority to the minority groups who did turn up. The Chinese, for example, who worked on the railroads in the nineteenth century, were maligned as cheap, opium-smoking drudges. As a result no Chinatowns of any size remain beyond the West Coast. The Indians were, of course, enclosed in reservations. The Japanese were forced into concentration camps in Colorado as well as elsewhere during World War II. Mexican migrant workers were—and are—despised as a race of menial laborers. The minuscule numbers of Jews and Italians who came West quickly assimilated without making the ethnic impact they had in other places. Lacking cultural diversity, the interior West has not fostered the pluralistic toleration that exists in liberal circles on both coasts. The Democrats don't need a balanced ticket to win in Montana or Colorado.

By tradition and by choice, then, the West is conservative. The traits   6 Kirkpatrick Sale in *Power Shift* attributed to the Sunbelt—fundamentalist religion, frontier morality, chaotic growth, a faith in the inviolability of the land, a recent past filled with violence, the influence of agricultural, mineral extraction, and defense money—can be identified as those of the mountain West as well. Put them all together and they spell conservative, whatever a person's party affiliation might be.

STUDY QUESTIONS

Organization and Content

1   Paragraph 1 brings out a contrast; which terms in sentence 6 specifically contrast with which terms in sentence 3?

2   How do sentences 4 and 5 contribute to the explanation?

3   What two kinds of Westerners does Lichtenstein mention in sentence 6? What use does she make of them in paragraphs 2 and 3?

4   If native Westerners believe that "that government is best which governs least" (paragraph 2, sentence 6), why are they necessarily opposed to the "traditional liberal domestic concerns" that Lichtenstein mentions in paragraph 1? Can you state the hidden

assumption in paragraph 1 that makes paragraph 2, sentence 6, apply in the argument?

5 According to paragraph 3 why do "new" Westerners tend to adopt a conservative position?

6 How do the concepts of "free enterprise" and "a fresh start" influence the views of young professional people?

7 In paragraph 4 Lichtenstein speaks of "the traditional values of land and free enterprise." What would contrasting non-traditional (liberal and Eastern?) values be?

8 Which of the "liberal domestic concerns" listed in paragraph 1 do the examples of paragraph 5 relate to?

9 A lack of cultural diversity produces what other lack in the attitudes of the people of the mountain West? Explain the reference to a balanced ticket in paragraph 5.

10 If you agree that Sale's traits of the Sunbelt enumerated in paragraph 6 "spell conservative," explain why this is so.

11 How does paragraph 6 function in the discussion?

12 Put into one sentence the issues on which Lichtenstein has tried to convince us that the mountain West is conservative.

Sentence Structure

1 In sentences 1 and 3 of paragraph 1, Lichtenstein uses dashes. What do they set off? Paragraph 2 also has sentences (3 and 5) with dashes. How does their use resemble and differ from that in paragraph 1?

2 The sentences in paragraph 1 are quite short. How does the author obtain enough variety to keep them from being monotonous?

3 Why use the parentheses in paragraph 2, sentence 2? Would other marks of punctuation serve equally well?

4 Most of Lichtenstein's sentences begin with the subject. What effect does such a sequence of sentences produce?

5 To what extent is sentence 4 of paragraph 3 a balanced sentence? Why does the author not use a conjunction or conjunctive adverb between the clauses?

6 Point out parallel elements in sentences 4 and 5 of paragraph 4.

7 Explain the function of the transitional device that starts off paragraph 5.

8 By what method is paragraph 5 largely developed? How is the structure of the sentences related to this method of development?

9 How does the author place emphasis on the *existing* condition in paragraph 5, sentence 8?

10 What purpose does paragraph 5, sentence 10, serve?

Diction

1 You may need to look up *constituency* (paragraph 1), *ultimate* (2), *anathema* (3), *innate, stratified, innovate* (4), *maligned, minuscule* (be sure not to misspell it) (5).

2 What difference is there between *civil liberties* and *civil rights*?

3 Explain the meanings of *ethnic impact, pluralistic toleration* (paragraph 5), *fundamentalist religion,* and *frontier morality* (6).

Assignment

1 Use evidence to show why the people of your community believe as they do about some political or social question, such as women's liberation, gun control, affirmative action programs, giving asylum to Cubans and Vietnamese, or putting controls on rents.
2 Use evidence to show why the people of the Sunbelt are the way they are described in Lichtenstein's final paragraph.
3 Use evidence to explain why some groups of people are Democrats or Republicans.
4 Certain areas in the United States are far more tolerant concerning such issues as gay liberation and more favorable toward abortion and birth control than others are. Why is this so? Give evidence to prove your theory.

For the Death Penalty

H. L. MENCKEN

Of the arguments against capital punishment that issue from uplifters, two are commonly heard most often, to wit: 1

That hanging a man (or frying him or gassing him) is a dreadful business, degrading to those who have to do it and revolting to those who have to witness it.   (1)

That it is useless, for it does not deter others from the same crime.   (2)

The first of these arguments, it seems to me, is plainly too weak to need serious refutation. All it says, in brief, is that the work of the hangman is unpleasant. Granted. But suppose it is? It may be quite necessary to society for all that. There are, indeed, many other jobs that are unpleasant, and yet no one thinks of abolishing them—that of the plumber, that of the soldier, that of the garbage-man, that of the priest hearing confes-sions, that of the sand-hog, and so on. Moreover, what evidence is there that any actual hang-man complains of his work? I have heard none. On the contrary, I have known many who delighted in their ancient art, and practised it proudly.   2

In the second argument of the abolitionists there is rather more force, but even here, I believe, the ground under them is shaky. Their fundamental error consists in assuming that the whole aim of punishing criminals is to deter other (potential) criminals—that we hang or electrocute A simply in order to so alarm B that he will not kill C. This, I believe, is an assumption which confuses a part with the whole. Deterrence, obviously, is *one* of the   3 aims of punishment, but it is surely not the only one. On the contrary, there are at least half a dozen, and some are probably quite as important. At least one of them, practically considered, is *more* important. Commonly, it is described as revenge, but revenge is really not the word for it. I borrow a better term from the late Aristotle: *katharsis. Katharsis,* so used, means a salubrious discharge of emotions, a healthy letting off of steam. A school-boy, disliking his teacher, deposits a tack upon the pedagogical chair; the teacher jumps and the boy laughs. This is *katharsis.* What I contend is that one of the prime objects of all judicial punishments is to afford the same grateful relief (*a*) to the immediate victims of the criminal punished, and (*b*) to the general body of moral and timorous men.

4   These persons, and particularly the first group, are concerned only indirectly with deterring other criminals. The thing they crave primarily is the satisfaction of seeing the criminal actually before them suffer as he made them suffer. What they want is the peace of mind that goes with the feeling that accounts are squared. Until they get that satisfaction they are in a state of emotional tension, and hence unhappy. The instant they get it they are comfortable. I do not argue that this yearning is noble; I simply argue that it is almost universal among human beings. In the face of injuries that are unimportant and can be borne without damage it may yield to higher impulses; that is to say, it may yield to what is called Christian charity. But when the injury is serious Christianity is adjourned, and even saints reach for their sidearms. It is plainly asking too much of human nature to expect it to conquer so natural an impulse. A keeps a store and has a bookkeeper, B. B steals $700, employs it in playing at dice or bingo, and is cleaned out. What is A to do? Let B go? If he does so he will be unable to sleep at night. The sense of injury, of injustice, of frustration will haunt him like pruritus. So he turns B over to the police, and they hustle B to prison. Thereafter A can sleep. More, he has pleasant dreams. He pictures B chained to the wall of a dungeon a hundred feet underground, devoured by rats and scorpions. It is so agreeable that it makes him forget his $700. He has got his *katharsis.*

5   The same thing precisely takes place on a larger scale when there is a crime which destroys a whole community's sense of security. Every law-abiding citizen feels menaced and frustrated until the criminals have been struck down—until the communal capacity to get even with them, and more than even, has been dramatically demonstrated. Here, manifestly, the business of deterring others is no more than an afterthought. The main thing is to destroy the concrete scoundrels whose act has alarmed everyone, and thus made everyone unhappy. Until they are brought to book that unhappiness continues; when the law has been executed upon them there is a sigh of relief. In other words, there is *katharsis.*

6   I know of no public demand for the death penalty for ordinary crimes, even for ordinary homicides. Its infliction would shock all men of normal decency of feeling. But for crimes involving the deliberate and inexcusable

taking of human life, by men openly defiant of all civilized order—for such crimes it seems, to nine men out of ten, a just and proper punishment. Any lesser penalty leaves them feeling that the criminal has got the better of society—that he is free to add insult to injury by laughing. That feeling can be dissipated only by a recourse to *katharsis,* the invention of the aforesaid Aristotle. It is more effectively and economically achieved, as human nature now is, by wafting the criminal to realms of bliss.

STUDY QUESTIONS

Organization and Content

1 This is a good example of the use of evidence to refute an argument. To what issues is Mencken directing his refutation?
2 How much space does he give to the first issue? how much to the second? Why does he devote so little attention to the first?
3 Explain how Mencken uses analogy in paragraph 2. What other method of refutation does he use in the last three sentences of paragraph 2?
4 What is the basis of his attack on his opponents' position in paragraph 3? How does he push his attack ahead in sentences 5–6, paragraph 3?
5 What contention in the last sentence of paragraph 3 is the main issue of Mencken's argument?
6 What relation does paragraph 4 have to paragraph 3?
7 What concesssions does Mencken make in sentences 6 and 7, paragraph 3? How does the second part of sentence 6 strengthen his position? What support do sentences 7–9 give to his argument?
8 What important function do sentences 10–21 perform?
9 Explain how paragraph 5 is parallel to paragraph 4 in the argument.
10 What limitation regarding the death penalty for lawbreakers is suggested in paragraph 6?

Sentence Structure

1 In paragraph 2, sentences 3, 4, and 8 are extremely short. Do they make Mencken's writing seem too conversational and informal? too lacking in seriousness? too crisp and efficient?
2 In sentence 6, paragraph 2, how does Mencken arrange the material so as to present his list of items at the end? How does he connect sentence 7 with sentence 6?
3 In sentence 2, paragraph 3, what method does Mencken use to introduce his example? What grammatical relation does the example have to the rest of the sentence?
4 Sentences 3–7, paragraph 3, all contain brief parenthetical modifiers. Which are used as slight interrupters between subject and

verb, and which are used as introductory modifiers? Which one serves an important transitional purpose?

5   In the example of A and B in paragraph 4, what kind of sentences does Mencken mainly use? Why do you think he uses such sentences?

6   At the end of paragraphs 4 and 5, what has Mencken done to emphasize an important word?

7   In sentence 3, paragraph 6, Mencken keeps the reader in suspense till the last word. How has he postponed the end of this periodic sentence? What is the effect of this kind of sentence in terms of emphasis?

Diction

1   You may need to look up *sand-hog* (paragraph 2); *salubrious, pedagogical, timorous* (3); *pruritus* (4); *dissipated* (6).

2   What is the relation between *katharsis* and *cathartic*?

3   What connotations do the following terms have, and what is their effect on the reader: *uplifters, frying* (paragraph 1); *hustle* (4)?

4   Do you feel a touch of humor (is it ironic?) in ''even saints reach for their sidearms'' (4) and ''wafting the criminal to realms of bliss'' (6)? What is there about the diction in these phrases that produces a special effect?

Assignment

Write a refutation of arguments for or against (1) habitual use of drugs; (2) habitual use of alcoholic drinks; (3) allowing unlimited possession of firearms in the United States; (4) legalizing of abortions; (5) prison reform.

Select, as Mencken did, only one or two key issues, and include at least one good example.

Women Discourage Other Women's Ambitions

SUSAN BROWNMILLER

One of the hardest things for a woman with aspirations to do in our so- 1
ciety is to admit, first to herself and then to others, that she has ambitions
that go beyond the routine—a good marriage, clever children. Early on, we
learn that men don't take kindly to the notion of a woman entering the
competitive lists. It is in the nature of power and position that those who
have it do not relinquish it graciously, as all colonial peoples and all minority groups discover at a certain stage in their development. Well, O.K. so be
it. But infinitely more damaging to our psyche is the realization that our
ambitions are met with equal hostility—pooh-poohed, sniffed at, scoffed at,
ignored, or worse, not taken seriously—by mothers, sisters, cousins, aunts,
and friends, who won't believe that we have set our sights on a different sort
of goal than *they* have envisioned, preferring instead to believe that our ambition is merely a "passing phase"—which, unfortunately, it often is because
of lack of encouragement.

Psychologists talk a great deal about the importance of the approbation 2
or approval of a peer group upon the individual. It is human nature to want
to fit in. The senior at college who sends away for law-school catalogues
while her dormitory mates down the corridor are sending away for catalogues of silver patterns is already conscious of swimming against the tide.
(How different the atmosphere must be in a man's dormitory!) The magazine researcher who took her job as a stepping-stone to becoming a writer,
but discovers that girl researchers are not encouraged to write by the magazine's male editors, will find little sympathy and understanding from other
researchers who have taken the job to mark time until their proper engage-
ments are properly announced in *The New York Times*. The peer-group
pressure on a young woman in her 20s—as opposed to the pressure on a
young man in his 20s—is decidedly against career.

STUDY QUESTIONS

Organization and Content

1   Sentences 1–4 are devoted to what idea? What contras
out in sentence 5? (Sentence 5 begins with an a f

ment—something that is even stronger in the discussion than what has already been stated.)

2 What evidence is presented in sentence 5?
3 What proposition presented in sentence 2, paragraph 2, supports the idea in sentence 1?
4 What two examples of "peer-group pressure" are given in paragraph 2 to provide evidence for the argument?
5 What is the function of the final sentence in paragraph 2?

Sentence Construction

1 How does sentence 4, paragraph 1, contrast in length and rhythm with sentences 3 and 5? What is the effect of sentence 4?
2 In sentence 5 the predicate comes before the subject of the main clause. What purpose does this inverted order have?
3 Are the verbs between dashes in sentence 5 arranged according to any principle?
4 How is the material after *friends* grammatically related to the rest of the sentence?
5 How, and why, is sentence 4, paragraph 2, given special emphasis? What is the purpose of the parentheses?
6 Sentence 5, paragraph 2, is quite long. Contrast its pattern of organization with that of sentence 5, paragraph 1.
7 What contrast do the two *who*-clauses of sentence 5, paragraph 2, bring out?
8 How is the contrast made between "a young woman" and "a young man" in sentence 6, paragraph 2?

Diction

1 What other commonly used words have the same Latin root as *aspirations?*
2 Does *psyche* as used here have any different meaning from the one that it had in Greek?
3 How can *peer* mean both an equal and a nobleman?
4 In sentence 5, paragraph 2, what are the connotations of *proper* and *properly?*
5 Some figurative language appears here: in sentence 2, paragraph 1; sentence 3, paragraph 2; and sentence 5, paragraph 2. Are the figures of speech more vivid, more economical, or more emphatic than nonfigurative language would have been?

Assignment

1 Writing on the same topic, use a different approach and different illustrations to support the argument.
2 Use evidence to prove that a young man may experience opposition to certain career choices.

3   Making use of evidence, argue that all people should be encouraged to achieve their aspirations in life.
4   Similarly argue that young women should be urged to broaden their aspirations.

Mechanization Means Less Freedom

ARNOLD J. TOYNBEE

Mechanization means the replacement of the use of human and animal   1
muscle-power by harnessing the inanimate forces of nature, which dwarf the physical power of any living creature in both potency and scale. Mechanization is now about 5,000 years old; for wind-power was harnessed at the dawn of civilization for the propulsion of ships, as an alternative to the muscle-power of oarsmen. Water-power was harnessed about 2,000 years ago. But it was not till 200 years ago that mechanization got up steam, and it is more recently still that the harnessing of steam-power has been followed by the harnessing of electricity-power, mineral-oil-power, and atomic power.

This progressive increase, through mechanization, in the potency of the   2
material power commanded by Man has necessitated a proportionate increase in the regimentation of human life, and this for several reasons. The more high-powered our machinery is, the more dangerous it is to life and limb, the greater the care and the precision that are required for operating it, the greater its cost and therefore the greater the economic pressure to get the most lucrative possible performance out of it, and, finally, the greater the scale of its operations. Each of these aspects of high-powered machinery calls for greater human discipline on a larger social scale; and the scale and discipline tend to set the stamp of the machine on the life of the machine-tenders. In contrast to a human being or a domesticated animal, machinery is impersonal. It is true, . . . that an element of impersonalness entered into human life already when, at the dawn of civilization, the size of human societies grew beyond the point at which a society could be held together by personal relations. The earliest use to which the art of writing was put was to serve as a medium for impersonal relations. It was used to compile lists of commodities and personnel, to record contracts, and to compose those official "forms" that descend upon us in such quantities in our time. In our

social life since then, personal relations have been supplemented, and over-shadowed, by impersonal institutions that can hold together human beings who have never met each other, and never will meet each other, face to face. This impersonal element has always been present in civilization. The social effect of the recent progress of mechanization has, however, enormously strengthened and accelerated this previously existing tendency.

3   The scale of operations that our advancing mechanization now demands, and the cost of operations on this scale, are now too great to be within an individual human being's capacity. The Iowa farmer who still manages to own and operate a farm personally by means of mechanization is a lonely survivor from the vanished age of individual private enterprise, and even he cannot expect to survive much longer, in spite of his technological and commercial prowess. He is doomed to be replaced by an impersonal cor-poration, and the corporation in its turn is doomed to become first the pen-sioner, then the creature, and finally one of the departments of a still more massive impersonal institution, the state. The structure of society that is presupposed in the Constitution of the United States and in the United Kingdom's Parliamentary Reform Bill of 1832 is one in which the typical citizen is a man who, on the economic level, is his own master. He is the farmer who owns his farm and stock, the storekeeper who owns his store and goods, and the professional man who charges a fee to his clients for his services. Between then and now, the typical citizen has come to be an em-ployee of a corporation or else of some local or national or international public authority. "State the name of your employer" is the first demand that is made nowadays on any form issued by any authority for any purpose. Oc-casionally the draftsman of the form has remembered to add in a footnote: "If you are self-employed, enter your private address in the space here pro-vided." Self-employed persons are unpopular with all public authorities, in-cluding those whose official ideology is Individualism, while private em-ployers are popular, even with Socialist régimes. A self-employed person is likely to be a nuisance to the officials through being unversed in the regula-tions, whereas a corporation can afford to employ, and finds it worthwhile to employ, experts in the regulations to deal with the public authorities, and these private experts can be constrained by the officials to do a good deal of the officials' work for them at the private employers' expense.

4   The trend towards regimentation in all fields within my life-time is sym-bolized, for me, in what has happened within my life-time on the roads. In the year 1899, when I was ten years old, I was at school in a village that was within a mile-and-a-quarter of the road from Dover to London, about half-way between Dover and Canterbury. I used this section of the London-Dover road as a convenient place for teaching myself to ride a (pedal-driven) bicycle. I spent hours on that road mounting, falling off into the thick layer of soft white dust that covered the road's surface, mounting again, and repeating the performance till I had acquired the art. If one of

my grandchildren were to try to learn to ride a bicycle on the same road today, she would be run down and killed before any of the traffic police had had time to order her off. In my day, of course, there were no traffic police, because there were no vehicles on the road that were capable of being a danger either to each other or to anyone else. During the hours that I spent on that road alternately mounting my bicycle and falling off it into the dust, I was passed by nothing more dangerous than a rare charabanc. The rest of the wheeled traffic, such as it was, consisted of farm-waggons, dog-carts, donkey-carts, and wheel-barrows. If a donkey-cart had collided with a wheelbarrow, the damage would probably have been slight. The slow average pace of that traffic was inefficient, but it was safe; and therefore anybody could do anything on the London-Dover road that he pleased—he could, for instance, learn to ride a bicycle on it, as I did. Since then the invention of mechanized vehicles has enormously speeded up the pace of the traffic, but this at the cost of proportionately increasing the risk. The public authorities have therefore had to step in. For safety's sake, they have had to deprive road-users of their former liberty. The traffic regulations grow ever stricter, and the penalties for violating them grow ever more severe; yet the toll of casualties continues to mount. This story of what has happened on the roads between 1899 and 1965 is the story of what has been happening in every department of life.

STUDY QUESTIONS

Organization and Content

1   What does sentence 1 imply as a reason why human beings have adopted mechanization?
2   Why does Toynbee find it necessary to present historical facts in the other three sentences of paragraph 1?
3   What double function does paragraph 2, sentence 1, have?
4   Why are paragraph 2, sentences 2 and 3, very important in the argument?
5   According to Toynbee, what proportion does the increase of regimentation in our lives bear to the increase of mechanical power in use?
6   What sets "the stamp of the machine on the life of the machine-tenders"? What is meant by the stamp of the machine?
7   When did impersonal relations begin to replace personal relations in human society? Why is there so much more impersonality in twentieth-century societies than in earlier ones?
8   In paragraph 3 the example of the Iowa farmer illustrates what arguments that Toynbee made in paragraph 2? What drastic change in our society does Toynbee prophesy in paragraph 3? Is such an extrapolation reasonable in the argument?

9   Paragraph 4 illustrates the same trend as do sentences 4–10, paragraph 3. What is the difference in these illustrations? Which one more effectively shows the increase of mechanization?

10   Reread paragraph 1. Which words there are most significant in view of Toynbee's argument?

11   In terms of argument, where does Toynbee employ logical reasoning to support his proposition? Then what kinds of evidence does he present?

12   At the beginning of paragraph 4 Toynbee uses the phrase "in all fields," and at the end, "in every department." Are such sweeping general terms justified by his argument?

Sentence Structure

1   What repeated words provide transition in the four sentences of paragraph 1?

2   Both sentences 2 and 4 have rather similar patterns. What different effects come from use of the semicolon in sentence 2 and that of the comma in sentence 4? Which sentence makes greater use of parallel structures?

3   Explain how the several parallel units are set up in paragraph 2, sentence 2.

4   Identify parallel elements in paragraph 2, sentence 7, and in paragraph 3, sentence 5.

5   What kind of structure has Toynbee used to make the last sentence in paragraph 3 so long?

6   In paragraph 4, sentences 1 and 2, point out all the prepositional phrases that Toynbee has used in these smoothly written statements.

7   Contrast the sentence structure in paragraph 4, sentences 4–8. Which ones begin with a phrase, which with a dependent clause, which with the subject? Show how the structure of sentence 10 differs from that of sentence 9.

8   How does Toynbee secure a climactic emphasis in sentence 14?

Diction

1   You may need to look up *inanimate, potency* (paragraph 1), *regimentation, lucrative, impersonal* (2), *charabanc* (4).

2   Are the verbs *dwarf* and *harnessed* used metaphorically in paragraph 1? Can you think of any good synonyms for them?

3   In paragraph 3, sentence 3, what are the connotations of *doomed, pensioner, creature,* and *massive*?

Assignment

Use evidence to support an argument for or against one of the following:

1   The more roads we build, the worse auto and truck traffic becomes.

2   The more handguns people have, the greater the number of murders committed.

3   The more pesticides that are used, the more the environment becomes contaminated.
4   The larger that cities grow, the worse the quality of life is in them.
5   The lower the death rate, the more diseased and defective people we shall have.

Nonconformity Means Social Health

BEN SHAHN

I have always held a notion of a healthy society as one in which the two opposing elements, the conservative and the creative (or radical, or visionary, or whatever term is best applied to the dissident), exist in a mutual balance. The conservative, with its vested interest in things as they are, holds onto the present, gives stability, and preserves established values (and keeps the banks open). The visionary, always able to see the configuration of the future in present things, presses for change, experiment, the venture into new ways. A truly creative artist is inevitably of this part of the society.

There takes place from time to time an imbalance between the stabilizing and the visionary elements in society. Conformity is then pressed upon everyone, and growth and change and art come to a standstill.

In the year 1573, the painter Veronese was summoned before the Inquisition to answer a charge of blasphemy. In a painting of the Last Supper he had created an outer scene of worldliness in contrast to the inner scene of solemnity. Among the figures of the outer scene was a dog, and it was the dog that constituted the blasphemy. Ten years earlier the Council of Trent had decided upon the proper iconography for this and other religious scenes; their decision was held to be final, and a dog was not among the items listed.

The painter sought to explain the formal considerations which had led to his arrangement. His explanation was disregarded and he was ordered to substitute a Magdalene for the dog or be subject to whatever penalty the Holy Tribunal should decide to impose. Veronese did not yield; he retained the dog and changed the title of the painting. But let us note that art itself did yield to the increased pressure for conformity. It was in an atmosphere

From *The Shape of Content* by Ben Shahn, Harvard University Press. Copyright © 1957 by the President and Fellows of Harvard College. Reprinted by permission.

of enforced acts of faith, of fear of heresy, of trial and ordeal, and of the increasing harshness of the Inquisition that three hundred years of Renaissance greatness came to a close in Italy.

5   In our own generation, there is a record of a Russian trial not dissimilar to that of Veronese. A Soviet painter named Nikritin was accused of decadent Western formalism in a painting which he had made of a sports event, the specific complaint being that he had employed symbolic devices at the expense of Soviet Realism. Defending himself before a tribunal made up of fellow-artists and a member of a cultural bureau, Nikritin explained the artistic reasons which had prompted his choice and arrangement of figures. His defense was unsuccessful. It was decided that such symbolic treatment as that which he had employed was not understandable to workers and was indeed an affront to them. One of his fellow-artists described him as "one of those fellows who want to talk at all cost about themselves ... an undesirable type of artist." The verdict: "What we see here is calumny; it is a class attack inimical to Soviet power. The picture must be removed and the appropriate steps taken."

6   Perhaps equally significant is a story related by my brother after he had returned from a trip to the Soviet Union. He was curious about the status of art there and arranged to meet a number of artists. After he had visited several studios he was struck by the fact that all the artists seemed to be working in groups rather than singly and to be producing more or less the same subject matter. After a great deal of inquiring he learned of one man who painted alone, and he made his way to this man's studio. There he found the solitary painter, the individualist, who in spite of hardships was carrying on. When my brother looked at his work he was astonished to find that this man was painting exactly the same subject matter—the idealized workers, anti-capitalist themes, and portraits of heroes which the collective artists were doing. Conformity is a mood and an atmosphere, a failure of hope or belief or rebellion.

7   I do not know of any trials which actually took place during the Hitler regime in Germany. But it is well known that the function of art was determined by edict during that time, that art was charged with carrying out the policies of the State. It was to be Nordic; it was to reject the so-called degenerate forms current in the Democracies; it was to be purged of Semitic influences. German Expressionism, one of the most brilliant art movements of modern times, came to an abrupt end. Its artists scattered across Europe and America—those that were fortunate enough to escape in time. And there arose in its place a cloying art of *kirche, küche,* and *kinder,* stillborn and unremembered.

8   Nonconformity is the basic pre-condition of art, as it is the pre-condition of good thinking and therefore of growth and greatness in a people. The degree of nonconformity present—and tolerated—in a society might be looked upon as a symptom of its state of health.

STUDY QUESTIONS

Organization and Content

1   Analyze paragraph 1. What relation do sentences 2 and 3 have to sentence 1? Why does sentence 4 logically follow from sentence 3?

2   According to Shahn—a noted American artist (1898–1969)— what condition results from the imbalance mentioned in paragraph 2?

3   Why was Veronese accused of blasphemy? What idea are the two paragraphs about Veronese intended to illustrate?

4   In what way did the trial of Nikritin resemble that of Veronese? What differences between the situations of the two artists can be pointed out?

5   What conclusion does Shahn draw on the basis of the examples in paragraphs 5 and 6?

7   What similarity is there between the situation in Nazi Germany and that in Soviet Russia?

8   Why did German Expressionism come to "an abrupt end"?

9   Do you believe, with Shahn, that "nonconformity . . . is the precondition of good thinking"? If so, why?

10   Does Shahn have an introduction to his discussion? Where does he tell us what proposition he is arguing for?

11   What issues does he try to prove?

12   What conclusion does he assert in paragraph 8? What is the relation of paragraph 8 to paragraph 2?

13   Make a two-level outline of Shahn's argument.

Sentence Structure

1   How are sentences 2 and 3, paragraph 1, very similar in structure? Why is their similarity suitable?

2   Show what Shahn does in paragraph 1, sentence 1; paragraph 2, sentence 2; and paragraph 3, sentence 1, to throw emphasis on the final word of each.

3   In paragraph 3, sentences 3 and 4, Shahn uses a sequence of independent clauses. Is this an effective pattern for the material presented? Is it an effective pattern for the material in paragraph 4, sentences 2 and 3?

4   How does Shahn distribute emphases in paragraph 4, sentence 5? What part do the parallel prepositional phrases play?

5   What part do the participial phrases of sentences 2 and 3 play in the variety of sentence structures that you find in paragraph 5?

6   Do you believe that the sentences of paragraph 6 have too much sameness of structure?

7   Comment on the effect that Shahn gets from the way he has constructed sentences 3 and 4, paragraph 7.

8   In paragraph 8, sentence 1, why does Shahn place its three main parts in the order that he uses?

9   Why does he include—and also set off with dashes— the "and tolerated" of his final sentence?

Diction

1 Learn the meanings of the roots of *dissident* (paragraph 1), *iconography* (3), *decadent* (5).
2 Do you think that *creative* or *radical* or *visionary* is the best term to apply to a dissident?
3 What does *vested interest* imply about the conservative element?
4 In his illustrations Shahn uses several historical references. If you do not have an exact knowledge of them, read up in an encyclopedia on the Inquisition, Council of Trent (3), and Expressionism (7).
5 The official doctrine of Nazi Germany was that women's activities should be limited to *kirche, küche, kinder* (church, kitchen, children). Do you agree with Shahn that an official art thus limited would be *cloying*?
6 Perhaps you will need to look up *Magdalene* (4), *affront, calumny, inimical* (5), *edict,* and *Semitic* (7).
7 This selection is from a lecture that Ben Shahn gave when he was Charles Eliot Norton Professor at Harvard University. Do you think that his vocabulary or other element of style shows any influence of the lecture platform?

Assignment

1 Using as many examples and illustrations as you can for evidence, write an argument demonstrating: the value of a good library to a college or a town; the value of a college to a town or city; the value of a lecture and concert series on a college campus; the value of a high school band or orchestra.
2 Similarly argue for the value of freedom of speech or religious freedom for a healthy society.
3 Similarly argue for the value of science or of the scientific attitude for a dynamic society.
4 Similarly argue for the value of tradition or of religion for a stable society.
5 Similarly argue for the value of Art or of Music or of Business to a society.

Cities Need Old Buildings

JANE JACOBS

Cities need old buildings so badly it is probably impossible for vigorous 1
streets and districts to grow without them. By old buildings I mean not
museum-piece old buildings, not old buildings in an excellent and expensive state of rehabilitation—although these make fine ingredients—but also
a good lot of plain, ordinary, low-value old buildings, including some run-
down old buildings.

If a city area has only new buildings, the enterprises that can exist there 2
are automatically limited to those that can support the high costs of new
construction. These high costs of occupying new buildings may be levied in
the form of rent, or they may be levied in the form of an owner's interest
and amortization payments on the capital costs of the construction. However the costs are paid off, they have to be paid off. And for this reason, enterprises that support the cost of new construction must be capable of paying a relatively high overhead—high in comparison to that necessarily
required by old buildings. To support such high overheads, the enterprises
must be either (*a*) high profit or (*b*) well subsidized.

If you look about, you will see that only operations that are well estab- 3
lished, high-turnover, standardized or heavily subsidized can afford, commonly, to carry the costs of new construction. Chain stores, chain restaurants and banks go into new construction. But neighborhood bars, foreign
restaurants and pawn shops go into older buildings. Supermarkets and shoe
stores often go into new buildings; good bookstores and antique dealers seldom do. Well subsidized opera and art museums often go into new buildings. But the unformalized feeders of the arts—studios, galleries, stores for
musical instruments and art supplies, backrooms where the low earning
power of a seat and a table can absorb uneconomic discussions—these go
into old buildings. Perhaps more significant, hundreds of ordinary enterprises, necessary to the safety and public life of streets and neighborhoods,
and appreciated for their convenience and personal quality, can make out
successfully in old buildings, but are inexorably slain by the high overhead
of new construction.

As for really new ideas of any kind—no matter how ultimately profitable 4
or otherwise successful some of them might prove to be—there is no leeway
for such chancy trial, error and experimentation in the high-overhead economy of new construction. Old ideas can sometimes use new buildings. New
ideas must use old buildings.

Even the enterprises that can support new construction in cities need old 5 construction in their immediate vicinity. Otherwise they are part of a total attraction and total environment that is economically too limited—and therefore functionally too limited to be lively, interesting and convenient. Flourishing diversity anywhere in a city means the mingling of high-yield, middling-yield, low-yield and no-yield enterprises.

STUDY QUESTIONS
Organization and Content

1 Regarding buildings in cities, what assumptions do many people make that may cause the author's first statement to be surprising and challenging?
2 Why does the author include sentence 2, paragraph 1?
3 In effect, the author says in sentence 1, paragraph 2: "Let us assume that a city area contains only new buildings." What conclusion follows from this assumption?
4 Indicate the steps in the reasoning from sentence 1 to sentence 5, paragraph 2.
5 Where does the author give examples of well-subsidized operations that can support costs of new construction? What kinds of operations are mentioned in sentences 2 and 4, paragraph 3?
6 What contrasts are brought out in sentences 3, 4, and 6, paragraph 3?
7 What function does paragraph 3 perform in the argument?
8 What assumptions and what reasoning lie behind the final statement of paragraph 4: "New ideas must use old buildings"?
9 How do the concepts of "total attraction" and "flourishing diversity" influence the argument in paragraph 5?
10 What is the main issue on which the success of this argument depends?

Sentence Structure

1 Most of the sentences in paragraphs 1 and 2 begin with introductory dependent elements. Which of them are used mainly for transition and which mainly because of the reasoning?
2 Why are there more sentences in paragraph 3 that begin with the subject?
3 Show how parallel construction, especially with groups of two or three examples, is used in paragraph 3.
4 Would it be better to use commas (less separation) or parentheses (greater separation) than the dashes to set off the interrupter in sentence 1, paragraph 4?
5 How is emphatic contrast achieved in sentences 2 and 3, paragraph 4?

Diction

1 Look up *museum-piece, amortization, inexorably.*
2 Is the author's vocabulary extremely formal, informal, or technical?

Assignment

Write an argument on one of the following topics: A person's wardrobe always needs some old clothes; a scientific curriculum needs courses in history of science; it is best to have friends with a diversity of age, interest, and occupation; it is best to have a balance of utility and beauty in a house.

Argue for certain means of achieving diversity in a flower garden; a personal collection of books; amusements; a recreational reading room in a library; house furnishings; diet.

Romance Is a Poor Basis for Marriage

DENIS DE ROUGEMONT
(*Montgomery Belgion, trans.*)

The better to see our situation, let us look at America—that other Europe 1 which has been released from both the routine practices and traditional restraints of the old. No other known civilization, in the 7000 years that one civilization has been succeeding another, has bestowed on the love known as *romance* anything like the same amount of daily publicity by means of the screen, the hoarding, the letterpress and advertisements in magazines, by means of songs and pictures, and of current morals and of whatever defies them. No other civilization has embarked with anything like the same ingenuous assurance upon the perilous enterprise of making marriage coincide with love thus understood, and of making the first depend upon the second.

During a telephone strike in 1947, the women operators in the county 2 town of White Plains, near New York, received the following call: "My girl and I want to get married. We're trying to locate a justice of the peace. Is it an emergency?" The women telephone operators decided forthwith that it

From *Love in the Western World,* revised and augmented edition, by Denis de Rougemont, translated by Montgomery Belgion. Copyright 1940, 1956, by Pantheon Books, Inc. Reprinted by permission of Pantheon Books, a division of Random House, Inc.

was. And the newspaper which reported the item headed it: "Love Is Classified as an Emergency." This commonplace newspaper cutting provides an example of the perfectly natural beliefs of Americans, and that is how it is of interest. It shows that in America the terms "love" and "marriage" are practically equivalent; that when one "loves" one must get married instantly; and, further, that "love" should normally overcome all obstacles, as is shown every day in films, novels, and comic-strips. In reality, however, let romantic love overcome no matter how many obstacles, and it almost always fails at one. That is the obstacle constituted by time. Now, either marriage is an institution set up to be lasting—or it is meaningless. That is the first secret of the present breakdown, a breakdown of which the extent can be measured simply by reference to divorce statistics, where the United States heads the list of countries. To try to base marriage on a form of love which is unstable by definition is really to benefit the State of Nevada. To insist that no matter what film, even one about the atomic bomb, shall contain a certain amount of romantic drug—and romantic more than erotic—known as "love interest," is to give publicity to the germs that are making marriage ill, not to a cure.

3   Romance feeds on obstacles, short excitations, and partings; marriage, on the contrary, is made up of wont, daily propinquity, growing accustomed to one another. Romance calls for "the faraway love" of the troubadours; marriage, for love of "one's neighbour." Where, then, a couple have married in obedience to a romance, it is natural that the first time a conflict of temperament or of taste becomes manifest the parties should ask themselves: "Why did I marry?" And it is no less natural that, obsessed by the universal propaganda in favour of romance, each should seize the first occasion to fall in love with somebody else. And thereupon it is perfectly logical to decide to divorce, so as to obtain from the new love, which demands a fresh marriage, a new promise of happiness—all three words, "marriage," "love," "happiness," being synonyms. Thus, remedying boredom with a passing fever, "he for the second time, she for the fourth," American men and women go in quest of "adjustment." They do not seek it, however, in the old situation, the one guaranteed—"for better, for worse"—by a vow. They seek it, on the contrary, in a fresh "experience" regarded as such, and affected from the start by the same potentialities of failure as those which preceded it. That is how divorce assumes in the United States a less "disastrous" character, and is even more "normal," than in Europe. There where a European regards the rupture of a marriage as producing social disorder and the loss of a capital of joint recollections and experiences, an American has rather the impression that "he is putting his life straight," and opening up for himself a fresh future. The economy of saving is once again opposed to that of squandering, as the concern to preserve the past is opposed to the concern to make a clean sweep in order to build something tidy, without compromise. But any man opposed to compromise is inconsistent in marry-

ing. And he who would draw a draft on his future is very unwise to mention beforehand that he wishes to be allowed not to honour it; as did the young millionairess who told the newspaper men on the eve of her marriage: "It's marvellous to be getting married *for the first time!*" A year later, she got divorced.

Whereupon a number of people propose to forbid divorce, or at least to **4** render it very difficult. But it is marriage which, in my opinion, has been made too easy, through the supposition that let there be "love" and marriage should follow, regardless of outmoded conventions of social and religious station, of upbringing and substance. It is certainly possible to imagine new conditions which candidates for marriage—that true "co-existence" which should be enduring, peaceable, and mutually educative—should fulfil. It is possible to exact tests or ordeals bearing on whatever gives any human union its best chances of lasting: aims in life, rhythms of life, comparative vocations, characters, and temperaments. If marriage—that is to say, lastingness—is what is wanted, it is natural to ensure its conditions. But such reforms would have little effect in a world which retained, if not true passion, at least the nostalgia of passion that has grown congenital in Western man.

When marriage was established on social conventions, and hence, from **5** the individual standpoint, on chance, it had at least as much likelihood of success as marriage based on "love" alone. But the whole of Western evolution goes from tribal wisdom to individual risk; it is irreversible, and it must be approved to the extent it tends to make collective and native destiny depend on personal decision.

STUDY QUESTIONS
Organization and Content

1   Why does the author focus paragraph 1 on America?
2   Why does he tell the story of the telephone operators in paragraph 2? Which sentence brings out his purpose?
3   In the second half of paragraph 2, what objection to romance does the author raise?
4   In sentence 10 of paragraph 2, what effect in the argument does the *either . . . or* statement have? Is it acceptable to you?
5   Paragraph 3 points out contrasts. List them.
6   Paragraph 4 shows the author rather dubious about reforms. Why?
7   To what extent does the author make concessions in paragraph 5?
8   The author uses specific examples, definitions, and reasoning from assumptions. Which of these means of argument is the most effective?

9   In what terms does the author define *romance* and *marriage?*
10   How are America and Europe represented? Does the effective-
     ness of the argument depend at all upon one's attitude toward
     America or Europe?
11   Set down De Rougemont's argument in the form of a syllogism,
     with major premise, minor premise, and conclusion.

Sentence Structure

1   Explain the reason for the structure of sentences 1 and 2 of para-
     graph 3.
2   Indicate by what means sentences 3–6 of paragraph 3 are linked.
3   What terms show that the author in sentences 3–6 is drawing
     conclusions from the ideas in sentences 1 and 2 of paragraph 3?
4   Why is the last sentence of paragraph 3 so short?
5   Are there too many "interrupters" in the sentences of paragraph
     4?

Diction

1   Look up *romance, hoarding, ingenuous, erotic, wont, propinquity,
     troubadour, obsessed, economy, nostalgia, congenital.*
2   Why do so many words have quotation marks around them?
3   Which of De Rougemont's terms are metaphors?

Assignment

De Rougemont's argument may make you wish to reply to it by
writing a defense of marriage based on romance. If you choose to
do so, state clearly on what issues you base your counterargu-
ment.

Perhaps you prefer to imitate the work of De Rougemont in an
argument that says *this* is better than (or preferable to) *that.* Some
possibilities:

1   A campus with plenty of grass and trees and without auto-
     mobiles is preferable to a campus with large areas given up
     to parking lots and many automobiles.
2   It is better to read much (100 books a year, for example)
     than to read little, as most Americans do.
3   It is better to play a musical instrument (or sing) than to at-
     tend concerts.
4   For nonscience students it would be better to read books
     about the history of science and the significance of science
     than to take a course in laboratory science.

Killing for Sport Is Pure Evil

JOSEPH WOOD KRUTCH

To me it is inconceivable how anyone should think an animal more inter-   1
esting dead than alive. I can also easily prove to my own satisfaction that
killing "for sport" is the perfect type of pure evil for which metaphysicians
have sometimes sought.

Most wicked deeds are done because the doer proposes some good to   2
himself. The liar lies to gain some end; the swindler and the thief want
things which, if honestly got, might be good in themselves. Even the murderer may be removing an impediment to normal desires or gaining possession of something which his victim keeps from him. None of these
usually does evil for evil's sake. They are selfish or unscrupulous, but their
deeds are not gratuitously evil. The killer for sport has no such comprehen-
sible motive. He prefers death to life, darkness to light. He gets nothing except the satisfaction of saying, "Something which wanted to live is dead.
There is that much less vitality, consciousness, and, perhaps, joy in the universe. I am the Spirit that Denies." When a man wantonly destroys one of
the works of man we call him Vandal. When he wantonly destroys one of
the works of God we call him Sportsman.

The hunter-for-food may be as wicked and as misguided as vegetarians   3
sometimes say; but he does not kill for the sake of killing. The rancher and
the farmer who exterminate all living things not immediately profitable to
them may sometimes be working against their own best interests; but
whether they are or are not they hope to achieve some supposed good by
their extermination. If to do evil not in the hope of gain but for evil's sake
involves the deepest guilt by which man can be stained, then killing for
killing's sake is a terrifying phenomenon and as strong a proof as we could
have of that "reality of evil" with which present-day theologians are again
concerned.

STUDY QUESTIONS

Organization and Content

1   Be sure to state correctly the proposition that Krutch
    Note that it is not: Sportsmen are bad men, or a law

passed protecting animals from sportsmen; the proposition of his argument is more abstract.

2   If sentence 1 is Krutch's major premise, what are the minor premise and conclusion of the syllogism he is relying on for support of his argument? (Krutch says "an animal"; presumably a proper example would be a leopard, rhinoceros, blacksnake, or bluejay.)

3   Krutch groups liar, swindler, thief, and murderer together because they have something in common. What is it? According to sentence 5, paragraph 2, what quality is absent from all of their deeds?

4   Paragraph 2 is divided into two parts. What is the main idea of each part, and how are the two parts related?

5   In Krutch's argument what are life and death to be equated with? In the argument, how are these equations related to sentence 1, paragraph 2?

6   What idea do sentences 11 and 12, paragraph 2, ironically illustrate? What contrast provides the basis for irony?

7   On what issues is the argument continued in paragraph 3? What is the significance of the final sentence?

8   To what extent is Krutch's argument based on evidence and to what extent on reasoning?

Sentence Structure

1   Why is the structure of sentence 2, paragraph 2, appropriate to the ideas expressed there? Why is the murderer named last and in a new sentence, and how does Krutch place emphasis on the murderer?

2   Sentences 6–8, paragraph 2, have the same basic structure. What is it, and why is it suitable? What transitional device links these three sentences?

3   Point out repetition and parallelism in sentences 11 and 12, paragraph 2. Why are these devices effective here?

4   How does Krutch gain strong contrast in sentences 1 and 2, paragraph 3?

Diction

1   Look up *metaphysicians, gratuitously, wantonly, Vandal, phenomenon, theologians.*

2   What do the words *gratuitously* and *wantonly* contribute to Krutch's argument?

3   Explain the allusion behind the meaning of *Vandal.*

Assignment

1   If you took the side of a "sportsman," could you suggest any "good" as he sees the matter, and formulate an argument opposing Krutch?

2   Perhaps you do not agree with Krutch's sentence 1. If so, justify your position.

3 Krutch condemns the sportsman for saying with satisfaction, "Something which wanted to live is dead." You might explore the questions: "Is every death an evil? What killings can be justified?" What proposition would you finally be willing to argue for?

4 Imitate Krutch by writing an argument on one of the following topics: Loss of freedom is the greatest evil; vivisection is an evil—or a good—in our society; a world that permits starvation is evil; a world that permits unlimited births is evil.

Photography Is as Much a Fine Art as Painting

DOUGLAS DAVIS

Is it really easier to make a superb photograph than a superb painting? 1 No, precisely because the act itself is so simple. Yes, anyone can "take" a picture—as virtually anyone can type. He who types doesn't necessarily write, however, and he who photographs isn't necessarily creating art. Photography is a language—much like verbal language—and photographs or paintings can lie, in the hands of the ungifted or the charlatan, as abjectly as words lie in the mouths of fakers and demagogues.

Both words and photographs are easily manufactured and easily used. 2 They are extensions of the self—and they reveal that self in ways that more sensuous, physically difficult mediums do not. Stieglitz once called the camera a means "to create with the brain"—which is precisely why its rewards and its difficulties are so great. Yes, "anyone" can produce a photograph—as "anyone" can wield a pencil—but few, very few can produce photographs with enduring structure and meaning. Photography—supposedly the most democratic of arts—is in fact the most aristocratic. It mercilessly lays bare dullness or insensitivity because there is no intervening layer of thick, gooey brush strokes or carefully modeled clay, to hide behind. At the last, as Stieglitz said, "the result is the only fair basis for judgment."

This is a standard that holds true across the board—across all the media. 3 The result counts, not how it is made. . . . I believe we are nearing the end of the day when photography—or the camera—can be seriously challenged as art. The achievement of an Atget or a Stieglitz is finally coming to be seen as comparable, in its scope and intellectual edge, to that of a Picasso or a Matisse.

STUDY QUESTIONS

Organization and Content

1   Sentence 1 is a rhetorical question that is immediately answered. According to sentence 2, what is the usual result of the simple act of "taking" a picture?

2   What analogy does Davis use in sentences 3 and 4?

3   What metaphor (or analogy) is expressed in the first clause of sentence 5? How is that analogy extended in the rest of the sentence?

4   If photographs reveal the self, as sentence 2, paragraph 2, says, what sort of self is most likely to be revealed in most photographs?

5   How does Stieglitz' statement (sentence 3, paragraph 2) show why both the rewards *and* the difficulties of the camera are great? What is it in sentence 4 that clinches the point?

6   How does sentence 6 demonstrate what sentence 5 says—that photography is not the most democratic but the most aristocratic of arts?

7   According to Stieglitz, how should the quality of any artist be judged?

8   How does sentence 2, paragraph 3, refute a prejudice that some people have had against photography?

9   Fill in each blank with one correct word: Instead of judging the quality of any piece of art by its_____, one should judge it by its_____.

10   Find out enough about Eugène Atget, Alfred Stieglitz, Pablo Picasso, and Henri Matisse so that you can understand the significance of the comparison in the last sentence. What criteria does Davis use in praising the work of the photographers?

11   Set down the issues on which Davis has focused his argument to prove the truth of his proposition.

Sentence Structure

1   In eight sentences Davis uses the dash. Explain for what purposes he uses it.

2   Do the sentences with dashes seem too jerky, too interrupted, or too loose?

3   In paragraph 2 Davis throws emphasis on the last part of several sentences. Explain how he does it.

4   Which sentence in each paragraph seems to you the most effectively constructed?

Diction

1   Does Davis do better to have "virtually anyone" in sentence 2 rather than *pretty nearly* or *almost* or *just about*?

2   What is the difference between a *charlatan* and a *demagogue* (paragraph 1)?

3 How does sentence 6, paragraph 2, illustrate the meaning of *sensuous* in sentence 2, paragraph 2?
4 Check the meanings of the Greek roots of *democratic* and *aristocratic.*

Assignment

1 From your observation of various teachers, could you argue that teaching is an art? If you argue that it is, to what other arts would you compare it?
2 Among different sports, is there any one that you think could qualify as an art? Explain why you would choose it, and construct an argument to convince readers that it would qualify.
3 Is there good reason to believe that cooking or designing clothing or raising children or even training animals might also be an art? If you think so, list pertinent issues and organize an effective argument around them.

For Zero Energy Growth

EDWARD ABBEY

All very well, the reader thinks, for a few thousand farmers and ranchers 1 [who oppose strip mining of coal] to want to save their homes and livelihoods, to preserve a charming but no doubt outmoded way of life. And it would be nice if we could keep the pure air, the wide-open spaces, the canyons and rivers and mountains free from pollution from a rash of new power plants. But America needs the energy. Our political and industrial leaders assure us that the very survival of America as a great world power may be at stake. We cannot let our future be dictated by a cartel of Arab potentates. We have more coal than the Arabs have oil. Let's dig it. The assumption is that we must continue down the road of never-ending economic expansion, toward an ever-grosser gross national product, driven by that mania for Growth with a capital *G* that entails, among other things, a doubling of the nation's energy production every ten years. "Expand or expire" is the essence of this attitude, exemplified in the words of President Ford in a statement to an Expo '74 audience: "Man is not built to vegetate or stagnate—we like to progress—zero-growth environmental policies fly in the face of human nature."

But a child can perceive that on our finite planet there must be, sooner or 2 later, a limit to quantitative growth. Any high-school math student can prove that if our production of electricity continued to grow at an exponential rate of 100 percent every ten years the result would be, in less than a century, a United States of America in which every square foot of land surface was preempted by mines and power plants, leaving no room at all for homes, cities, farms, living space, or even graveyards. Growth for the sake of growth *is* the ideology of the cancer cell.

3   Far ahead of their so-called leaders, as usual, the American people as a whole have already begun putting into practice the obvious need for zero population growth. If the trend continues, the population of the U.S. should level off at about 250 million by the year 2000. Even that is far too many bodies for a free society, but better than the overcrowding typical of European nations. Beyond that point the goal would be an eventual reduction of the population (through normal attrition, of course) to something like 100 million, a rational figure if we desire our grandchildren to live in a green and spacious America.

4   An immediate and required step forward is stabilization of the energy growth rate. This will be forced upon us sooner than expected in any case. As some economists (though still a minority in that dismally obtuse profession) and most ecologists have pointed out, it takes energy to produce energy. The law of diminishing returns is now in operation. When oil could be pumped from a sixty-nine-foot well in Titusville, Pennsylvania, in 1859, it was a cheap commodity. When it has to be piped 800 miles across Alaska, or extracted from the continental shelf, or shipped in super-tankers all the way from the Persian Gulf, oil becomes an expensive luxury.

5   If we are driven to manufacture synthetic fuels from coal or to squeeze oil from shale rock—a silly proposition on the face of it—we shall find ourselves expending as much energy as we gain; the net profit becomes marginal. This is the reason the power companies and oil corporations are demanding subsidies from the government. Nor will nuclear energy solve the problem. The available evidence indicates that the construction of nuclear power plants and the mining and processing of reactor fuel will require in themselves more electrical energy than these proposed plants could produce for the next forty to fifty years.

6   Nuclear fusion offers the last best hope of the technophiles. But nuclear fusion remains at least a generation away, perhaps farther, perhaps forever out of reach. Even if it can be developed someday, fusion will doubtless prove to involve hazards now unforeseen. Any form of cheap and unlimited power, if placed in the hands of humanity as we know it today, would probably lead, not to a free and abundant life for all, but to the rapid transformation of our planet into a gigantic dormitory and food factory. Earth would become a ball of passive flesh, alive perhaps but scarcely human, wobbling slowly around the sun.

7   The way to zero energy growth has been outlined for us by the report of the recent Energy Policy Project sponsored by the Ford Foundation. Two

years in the making, *A Time To Choose: America's Energy Future* is the work of a professional staff of economists, ecologists, physicists, engineers, and research specialists, with a panel of supporting consultants including such distinguished names as Barry Commoner, René Dubos, Harrison Brown, Kenneth E. Boulding, Daniel Bell, Alan Poole, Ben J. Wattenberg, and Robert H. Socolow and an advisory board consisting of leaders from the world of science, conservation, law, and industry. *A Time To Choose* presents various scenarios for the future, including the option of zero energy growth, which can be accomplished, according to this study, without lowering the American standard of living; indeed, providing for continuing economic growth by assigning first priority to the fields of medicine, education, the arts, and sciences, and to basic human needs such as decent housing, adequate nutrition, livable cities, a clean, attractive, healthy environment.

STUDY QUESTIONS

Organization and Content

1   In the 1970s Abbey traveled through Montana and Wyoming investigating mining activities there. This part of his report comes after his account of how ranchers there have been fighting to save their land from mining companies. According to paragraph 1, what attitude are most Americans likely to adopt on preserving the Western environment?

2   What gives importance to sentence 3 in Abbey's discussion? What arguments favor strip mining of coal?

3   What widely held assumption is illustrated by the quotation from Gerald Ford?

4   What is Abbey's first issue in the argument? What part does mathematics play in his discussion of the issue? What effect does he gain by his analogy of the cancer cell?

5   How does the issue raised in paragraph 3 work in terms of the opposing argument? What is Abbey's position on this issue?

6   What issue does Abbey take up in paragraphs 4 and 5? What illustrations does he use as evidence for his opinion?

7   What three means of producing more energy does he consider in paragraph 5?

8   How is paragraph 6 related to paragraph 5? What objections does Abbey raise to our depending on nuclear fusion? What conclusion does he reach in paragraph 6, sentences 3 and 4?

9   In paragraph 7 Abbey cites authorities in favor of his argument. How are you impressed by his account of *A Time to Choose* and the persons who produced it? Is his appeal to authority more, or less, convincing than his arguments in paragraphs 2–5?

10 According to paragraph 7 how does Abbey answer a person who thinks that a policy of zero energy growth would be bad for business and lead to a loss of jobs?

11 Make a two-level outline of Abbey's argument.

Sentence Structure

1   Contrast the structure, rhythm, and tone of sentences 1–2 with those of sentences 3–7. What kind of person seems to be speaking in sentences 3–7?
2   Paragraph 2, sentence 2, is a sentence of the climactic, or periodic, type. How far do we read before the sentence makes complete sense? What structural arrangements cause so long a postponing of completion?
3   Point out the parallelism of sentences 5 and 6 in paragraph 4.
4   Both paragraph 6, sentence 4, and paragraph 7, sentence 3, are long sentences with interrupters. Explain how the interrupters are tucked away inside the larger grammatical units.
5   Show how in paragraph 7, sentence 3, Abbey uses parallel items in series.

Diction

1   You may need to check the meanings of *cartel, potentates* (paragraph 1), *exponential, preempted* (2), *attrition* (3), *obtuse* (4), *synthetic* (5), *scenarios* (7)
2   *Nice* is an interesting word which has had several different meanings. Look it up.
3   Is *mania* used in an exact sense in paragraph 1, sentence 8? Is it an effective word in the argument?
4   What is the effect of ending paragraph 2, sentence 2, with ''living space, or even graveyards''?
5   Learn the meanings of the roots of *finite* (paragraph 2) and *technophiles* (6).
6   Why do you think Abbey uses such general terms at the end of paragraph 7?

Assignment

1   Write an argument in favor of the conservation of gasoline or electricity in the United States.
2   Write an argument to persuade a friend to change from one make of automobile to another which you believe to be better, or, similarly, from one type or brand of clothing to another.
    Get in as much specific evidence as you can.

A Rebuttal of Antitechnologists

SAMUEL C. FLORMAN

Another atrocity of which technology is accused is cutting man off from 1
the natural world in which he evolved. "Man was created," says Ellul, "to
have room to move about in, to gaze into far distances, to live in rooms
which, even when they were tiny, opened out on fields. See him now . . . in
a twelve-by-twelve closet opening out on an anonymous world of city
streets." Mumford avers that "a day such as millions spend in factories, in
offices, on the highway, is a day empty of organic contents and human rewards." This could have disastrous results, as he sees it, since the human
species came into being amidst the abundant variety of the natural world,
and if contact with that natural world is not maintained, "then man himself
will become . . . denatured, that is to say, dehumanized."

To Dubos, also, the decrease in contact with nature has been devastating: 2

> Modern man is anxious, even during peace and in the midst of economic
> affluence, because the technological world that constitutes his immediate
> environment, by separating him from the natural world under which he
> evolved, fails to satisfy certain of his unchangeable needs.

Reich mourns the disappearance from our lives of such vital experiences 3
as "living in harmony with nature, on a farm, or by a sea, or near a lake or
meadow, knowing, using, and returning the elements." Roszak is concerned
that "the whole force of urban industrialism upon our tastes is to convince
us that artificiality is not only inevitable, but better—perhaps finally to shut
the real and original out of our awareness entirely."

This subject seems to cause the antitechnologists particular distress. 4
Dubos and Reich compare modern man to a wild animal spending its life in
a city zoo. The architecture of modern cities they find "blankly uniform"
(Mumford), "lifeless and gleamingly sterile" (Roszak). As for the attempts
of city dwellers to make some small contact with nature, Ellul scorns "a
crowd of brainless conformists camping out," while Dubos refers to the
"pathetic weekend in the country."

Not only weekend outings, but all of modern man's leisure activities, are 5
subjected to the most critical scrutiny by the antitechnologists. Predictably,
they view these activities with pity and contempt. Television, according to
Ellul, is enjoyed because man seeks "a total obliviousness of himself and his
problems, and the simultaneous fusion of his consciousness with an omni-

Pp. 52–53, 66–68 from *The Existential Pleasures of Engineering* by Samuel C. Florman,
St. Martin's Press, Inc.

present technical diversion." Are spectator sports popular with the average citizen? Mumford tells us that they are "watched by thousands of overfed and underexercised spectators whose only way of taking active part in the game is to assault the umpire." As for such innocuous amusements as a pinball game and a jukebox, Mumford labels them "disreputable" because they do not "promote human welfare, in the fullest sense." Does the common man enjoy riding in his automobile? Dubos tells us it "represents our flight from the responsibility of developing creative associations with our environment."

6   Reich speaks of the "pathos" of an old-fashioned ice cream parlor where families amuse themselves "amid a sterile model of the past." He tells of a young couple who ski, play tennis, and sail, but only "think" they enjoy these pastimes, when they are really playing out roles copied from the mass media. Roszak is irritated by people "devouring hot dogs and swilling soft drinks" while waiting to see Old Faithful erupt. He observes with disgust that "their eyes vanished behind their cameras" and that one young boy said, "Disneyland is better."

7   Next we must confront the charge that technology is cutting man off from his natural habitat, with catastrophic consequences. It is important to point out that if we are less in touch with nature than we were—and this can hardly be disputed—then the reason does not lie exclusively with technology. Technology could be used to put people in very close touch with nature, if that is what they want. Wealthy people could have comfortable abodes in the wilderness, could live among birds in the highest jungle treetops, or even commune with fish in the ocean depths. But they seem to prefer penthouse apartments in New York and villas on the crowded hills above Cannes. Poorer people could stay on their farms on the plains of Iowa, or in their small towns in the hills of New Hampshire, if they were willing to live the spare and simple life. But many of them seem to tire of the loneliness and the hard physical labor that goes with rusticity, and succumb to the allure of the cities.

8   It is Roszak's lament that "the malaise of a Chekhov play" has settled upon daily life. He ignores the fact that the famous Chekhov malaise stems in no small measure from living in the country. "Yes, old man," shouts Dr. Astrov at Uncle Vanya, "in the whole district there were only two decent, well-educated men: you and I. And in some ten years the common round of the trivial life here has swamped us, and has poisoned our life with its putrid vapours, and made us just as despicable as all the rest." There is tedium in the countryside, and sometimes squalor. No poet has sung the praises of Tobacco Road.

9   Nevertheless, I personally enjoy being in the countryside or in the woods, and so feel a certain sympathy for the antitechnologists' views on this subject. But I can see no evidence that frequent contact with nature is *essential* to human well-being, as the antitechnologists assert. Even if the human

species owes much of its complexity to the diversity of the natural environment, why must man continue to commune with the landscapes in which he evolved? Millions of people, in ages past as well as present, have lived out their lives in city environs, with very little if any contact with "nature." Have they lived lives inherently inferior because of this? Who would be presumptuous enough to make such a statement?

The common domestic cat evolved in the wild, but a thousand genera- **10** tions of domesticity do not seem to have "denatured" it in the least. This is not the place to write the ode to my cat that should someday be written. Suffice it to say that although she never goes out of doors, she plays, hunts, loves, and eats with gusto, and relaxes with that sensuous peace that is uniquely feline. I submit that she is not more "alienated" than her wild sister who fights for survival in some distant wood.

The antitechnologists talk a lot about nature without clearly defining **11** what they mean by the word. Does nature consist of farms, seashores, lakes, and meadows, to use Reich's list? Does not nature consist also of scorched deserts, fetid tropical forests, barren ice fields, ocean depths, and outer space—environments relentlessly hostile to human life? If farms and meadows are considered "natural" even though they have been made by men out of the stuff of the universe, what is "unnatural"? A stone wall and a farm cottage are still "good," I suppose, but a bridge and a dam become "bad," and a glass building façade becomes unnatural and dehumanizing, even though the glass has been made by man out of the sands of the earth.

Must one be in the wilds to be in touch with nature? Will not a garden **12** in the back yard suffice? How about a collection of plants in the living room? Oriental artists have shown us how the beauty of all creation is implicit in a single blossom, or in the arrangement of a few stones. The assertion that men are emotionally crippled by being isolated from the wilds is, as I have said, unwarranted because of lack of evidence. But more than that, it does not take into account the multitude of ways in which "nature" can be experienced.

If pressed, the antitechnologists might grudgingly admit that the harm of **13** being separated from nature can be mitigated if the separating medium is graceful and in harmony with natural principles, say like the Left Bank in Paris, or the Piazza Navone in Rome. But they point to the modern city as the epitome of everything that is mechanical and antihuman

I will not here embark on a discussion of functionalism and modern ar- **14** chitecture. But I will note in passing that there are millions of families who have lived happy years in nondescript high-rise apartments, and millions of people who have spent pleasant working lifetimes in the most modern office buildings. To claim that such passive environments are emotionally crippling is not to state a general truth, but rather to exhibit a personal phobia.

I have seen early-morning crowds pouring into a Park Avenue office **15** building, into a spacious lobby, via a smooth-riding elevator to comfortable offices with thick carpets and dazzling window views. I have heard them chattering of personal concerns, a boyfriend who called, a child who scratched his knee, a movie seen, an aunt visiting from out of town. These people are no more dehumanized by their environment than are a group of native women doing their laundry on the bank of a river. I have seen them at their work, remarkably free to move about, exchange gossip, and gather at the water cooler. I have seen them promenading at lunch hour, looking into gaily decorated store windows, boys and girls eyeing each other, in time-honored fashion. I have shared in coffee breaks, drinking lukewarm coffee out of traditional cardboard and plastic cups with as much gusto as a peasant drinking his *vin ordinaire*.

16   · I have also seen these office workers on a Monday morning comparing sunburns and trading tales about picnics, hikes, fishing trips, and various other sorties into the out-of-doors. The average person is not as isolated from nature as the antitechnologists would have us suppose.

STUDY QUESTIONS

Organization and Content

1   In the early part of his argument Florman uses a technique rather similar to Abbey's. Point out the similarity.

2   Why does Florman quote so much in paragraphs 1–6? What do the writers from whom he quotes have in common?

3   In terms of content, how do paragraphs 5–6 differ from 1–4?

4   What issue does Florman begin to deal with in paragraph 7?

5   What is his first answer to antitechnologists in paragraph 7? What rebuttal does he use in reply to Roszak?

6   What different approach does Florman take in paragraph 9? Is sentence 4 real evidence or merely a personal opinion? How do the three questions asked in paragraph 9 function in the argument?

7   What does Florman's cat (paragraph 10) have to do with the issue being argued? Whose statements is Florman rebutting in paragraphs 9 and 10?

8   In paragraphs 11–12 what shortcomings of the opposing arguments does he attack? What is the tone of paragraph 11?

9   What further aspect of the argument does Florman introduce in paragraph 13?

10   What is the value for refutation of paragraph 14?

11   How does paragraph 15 differ as evidence from paragraph 14? How are the two paragraphs related? Which sentence of paragraph 15 is most effective in the rebuttal?

12   What general conclusion does Florman come round to in paragraph 16?

13   If you care to speculate, what opinion do you think Florman would

have of strip mining in the West to increase supplies of energy for Denver, Salt Lake City, and Las Vegas?

Sentence Structure

1   Note the variety of ways in paragraphs 1–6 by which Florman introduces quotations into his writing. How many are there? What different verbs are used in introducing the quotations?
2   In paragraph 7 how has Florman handled sentences 4–7 for cumulative effect by similarity of structure?
3   On what words does the emphasis fall in paragraph 8, sentences 5 and 6?
4   Why does Florman begin paragraph 9, sentence 1, with *nevertheless* and sentence 2 with *but?*
5   Why is the word order in paragraph 9, sentence 3, a good one? Where does emphasis fall in sentence 4?
6   Why is the sentence pattern in paragraph 11, sentences 2 and 3, effective in Florman's rebuttal?
7   In paragraph 14, sentence 2, parallel elements are linked to show similarity, but in sentence 3 they are contrasted. Show how both patterns are suitable for Florman's purpose.
8   Is the repetition in several sentences of paragraph 15 effective or not? What purpose is it intended to fulfill?

Diction

1   If you need to, look up *atrocity* (paragraph 1), *obliviousness, innocuous* (5), *malaise* (8), *presumptuous* (9), *fetid* (11), *implicit* (12), *mitigated, epitome* (13), *functionalism, nondescript, phobia* (14), *vin ordinaire* (15), *sorties* (16).
2   Why should a day filled with *organic contents* (paragraph 1) appear favorable? Does *organic* have the same meaning here as in the selection by Powys?
3   Is there a connection between *allure* (7) and *lure?*
4   When and where did Chekhov (8) write plays? Why is Tobacco Road (8) a suitable allusion at the end of paragraph 8?
5   Are the connotations of *sensuous* (10) favorable or unfavorable? Compare *sensual.*
6   Why should the Left Bank of the Seine in Paris be favored over the Right Bank?

Assignment

1   Write an argument as a rebuttal of beliefs held by environmentalists or by anti-environmentalists.
2   Similarly write a rebuttal of one of the following beliefs: all children should have free public education; democracy is the best form of government; everyone should run five miles a day; everyone needs a college education; being reared in a small community is

wholesome and beneficial; being reared in a small community is stultifying and harmful; the "hippies" of the 1960s were all bad.

3   Similarly write a rebuttal of some belief uncritically held by many people. Some suggestions: women are generally less capable than men; young people today are generally wicked and destructive; human beings live happier lives than other animals; fraternity or sorority membership is a criterion of excellence; a strong athletic program indicates that a university is excellent; young people have a dangerous amount of influence and power in the modern world.

We Have a Responsibility to Take Care of Ourselves, Not Others

GARRETT HARDIN

1   [Rejecting the metaphor of Spaceship Earth], let us look at an alternative metaphor, that of a lifeboat. In developing some relevant examples the following numerical values are assumed. Approximately two-thirds of the world is desperately poor, and only one-third is comparatively rich. The people in poor countries have an average per capita GNP (Gross National Product) of about $200 per year; the rich, of about $3,000. (For the United States it is nearly $5,000 per year.) Metaphorically, each rich nation amounts to a lifeboat full of comparatively rich people. The poor of the world are in other, much more crowded lifeboats. Continuously, so to speak, the poor fall out of their lifeboats and swim for a while in the water outside, hoping to be admitted to a rich lifeboat, or in some other way to benefit from the "goodies" on board. What should the passengers on a rich lifeboat do? This is the central problem of "the ethics of a lifeboat."

2   First we must acknowledge that each lifeboat is effectively limited in capacity. The land of every nation has a limited carrying capacity. The exact limit is a matter for argument, but the energy crunch is convincing more people every day that we have already exceeded the carrying capacity of the land. We have been living on "capital"—stored petroleum and coal—and soon we must live on income alone.

3   Let us look at only one lifeboat—ours. The ethical problem is the same

Reprinted, with permission, from *Bioscience,* 24 (1974), 561–568, published by the American Institute of Biological Sciences. Reprinted, also, with permission of the author.

for all, and is as follows. Here we sit, say 50 people in a lifeboat. To be generous, let us assume our boat has a capacity of 10 more, making 60. (This, however, is to violate the engineering principle of the "safety factor." A new plant disease or a bad change in the weather may decimate our population if we don't preserve some excess capacity as a safety factor.)

The 50 of us in the lifeboat see 100 others swimming in the water outside, asking for admission to the boat, or for handouts. How shall we respond to their calls? There are several possibilities. 4

One. We may be tempted to try to live by the Christian ideal of being 5
"our brother's keeper," or by the Marxian ideal (Marx 1875) of "from each according to his abilities, to each according to his needs." Since the needs of all are the same, we take all the needy into our boat, making a total of 150 in a boat with a capacity of 60. The boat is swamped, and everyone drowns. Complete justice, complete catastrophe.

Two. Since the boat has an unused excess capacity of 10, we admit just 10 6
more to it. This has the disadvantage of getting rid of the safety factor, for which action we will sooner or later pay dearly. Moreover, *which* 10 do we let in? "First come, first served?" The best 10? The neediest 10? How do we *discriminate?* And what do we say to the 90 who are excluded?

Three. Admit no more to the boat and preserve the small safety factor. 7
Survival of the people in the lifeboat is then possible (though we shall have to be on our guard against boarding parties).

The last solution is abhorrent to many people. It is unjust, they say. Let 8
us grant that it is:

"I feel guilty about my good luck," say some. The reply to this is simple: 9
Get out and yield your place to others. Such a selfless action might satisfy the conscience of those who are addicted to guilt but it would not change the ethics of the lifeboat. The needy person to whom a guilt-addict yields his place will not himself feel guilty about his sudden good luck. (If he did he would not climb aboard.) The net result of conscience-stricken people relinquishing their unjustly held positions is the elimination of their kind of conscience from the lifeboat. The lifeboat, as it were, purifies itself of guilt. The ethics of the lifeboat persist, unchanged by such momentary aberrations.

STUDY QUESTIONS
Organization and Content

1. In his argument based on a metaphor, Hardin is using a term (lifeboat) that denotes one thing in place of another and quite different thing, in order to show a limited likeness, or analogy, between them. What is he thus comparing to a lifeboat? (Hardin rejects the widely used metaphor of Spaceship Earth.)

2   In what limited respects can the two things be said to resemble each other?

3   What are the topic sentences of paragraphs 1 and 2?

4   What basic assumptions does Hardin state in paragraphs 2 and 3?

5   What problem is stated in paragraph 4? What is the function of sentence 3, paragraph 4?

6   In which paragraphs does Hardin make use of enumeration? What is he enumerating?

7   Why does the solution proposed in paragraph 5 seem unsatisfactory?

8   In paragraph 6 Hardin raises three objections. What are they? Translate the third one from a question to a statement. What is the key word in your statement?

9   What choice among ways of "lifeboat operation" does Hardin favor?

10   In paragraph 8 what does he concede to opponents?

11   What is Hardin's advice to those who are not willing to act unjustly? How does this advice work to uphold his argument in spite of his concession in paragraph 8?

12   What does Hardin mean by "ethics of the lifeboat"? How is it that, according to paragraph 9, the "ethics" remain unchanged?

13   Hardin uses rhetorical questions in paragraphs 1, 4, and 6. Explain how they function in the discussion.

14   State the proposition that Hardin is arguing for.

15   State the issues that support his argument.

16   Is the use of metaphor an efficient, time-saving way to bring out the main point? to bring the discussion into focus?

17   Are there any significant differences between the metaphorical situation and the real situation? If there should be, would they seriously weaken Hardin's argument?

18   Hardin says that those "in the lifeboat see 100 others swimming in the water outside." To what actual people do these metaphorical swimmers correspond? Would real people be willing to die of starvation just as Hardin's metaphorical people drown? If we follow Hardin's analogy, is there any reason why we should not let poor people who cannot support their large families, say in New York City, starve to death?

Sentence Structure

1   Are most of Hardin's sentences short or long?

2   How many of them are compound, with clauses connected by *and* or *but*? How do such sentences function in the discussion?

3   When Hardin uses short simple sentences, what is their effect? Do you feel that they are unpleasantly abrupt? that they suggest a cocksure, know-it-all attitude in the author? that he is bossy, authoritarian, or even brutal? that they are factual and businesslike? that they represent a detached, scientific approach to problems?

4   The last sentence of paragraph 5 is very short and succinct, and it has fine parallelism. But it has no verb. How would it read if you expanded it into a complete statement?

5 Sentences 4, 5, and 6 of paragraph 6 are also grammatically incomplete. Why?

Diction

1 Look up the roots of *decimate* (paragraph 3), *abhorrent* (8), and *aberrations* (9).
2 Look up *relevant, ethics* (paragraph 1), *catastrophe* (5), *discriminate* (6).
3 What is the meaning of *crunch* as used in paragraph 2?
4 Judged by the diction, does this selection seem formal in tone, or colloquial?

Assignment

Develop an argument by analogy. If no analogical argument comes to your mind, here are some possible topics:

1 It was proper for the federal government to give financial help to New York City just as anyone would help a neighbor save his or her burning house, to prevent the fire from doing damage to one's own house.
2 People are the only animals that have developed a custom of watching other people play. Other animals, though many of them play themselves, are never simply spectators of the play of animals. Spectator sports therefore represent an unnatural, unhealthful departure from the sound ways of nature.
3 Informal education is more natural and effective than formal education. Children need only to be trained by their parents just as the young of cats, tigers, and wolves are.
4 Education should be carefully controlled; teachers should know exactly what operations to perform day by day and hour by hour, for educating a person is like turning out a product in a factory.

Law as the Means to Freedom

A. DELAFIELD SMITH

1   We need to see what the true meaning and function of law is, not in terms of authority, which is so commonly mistaken for law, but in terms of the rule of law in the ideal sense as a guide and challenge to the human will.

2   The best example of how law, in the ideal sense, works, how it evokes the sense of freedom and stimulates the individual is the survey of a game. Have you ever asked yourself why the participation in a game is so excellent a medium for self-expression and character development? This question is often superficially answered in terms of the rein given to the competitive instincts of the individual and his "zest" for conquest. But have you ever considered that here, in a game, and perhaps here alone, we human beings really do act almost completely under the aegis of law? That, rather than competition, is the real source of the game's restorative value for the human spirit. Analyze the process step by step and you must be convinced that this is the truth.

3   Your first step upon entering a game is the assumption of a distinct personality. You become clothed in a personality defined by the rules of the game. You assume a legal or game personality. You may describe yourself as a first baseman, as a right guard, or as a dealer. But however you describe yourself you will see that what you have described is a legal status—one of the focal points in a legal pattern with rights and obligations suitable to the position. These rights and duties are defined by the rules under whose empery you have thus put both yourself and all others with whom you have dealings. Your status, your rights, your obligations, all are secure, for the rules of the game are almost sure to be followed. The game indeed is defined by its rules. These are purely abstract. They are wholly free of will and dictation. They are pure rules of action composed usually in some physical setting which they serve to interpret and fashion till it becomes an arena of human action, just as, for example, the rules of the highway, in relation to the highway pattern itself, provide individuals with an arena on which they can operate successfully. Now the rules of the game have many functions. They, in fact, define the very goals that the players seek. One wins only in the context of the rules of the game. They determine inexorably the consequences of the player's action, every play that he makes. He acts solely in relation to the rules. Their empery is accepted like a fact or a circumstance.

From *The Right of Life: A Legal Approach to Society's Responsibility to the Individual* by A. Delafield Smith. © 1955 The University of North Carolina Press. Reprinted by permission of the publisher.

Finally, they challenge and stimulate him for he uses the rules to win. The game is otherwise unmanaged. An umpire or a referee is but an interpreter of the rules. He *can* be wrong. Such is the conception. This, then, may furnish an introduction to the real function of law in society.

Law gave birth to the concept of freedom. True it is that you can have no **4** security in a situation in which every person and everything around you acts capriciously, unpredictably, or, in other words, lawlessly; but the point I wish to make is that while you would have no security in such an environment, it is more significant that you would have no freedom in such an environment. The reason you could not be free in such a situation is that you could not get anywhere you wanted to go or successfully do anything you wanted to do. You could make no plan in the expectation of carrying it out. You cannot possibly carry out any aim or goal of your own unless you have some basis for calculating what results may follow from any given act or activity of your own. Unless you can determine in advance what are the prospects and limitations of a given course of behavior, you cannot act intelligently. Whatever intelligence you may have will do you no good. You cannot adjust your own step to anyone else's step nor can you relate your conduct to any series of events or occurrences outside yourself except to the extent that they follow a pattern that you can learn about in advance of your action.

The only way to promote freedom is to devise a set of rules and thus construct **5** a pattern which the various members of that society can follow. Each can then determine his own acts in the light of his knowledge of the rules. On this basis each can predict his field of action in advance and what results are likely to ensue from his acts; and so he gains freedom to plan and to carry out his plans. The more you attempt to administer society, however, the less free it becomes. There is opportunity for freedom of choice only in acting subject to the rules, and then only if the rules are freed of any element of will or dictation. If these rules are just rules that tell you what method or act will yield what results, like the rules of a game, you can then freely determine your own play. You can use the rules to win the game. The more abstract and objective the rule, the freer is the individual in the choice of his alternatives. The rules must be so written as to cover every possible eventuality of choice and action.

STUDY QUESTIONS
Organization and Content

1 The assignment that Smith gave himself may look quite difficult: to convince people, most of whom have probably thought of law in terms of restriction, that law is the means to freedom; many people would think this a paradoxical idea. Smith approaches this

challenging assignment by means of an analogy. In which sentence does he announce that he is going to make use of the analogy?

2   Paragraph 1 has what function?
3   In order to ''clear the ground,'' what false idea does the author try to eliminate in paragraph 2?
4   What is he ready to do in paragraph 3?
5   Paragraph 3 has more than twenty sentences. To what are they devoted?
6   Which sentence is the topic sentence of paragraph 3? Why does the author mention the ''rules of the highway''?
7   Explain the analogy used by Smith. Does his analogy hold? Are there important likenesses between the analogy and the situation he is discussing? Are there any significant differences?
8   How important is this analogy to his argument?
9   What idea essential to the argument is brought out in paragraph 4?
10   Does paragraph 4 have any connection with the analogy?
11   Is the first sentence of paragraph 5 a conclusion drawn from the preceding discussion, or is it simply an assertion of the proposition that the author is trying to prove?
12   On what evidence is he justified in saying, ''The more abstract and objective the rule, the freer is the individual in the choice of his alternatives''?
13   He also says in paragraph 5, ''The more you attempt to administer society, . . . the less free it becomes.'' Is this idea brought out in, or covered by, the analogy?

Sentence Structure

1   Many of the sentences of this selection are addressed to ''you.'' Why? What is the effect of thus addressing the reader? Is there any advantage for the author in doing so?
2   Indicate how repetition of certain terms supplies transition in paragraphs 3 and 4.
3   Compare Smith's sentence style with that of Hardin or of Abbey. Which is the more formal, the more lively, the more dignified, the more concrete, the more emotional, the more complex, the more demanding?

Diction

1   Look up *aegis, assumption, empery, abstract, arena, context, inexorably, administer, objective, eventuality.*
2   Smith was trained as a lawyer. To what extent has his legal training influenced his choice of diction?

Assignment

Write an argument in which you, like Smith, use an analogy. Some suggestions are:

1 Education is best when students have much freedom (for education is like the growth of a tree; all the tree needs is a chance at things that are good for it, without unnecessary obstacles).

2 Students should have (or not have) freedom in choosing courses (for a college is like a great city with a wealth of things and experiences at the disposal of the inhabitants).

3 Students should have freedom in choosing courses (for studying some subject that one dislikes is like climbing a mountain).

4 It is good (or not good) to make oneself into a sophisticated person (for doing so is like baking and decorating a cake, or trimming a Christmas tree).

5 We should encourage more discipline in every phase of our society (for in Japanese flower-arranging, effects of grace and simplicity are obtained by disciplined training; or, as Alexander Pope wrote:

> True ease in writing comes from art, not chance,
> As those move easiest who have learned to dance).

6 No politician can be a completely good man; a politician should be prepared to have to make compromises and even to do some things that he knows are not good, in order to be able to accomplish the good things that he regards as most important (for a basketball player though committing many fouls may make enough goals to ensure that his team will win).

Why All Should Have a Liberal Education

BERTRAND DE JOUVENEL

If one reflects on the career of a hypothetical young man who goes to work at the early age of seventeen, he has a long career of work stretching before him. We may make some revealing calculations. He can look forward to fifty-three years of life, of which he can expect to spend ten after retirement. The very most he can expect to spend at work each year, assuming forty-three years of work, is approximately 1900 hours per year. Taking these figures, which surely do not err on the side of optimism, the most our young man can expect to spend at work is less than 18 percent of the time

From "Toward a Political Theory in Education" by Bertrand de Jouvenel from *Humanistic Education and Western Civilization* edited by Arthur A. Cohen. Copyright © 1964 by Holt, Rinehart and Winston. Reprinted by permission of Holt, Rinehart and Winston.

of life he has before him. If he assumes that during the coming forty-three years, the average time worked will be forty-eight weeks and thirty-five hours per week (1680 hours per year), then the share of the time at work during his lifetime falls to 15.7 percent. I think it is permissible to state that work-time will absorb one-sixth of the time he has before him.

2   Assuming that sleep will absorb one-third of the remaining time, our young man has one-half of his prospective life unconsumed by work or sleep. In more striking terms, a man's waking hours (two-thirds of his whole mature life) will be divided one-quarter for work and three-quarters for free time. I find it surprising that people seldom make such simple arithmetical calculations—calculations, moreover, which are likely to shed light on pressing problems.

3   Let us by all means so educate our young man so that his hours of work will be more productive. Of course, if we delay his entry into work by one year, it will mean so many hours less (possibly as much as 1900 hours) available to him in his lifetime. At the same time it may well be that the loss of one year of work consumed by education might add to his economic capability in such a way that the life-product for the total hours remaining will be increased, not diminished—and, indeed, so increased that the shortening of the normal work year to come may ensue. All this is quite right.

4   But what seems very wrong is to educate our hypothetical young worker for one-quarter of his waking hours to come, and not for the other three-quarters! I am quite willing to recognize that not all of the three-quarters is, in fact, available time: much of it is taken up by travel to and from work—but even during this trip the fruits of education may appear. Using public means of conveyance, one may as well read Pascal as look at comic strips. In short, all the waking hours ahead of us—those hours not consumed by work—depend for their use upon the education we receive.

5   Let me put it another way—and for this purpose I shall provisionally adopt the vocabulary of aristocratic civilizations which contrast the laborer bent upon his task, and the gentleman of leisure who bears his head high, *os sublime.* In our day the man who is all the time a "gentleman of leisure" has utterly disappeared. But the laborer who was nothing but laborer, a mere "hand," has also disappeared. The man of our day is part laborer, part gentleman of leisure. If we want to call work "slavery," then the contemporary is a good deal less than "half-slave" and a good deal more than "half-free": look to the foregoing figures.

6   The case for developing the average man's skill as a laborer is unanswerable, since among the benefits procured, despite the loss of work-time, is the progressive enlargement of that share of time during which he is a freeman, a "gentleman." But the greater the share thus liberated, the more pressing it becomes to educate man for the fruitful use of this free time. Sebastian de Grazia put things very nicely when he used the term "free time" negatively, to signify that part of time which is "saved from the job," while reserving

the term "leisure" to signify something positive, "a state of being in which activity is performed for its own sake or as its own end." And he says: "To save time through machines is not easy. To transform free time into leisure is not to be easy either."

While the contrast here drawn between "free time" and "leisure" may   7 well be deemed excessive, it does point to a major problem of our times which is well expressed in the popular expression: "How shall I spend my time?", or even better the childish question: "What shall I do with myself?" According to the way we spend our time, we improve or harm ourselves— and it is truly a question of *ourselves* and not of such externals as our job or status.

No term is clearer than that of "culture": it means something done to us   8 for our improvement, and something we do to ourselves for improvement. There is a wealth of examples to show that a man who has not been culti- vated can, later in life, cultivate himself. But it would be optimistic to be- lieve that more than a small minority are capable of this—most of us de- pend for our cultivation upon the good start given us by our teachers.

In short, future generations, which can look forward to an increasingly   9 lighter burden of work, and to an increasing share of free time, require a liberal education.

STUDY QUESTIONS

Organization and Content

1   What conclusions about work time and free time does De Jouvenel reach in paragraphs 1 and 2?

2   What effect on free time does he suggest in paragraph 3 will be the result of education for more productive work?

3   What ideas regarding education are put forth in paragraph 4? Why does De Jouvenel criticize a vocation-oriented education?

4   Would De Jouvenel's concept of leisure, as suggested by para- graphs 5 and 6, correspond to that of Adler (see pp. 207–209)? Using De Grazia's distinction, describe the difference between lei- sure and free time.

5   State in your own words the problem of "free time" for great num- bers of people. Can free time actually cause us to "harm our- selves"?

6   Why does De Jouvenel, in paragraph 8, advocate the cultivation of mankind? What is the value of culture? Relate paragraph 8 to sen- tence 4, paragraph 4. Why is sentence 3, paragraph 8, particularly important?

7   What is the proposition, announced in paragraph 9, that De Jou- venel is arguing for—the proposition for which the preceding mate- rial provides support?

8   In what ways does Kemelman's "Education and Training" (pp.

150–151) support De Jouvenel's view on the value of liberal education?

9   State the essence of De Jouvenel's argument in one sentence.

Sentence Structure

1   Paragraph 1 comprises seven sentences. Which ones have introductory subordinate material, which have subordinate material at the end, and which have such material in the middle? Are any of them simple sentences? How much variety of structure and of length do the seven sentences have?

2   Point out how De Jouvenel has secured strong emphasis in sentences 1 and 4 of paragraph 4.

3   What is the function of the colon in sentence 2, paragraph 4? Why did De Jouvenel use a dash instead of a comma after *work* in this sentence?

4   What special function do the dashes have in sentences 2, paragraph 7, and sentence 3, paragraph 8?

5   Comment on the skillful construction of the one sentence in paragraph 9. Why should paragraph 9 consist of only one sentence?

Diction

1   De Jouvenel's vocabulary is easy to understand. In what special sense is he using *pressing* (paragraphs 2, 6), *life-product* (3), *the contemporary* (5), *wealth* (8)?

2   What is the significance of the allusion to Pascal in paragraph 4? As an American, what names would you suggest to perform the same function as Pascal's in the argument?

Assignment

1   Argue that some special type of activity is the best possible thing for which leisure can be used.

2   Argue for or against ''spectator sports'' as a valuable way to use one's free time or one's leisure.

3   Argue for or against watching television as a profitable use of free time or leisure.

4   Argue for or against play, reading, or travel as a sound use of leisure.

Love Declines

STAFFAN BURENSTAM LINDER

Another ancient and well-established pleasure is physical love—if this cir- 1
cumspect, clinical term can be accepted by those who would prefer a lustier
expression. In view of the enormous amount of "sex" that is believed to
characterize our age, it is perhaps somewhat provocative to suggest that we
are devoting less and less time to it. However, there are very good grounds
for such an assertion.

To treat sexual matters in a work on economics is no innovation. Econo- 2
mists have discussed sex as a conceivable obstacle to economic growth,
while I shall be discussing economic growth as a conceivable obstacle to
sex. Even since the time of Malthus, a certain aversion to sex has been noticeable in the economic literature, since it is practices of this kind that give
rise to the enormous problem of overpopulation. The development of con-
traceptive methods, however, has made it possible for economists and others
to worry about population problems without having to accept Malthus'
"positive controls." Economists, if asked, would probably say that economic
growth has had a stimulating effect on sexual activities. High levels of education, a result of economic growth, have eliminated much superstition and
permitted a freer flow of emotions. Also, thanks to economic growth, con-
traceptives have become not only technically but also financially available.

Such arguments are probably correct enough in themselves. Certain 3
forces, however, are acting in the contrary direction. Love takes time. To
court and love someone in a satisfactory manner is a game with many and
time-consuming phases. To illustrate how economic growth affects the allo-
cation of time to love, we can observe that the pleasure achieved by an embrace can hardly be intensified by increasing the number of goods consumed
during the period in question. Goods in fact would only be in the way, beyond the minimum requirement in respect of furniture. In this respect love
differs from most other activities, and it is this that has made its status so
vulnerable. A moralist may be glad to learn that love has a negative income
elasticity. It is an "inferior" activity—although inferior in another sense
than that employed by the moralist.

One can distinguish three different ways in which efforts to save time in 4
our love life manifest themselves. Affairs, which by their very nature occupy
a great deal of time, become less attractive; the time spent on each occasion
of love-making is being reduced; the total number of sexual encounters is
declining.

To keep a mistress is an institution requiring considerable time. Disraeli 5

From S. B. Linder: *The Harried Leisure Class.* New York: Columbia University Press,
1970, pp. 83–89, by permission of the publisher.

devoted much attention—perhaps mainly of a Platonic nature—to Lady Chesterfield, at times when our non-Victorian Prime Ministers and Presidents address themselves energetically to hard work. People in exalted—and even less exalted—offices should now, it is thought, be on the job from morning to night. The mistress, as an institution, is disappearing. Who has time these days for intimate lunches in conversation with an attractive woman? The French institution of the *cinq-à-sept*—two hours for which love-seeking husbands do not always feel bound to account—is reported to be disappearing in the increased hustle of life even in France. On the whole, it is probable that conjugal fidelity is increasing, if not in thought, at least in practice. It takes too much time to establish new contacts, as compared with relaxation in the home. For the same reason, perhaps, young and energetic people tend to marry early and cut down on the time-consuming process of search.

6   Of course, new sexual contacts are still being established, and on a large scale, particularly among the unmarried. The increasing scarcity of time should in this case lead to these contacts being after increasingly brief preliminary approaches. Since there is no time for repeated lunches, during which one reconnoiters the lay of the land, one has to show one's inclinations more directly. Modern love affairs are reminiscent, according to Sebastian de Grazia, of business agreements: "No frills, no flowers, no time wasted in elaborate compliments, verses, and lengthy seductions, no complications, and no scenes, please." Such a system is designed to save time, and it presupposes what we mean by "sexual freedom." Those who complain that girls these days are "easy" fail to understand that in a hectic age girls must accelerate to save time, both for themselves and for their male friends. It would be inconceivable, for reasons of time, that a modern young lady should require her presumptive lover—as she did in a Noh play I once had the pleasure of seeing—to appear for one hundred evenings and wait outside her door, to be admitted on the hundred-and-first. The smooth character parodied in the well-known film *The Knack* is described as requiring only "two minutes from start to finish." This is much more typical behavior in an age with an increasing scarcity of time.

7   Modern people do not only try to save time in the actual establishment of contact. The man in *The Knack* obviously saved time on every lap of the course. It is only to be expected that people who are in a hurry should become the devotees of instant love. The ultimate way of saving time, of course, is to refrain entirely from this pleasure, or at least to such degree as may be possible without disrupting psychological effects. Such a method is obviously not alien to people today. As a by-product of a sociological study of some eighty-three hundred business executives, W. Lloyd Warner and James C. Abegglen were able to make a number of interesting observations on the situation of their wives. We learn, for instance, that the wife of an executive "must not demand too much of her husband's time or interest.

Because of his single-minded concentration on the job, even his sexual activity is relegated to a secondary place."

Even individuals belonging to less harried classes seem to save time in the **8** same way. It may surprise some readers to learn that, according to an article in *Gaudeamus*—the Stockholm University student newspaper—female students are complaining that their male colleagues fail to take time off for love. They are so engrossed in their studies. The female students—and how, by the way, do they come to have more time?—are obliged to turn to foreign students or "ordinary" young men.

When we leave the executive world and student life, we can still find **9** signs that love is suffering from the competition of other activities. It is well known that the big blackout in New York in November 1965 was followed, nine months later, by a spectacular rise in the birth-rate. With nothing else to do, people did what could be done in the dark.... Some may have groped their way from the television set to the bed to seek support in what must have been a moment of fear. A boring lack of alternatives, however, must surely have played its part. This at any rate would seem to explain why the birth rate in Chicago rose by 30 per cent nine months after the worst snowstorm in memory (in January 1967). In underdeveloped countries, the birth rate reportedly falls in villages when electricity is installed. The pleasures of the night suffer competition from the extended day. To add to our list of empirical guesses, we may perhaps suggest that the phenomenon of shipboard romances is due simply to the abnormal amount of time available.

In various ways, the increasing scarcity of time can thus divert time from **10** Venus. Only insofar as our Victorian inhibitions have been dissipated and love is now in favor is there any force to offset the effects of the time scarcity. The counterforce is probably not sufficient to have created any movement in the direction of more love, particularly since there also exist changes in taste which have thinned our desires.

... Anyone who cares to study a sexual manual will find that great em- **11** phasis is placed on the ruinous effects of chronological shortcuts. Yet perhaps the writers of these books, as members of the harried leisure class, have also fallen victim to the cooling effects of the time scarcity on appetite. David Riesman in *The Lonely Crowd* makes the following observation: "The older marriage manuals, such as that of Van der Velde (still popular, however), breathe an ecstatic tone, they are travelogues of the joy of love. The newer ones, including some high school sex manuals, are matter of fact, toneless, and hygienic—Boston Cooking School style."

"Sex is Dead" proclaimed a well-written and amusing article in the *Chris-* **12** *tian Century* in 1966, presenting a variety of evidence that the taste for love has declined. Obviously, this obituary does not mean, any more than does our argument of the increasing scarcity of time, that physical love has been entirely eliminated. People have not stopped making love, any more than they have stopped eating. But—to extend the surprisingly adequate parallel with the joys of gastronomy—less time is devoted to both preparation and savoring. As a result, we get an increasing amount of frozen nutrition at rapid sittings—the time, on occasion, being too short for any effort to be made at all at stilling the hunger. A pleasure has been turned into the satisfaction of a basic need—"a grocer's orgy"—a maintenance function—a conjugal duty.

13   Interestingly enough, such a status of love is in itself compatible with the doctrines voiced by certain schools of thought within the Christian Church: physical love is required for the multiplication of souls, and as such it is therefore acceptable as long as it is quick, not particularly frequent, and always within the family. In this lies a perfect irony. Just as medieval regulations in the economic sector were abolished to permit the Industrial Revolution, so have various inhibiting rules in the social and ethical sector been crushed by an age inspired by the philosophy of pleasure. Yet the supposedly amoral members of this irreligious age have found no cause to avail themselves of their erotic freedom, and they behave in practice more in conformity with the previous moral laws than those who originally formulated them.

14   Even if all this is worth saying and may seem plausible enough, are there not clear signs to the contrary? Has not our age actually been called oversexed? The phenomena, however, that have led to this epithet do not conflict with the idea that economic growth has led to certain efforts to save time in the erotic sector. Let us consider in more detail three phenomena which are customarily taken as a sure sign that modern people are a lusty lot. The first is that sexual contacts are being made at an increasingly early age. What this implies is simply that young people, who have not yet achieved the income level of the harried leisure class, have exploited the freedoms originally created with a view to adult welfare. Another sign often quoted is that sexual unions are becoming casual, i.e., the result of increasingly short acquaintanceship. The fact, however, that people take less time is rather an indication that they spend less time on loving. They are in a hurry, and so each contact must proceed faster. Thirdly, all pornography is taken as evidence of great sexual activity. This, however, may be a case of smoke without fire. Pinups and other manifestations of quasi sex serve to give satisfaction from looking, rather than from doing. A love life consisting of a series of extremely quick encounters tends to be frustrating. In this situation, a few lively films can function as a rapid and convenient manner of experiencing certain sensations. The change in female ideals is probably indicative of modern ways of life. The mystique of a Marlene Dietrich has little to give a generation that is not interested in doing it and doing it well. Contemporary sex queens are more conducive to satisfaction from just looking, or possibly hoping for a quick "touch-and-go."

STUDY QUESTIONS

Organization and Content

1 What important function does paragraph 1 have in Linder's argument? What specific proposition is he maintaining?

2 Linder is an economist. What idea, held by other economists, does he feel that he has to oppose?

3 What concession to other economists does he make in paragraph 3?

4 What issue, however, does he insist is far more important for the proposition he is arguing for?

5 How does paragraph 4 function in Linder's argument?

6 How are paragraphs 5, 6, and 7 related to paragraph 4?

7 What specific examples in paragraphs 7–9 illustrate the idea announced in paragraphs 4 and 7?

8 Paragraph 10 serves as a transitional paragraph. Explain the connections of each of its three sentences with the development of the argument.

9 What amusing analogy does Linder use in paragraph 11 to show that love is not so engaging a pleasure as it formerly was?

10 What ironic development does he point to for his argument in paragraph 12?

11 In paragraph 14 Linder deals with the possibility that he is wrong and that our age is oversexed. What rebuttal does he make to each of the pieces of evidence supposed to give support to his opponents?

Sentence Structure

1 Notice that, although he writes smoothly, Linder includes numerous interrupters in his sentences. What interrupters do you find in sentences 4–6, paragraph 2? What different grammatical construction does each one represent?

2 Similarly identify and explain the interrupters in paragraph 5.

3 Explain the functions, organization, and punctuation of the two sentences in paragraph 4.

4 Explain how the first element in the first sentence of paragraphs 8, 9, and 10 ensures smooth transition by relating to the preceding paragraph.

Diction

1 Identify *Malthus* (paragraph 2), *Disraeli* (5), *Venus* and *Victorian* (10).

2 Look up the meanings and learn the roots of *innovation, aversion* (paragraph 2), *fidelity* (5), *disrupting* (7), *dissipated* (10).

3 Look up any of these words that are unfamiliar to you: *circumspect* (paragraph 1), *obstacle* (2), *vulnerable* (3), *Platonic, ex-*

alted, conjugal (5), reconnoiters, presumptive (6), relegated (7), harried (8), empirical (9), inhibitions (10), obituary, gastronomy (11), compatible, amoral, erotic, conformity (12), plausible, epithet, quasi, mystique (13).

Assignment

1   Argue that the increased leisure which many people have constitutes a serious problem.
2   Argue that because of the women's liberation movement lasting and successful marriages are now on the decline.
3   Argue that "male chauvinism" is a serious obstacle to lasting and successful marriage.
4   Argue that love has more important requirements than ample time.

Order in The Classroom!

NEIL POSTMAN

1   William O'Connor, who is unknown to me in a personal way, was once a member of the Boston School Committee, in which capacity he made the following remark: "We have no inferior education in our schools. What we have been getting is an inferior type of student."

2   The remark is easy to ridicule, and I have had some fun with it in the past. But there are a couple of senses in which it is perfectly sound.

3   In the first place, a classroom is a technique for the achievement of certain kinds of learning. It is a workable technique provided that both the teacher and the student have the skills and, particularly, the attitudes that are fundamental to it. Among these, from the student's point of view, are tolerance for delayed gratification, a certain measure of respect for and fear of authority, and a willingness to accommodate one's individual desires to the interests of group cohesion and purpose. These attitudes cannot be taught easily in school because they are a necessary component of the teaching situation itself. The problem is not unlike trying to find out how to spell a word by looking it up in the dictionary. If you do not know how a word is spelled, it is hard to look it up. In the same way, little can be taught in school unless these attitudes are present. And if they are not, to teach them is difficult.

Obviously, such attitudes must be learned during the years before a child **4** starts school; that is, in the home. This is the real meaning of the phrase "pre-school education." If a child is not made ready at home for the classroom experience, he or she usually cannot benefit from any normal school program. Just as important, the school is defenseless against such a child, who, typically, is a source of disorder in a situation that requires order. I raise this issue because education reform is impossible without order in the classroom. Without the attitudes that lead to order, the classroom is an entirely impotent technique. Therefore, one possible translation of Mr. O'Connor's remark is, "We have a useful technique for educating youth but too many of them have not been provided at home with the attitudes necessary for the technique to work." There is nothing nonsensical about such an observation. In fact, it calls to mind several historical instances when some magnificent technology was conceived, only to remain undeveloped because the conditions for its creative use did not exist. The Aztecs, for example, invented the wheel, but applied it only to children's toys because the terrain on which they lived made it useless. In other words, the classroom—even the traditional classroom—is not to be abandoned because some children have not learned to use it.

In still another way Mr. O'Connor's remark makes plain sense. The elec- **5** tronic media, with their emphasis on visual imagery, immediacy, non-linearity, and fragmentation, do not give support to the attitudes that are fundamental to the classroom; that is, Mr. O'Connor's remark can be translated as, "We would not have an inferior education if it were the nineteenth century. Our problem is that we have been getting students who are products of the twentieth century." But there is nothing nonsensical about this, either. The nineteenth century had much to recommend it, and we certainly may be permitted to allow it to exert an influence on the twentieth. The classroom is a nineteenth-century invention, and we ought to prize what it has to offer. It is one of the few social organizations left to us in which sequence, social order, hierarchy, continuity, and deferred pleasure are important.

The problem of disorder in the classroom is created largely by two factors: **6** a dissolving family structure, out of which come youngsters who are "unfit" for the presuppositions of a classroom; and a radically altered information environment, which undermines the foundations of school. The question, then, is, What should be done about the increasing tendency toward disorder in the classroom? . . .

The school ought not to accommodate itself to disorder, to the biases of **7** other communication systems. . . . The school is not an extension of the street, the movie theater, a rock concert, or a playground. And it is certainly not an extension of the psychiatric clinic. It is a special environment that requires the enforcement of certain traditional rules of controlled group interaction. The school may be the only remaining public situation in which requires the enforcement of certain traditional rules of controlled group interaction. The school may be the only remaining public situation in which such rules have any meaning, and it would be a grave mistake to change those rules because some children find them hard or cannot function within them. Children who cannot ought to be removed from the environment in the interests of those who can. . . .

8   At this point I should like to . . . indicate some particulars of my own.

9   Let us start, for instance, with the idea of a dress code. A dress code signifies that school is a special place in which special kinds of behavior are required. The way one dresses is an indication of an attitude toward a situation. And the way one is *expected* to dress indicates what that attitude ought to be. You would not wear dungarees and a T-shirt that says "Feel Me" when attending a church wedding. That would be considered an outrage against the tone and meaning of the situation. The school has every right and reason, I believe, to expect the same sort of consideration.

10   Those who are inclined to think this is a superficial point are probably forgetting that symbols not only reflect our feelings but to some extent create them. One's kneeling in church, for example, reflects a sense of reverence but also engenders reverence. If we want school to *feel* like a special place, we can find no better way to begin than by requiring students to dress in a manner befitting the seriousness of the enterprise and the institution. I should include teachers in this requirement. I know of one high school in which the principal has put forward a dress code of sorts for teachers. (He has not, apparently, had the courage to propose one for the students.) For males the requirement is merely a jacket and tie. One of his teachers bitterly complained to me that such a regulation infringed upon his civil rights. And yet, this teacher will accept without complaint the same regulation when it is enforced by an elegant restaurant. His complaint and his acquiescence tell a great deal about how he values schools and how he values restaurants.

11   I do not have in mind, for students, uniforms of the type sometimes worn in parochial schools. I am referring here to some reasonable standard of dress which would mark school as a place of dignity and seriousness. And I might add that I do not believe for one moment the argument that poor people would be unable to clothe their children properly if such a code were in force. Furthermore, I do not believe that poor people have advanced that argument. It is an argument that middle-class education critics have made on behalf of the poor.

12   Another argument advanced in behalf of the poor and oppressed is the students' right to their own language. I have never heard this argument come from parents whose children are not competent to use Standard English. It is an argument, once again, put forward by "liberal" education critics whose children *are* competent in Standard English but who in some curious way wish to express their solidarity with and charity for those who are

less capable. It is a case of pure condescension, and I do not think teachers should be taken in by it. Like the mode of dress, the mode of language in school ought to be relatively formal and exemplary, and therefore markedly different from the custom in less rigorous places. It is particularly important that teachers should avoid trying to win their students' affection by adopting the language of youth. Such teachers frequently win only the contempt of their students, who sense that the language of teachers and the language of students ought to be different; that is to say, the world of adults is different from the world of children. . . .

I raise this point because the school is one of our few remaining institu- 13 tions based on firm distinctions between childhood and adulthood, and on the assumption that adults have something of value to teach the young. That is why teachers must avoid emulating in dress and speech the style of the young. It is also why the school ought to be a place for what we might call "manners education": the adults in school ought to be concerned with teaching youth a standard of civilized interaction. . . .

School . . . is a social situation requiring the subordination of one's own 14 impulses and interests to those of the group. In a word, manners. As a rule, elementary school teachers will exert considerable effort in teaching manners. I believe they refer to this effort as "socializing the child." But it is astonishing how precipitously this effort is diminished at higher levels. It is certainly neglected in the high schools, and where it is not, there is usually an excessive concern for "bad habits," such as smoking, drinking, and, in some nineteenth-century schools, swearing. But, as William James noted, our virtues are as habitual as our vices. Where is the attention given to the "Good morning" habit, to the "I beg your pardon" habit, to the "Please forgive the interruption" habit?

The most civilized high school class I have ever seen was one in which 15 students and teacher said "Good morning" to each other and in which the students stood up when they had something to say. The teacher, moreover, thanked each student for any contribution made to the class, did not sit with his feet on the desk and did not interrupt a student unless he had asked permission to do so. The students, in turn, did not interrupt each other, or chew gum, or read comic books when they were bored. To avoid being a burden to others when one is bored is the essence of civilized behavior. . . .

I trust that the reader is not misled by what I have been saying. As I 16 see it, nothing in any of the above leads to the conclusion that I favor a classroom that is authoritarian or coldhearted, or dominated by a teacher insensitive to students and how they learn. I merely want to affirm the importance of the classroom as a special place, aloof from the biases of the media; a place in which the uses of the intellect are given prominence in a setting of elevated language, civilized manners, and respect for social symbols.

STUDY QUESTIONS

Organization and Content

1   Is there any advantage in Postman's beginning his discussion with a quotation from William O'Connor?

2   What are the two senses in which Postman thinks that O'Connor's remark is "perfectly sound"?

3   Is it reasonable to call a classroom a "technique"?

4   What are some specific things that would make this technique unworkable? What twentieth-century situations or developments have increased classroom disorder?

5   How do the references to looking up words in a dictionary and to the Aztec invention of the wheel contribute to Postman's argument?

6   Explain why Postman thinks that the twentieth-century electronic media "do not give support to the attitudes that are fundamental to the classroom," as he says in paragraph 5. Even if Postman is right, do you agree that the electronic media have enough influence on children to create a classroom problem?

7   Why are the items mentioned at the end of paragraph 5 significant for classroom teaching?

8   What is the function of paragraph 6?

9   Point out the contrast of the negative and the positive in paragraph 7. If we regard Postman's statement about the school in paragraph 7 as a definition, what terms in it are especially significant? On the basis of this statement, what conclusion does Postman draw?

10   What evidence or reasoning does Postman use to convince us that he is right on the issue of a dress code?

11   What analogies does Postman employ in paragraphs 9 and 10 of his argument?

12   How does Postmen support his belief (paragraph 12) that the language of both students and teachers should be "relatively formal and exemplary"?

13   Even if "the world of adults is different from the world of children," should the language of teachers differ from that of students? If so, in what ways?

14   In paragraph 13 how does Postman justify his advocacy of "manners education" in schools?

15   What educational advantages might come, in terms of "group interaction," in classrooms where traditions of "civilized behavior" were upheld?

16   What negative and positive aspects of the classroom situation does Postman bring out in his final paragraph? What does he finally stress the most?

17   What assumptions has he made that are basic to his argument?

Sentence Structure

1   Postman's first sentence is gracefully written. Explain how the author has arranged his two relative clauses and the quotation to make it so.

2   Point out how in paragraph 3, sentences 2–4, and paragraph 4, sentences 4–6, Postman has made good, clear transitions.

3   What special transitional devices has he used in paragraph 4, sentences 9–11?

4   Give reasons for the punctuation of sentence 1, paragraph 6.

5   Show the importance of parallelism and repetition for the structure of sentences 1–3, paragraph 7.

6   All the sentences of paragraph 9 are relatively short. What is their effect in the paragraph? How do Postman's last two sentences (paragraph 16) differ in length, structure, and effect from those of paragraph 9?

Diction

1   You may need to look up *gratification* (paragraph 3), *terrain* (4), *hierarchy* (5), *radically* (6), *biases, psychiatric* (7), *engenders, acquiescence* (10), *condescension* (12), *emulating* (13), *precipitously* (14), *essence* (15), *aloof* (16).

2   What are ''electronic media'' (paragraph 5)? In what sense does Postman use *immediacy, non-linearity,* and *fragmentation*?

3   To what other words is *exemplary* related (paragraph 12)? What is their root?

4   Should a school be a *rigorous* place?

Assignment

1   Write an argument opposing Postman's and trying to refute him on one or more of the same issues.

2   Argue that order (or discipline) is needed in American life today, or in some phase of it.

3   Argue that because the United States has become monotonously standardized, American life needs the spice of variety.

4   Argue that people in many towns live lives that are far too highly organized.

5   Write an argument opposing the lecture system as a means of instruction.

Check Point

5

At the end of this course you should be able to produce a full-length theme with paragraphs that are properly linked and substantial. Your study of argument should enable you to identify issues and in your own writing to create cogent examples of argument supported by evidence and convincing through their logic. You should be able to use analogies, aware of both their value and their limitations. In your arguments you should have made appropriate use of the other types of writing you have studied: comparison, definition, analysis, enumeration, and description. The cumulative effects of this whole apprenticeship should now become apparent. We may hope that your sentences will be clear, stimulating to read, and, when occasion requires, even elegant. The language you use should show that you can avoid the commonplace and, with some sensitivity, take into account the connotations of words. Finally, without having been made a slave to imitation, you will probably appreciate that, as Alexander Pope said, "True ease in writing comes from art, not chance."

Glossary

Abstract–Concrete Abstract terms represent ideas, such as *marriage, liberty,* or *crime,* that cannot be seen or felt. Concrete terms are the opposite, like *hubcap, red oak tree,* or *kid glove,* which have sense appeal. Abstract terms are necesary for the discussion of broad principles or large areas of experience: for example, "Marriage rates increase during prosperity, decrease during depression." But concrete details, with their emphasis on the physical, which creates sensory images, do much to make writing vivid, appealing, convincing, and easy to understand.

Allusion An allusion is a reference to some person or event, generally in literature, history, or the arts, that is well known and can rapidly clarify and enrich an idea, like the patience of Job, the spirit of Valley Forge, a Marilyn-Monroe-like smile, or the words from William Jennings Bryan's speech of 1896: ". . . you shall not crucify mankind upon a cross of gold."

Analogy See pages 223–24.

Analysis See pages 78–79.

Argument See pages 215–26.

Atmosphere See *Tone.*

Audience Writers need to take into account the audience that they are writing for. The age, educational level, interests, and experience of the projected audience are significant points to consider, as well as their technical knowledge and training. Writing about art for scientists or about science for artists is different from writing about these matters for specialists in the field. Whether to use technical or scientific terms, whether to use formal or informal English, whether to use many examples, illustrations, and specific details or to cover much ground rapidly with general statements—these decisions all have to be made according to the audience one has in mind. It is one thing to write for friends and classmates with whom one can be relaxed and even amusing but quite another thing to write for the whole American public or, say, for the trustees of a university. One's language, tone, sentence structure—perhaps one's thesis and even one's plan of organization—will be influenced to some extent by considering one's audience.

Classification   See pages 78–79.

Cliché   See *Triteness.*

Climax   Climax is from a Greek word meaning *ladder;* thus it suggests a going up—to the highest point of tension, where suspense is broken, in a narrative or a play. (See page 4.) When we use the *climactic order,* we place the most important, or most striking, item last. *Anticlimax* is the opposite of climax, as in "He gave her a mink coat, a Cadillac, and a box of chocolates." We need to guard against an anticlimactic effect in sentences, paragraphs, and themes.

Coherence   Coherence, an essential element in writing, means "sticking together." *Coherent* writing is a clear and logical sequence of elements—parts of sentences, sentences, paragraphs, chapters—so arranged and linked together that a reader can understand it without experiencing any confusion of meaning. See *Transition.*

Comparison–Contrast   See pages 132–33.

Conclusions   At the end of a discussion it is often effective to remind the reader of the main point or points by closing with a brief summary. See the selections by Florman (page 111), Podhoretz, Hauser, Hemenway, Postman. Writers often conclude with a restatement—again to make a final impression upon the reader (see *Restatement*). See selections by Drucker, Kemelman, Russell, Twain, Catton, Lichtenstein, A.D. Smith, De Jouvenel.

Sometimes it may be appropriate to end with a persuasive comment going back to a thesis statement. See selections by Young, Ramírez, H.N. Smith, Pirsig, Shahn, Davis. Or on the basis of the discussion one may make a recommendation; see Gundry.

One may also conclude by indicating results. See selections by E. White, Lamar, Twain, Von Hagen, De Rougemont, Hardin. It is of course effective to end with a reiterative statement that is climactic as well. See Amory, Jacobs, Krutch.

Often, however, one does not need to compose any special conclusion; in a time-sequence or an enumeration, one can simply show the last thing that happened or present the last item, and then *quit.* See selections by Defoe, Didion, Keats, Sontag, Maraini, Padilla, Charteris. A writer should not assume that he needs mechanically to create a formal conclusion for every piece of writing.

Concrete   See *Abstract—Concrete.*

Connotation   Connotation is the special, extra, or suggestive meaning that some words have which makes them especially appropriate or not appropriate to be used in particular contexts. An example is *nag, steed,* and *horse,* each with its own suggestion of quality or use. *House* and *home* have different connotations. It would not sound proper to say in a marriage ceremony, "Do you, Jane, take this *guy* to be your husband?" Because of connotation a word often conveys a sense of dignity, lack of dignity, or a special atmosphere, as in Shakespeare's "*Golden* lads and girls all must,/As chimney-sweepers, come to dust." See *Denotation.*

Deduction-Induction   See pages 218–21.

Definition   See pages 180–82.

Denotation   Denotation is the exact or "dictionary" meaning of a word. For example, *gold* is "a malleable, ductile, yellow metallic element." See *Connotation.*

Description   See pages 1–4.

Development   Development means going into detail in one or more ways so as to provide enough material to satisfy a reader's curiosity or need for information. The apprentice writer is frequently guilty of inadequate development of paragraphs and of themes. A paragraph is well developed when it has abundant material to convince a reader that the topic sentence is a true statement. Ideas are developed according to the patterns, such as analysis and comparison-contrast, presented in the descriptive and expository sections of this book. But within these patterns writers generally develop ideas by means of examples and illustrations. An example is usually thought of as a single item that explains or illustrates a point; an illustration, as a more sustained or detailed example, such as an account of an incident.

Diction   Diction means choice of words. A writer should choose words for precision and suitability. This means choosing according to levels of usage (see *Standard English*); according to connotations; and according to the degree of abstractness or concreteness. Whatever effect a piece of writing has upon a reader comes about because of words alone. Whether the writer be Shakespeare or Hemingway, Daniel Defoe or Joan Didion, effects take place entirely through words. Therefore, diction is all-important.

Economy of Expression   Writers should strive for direct and economical writing. They ought not to use unnecessary details, roundabout expressions, tautological expressions, or general wordiness. As Alan Simpson says, "Every slaughtered syllable is a good deed." Students should avoid the weak passive voice and should write in the active voice as much as possible. They might well experiment by removing from their themes every word that can be omitted. By doing so, they will usually find that they have strengthened their papers. A good test for economy is to examine every sentence in a paragraph, questioning whether or not it contributes to the development of the topic sentence, and, if not, striking it out.

Emphasis   Through emphasis one brings to notice the special importance of some term or idea. One can do this by simple, mechanical means such as an exclamation point or underlining. But skillful writers more often obtain emphasis by repetition of key words, by using parallel constructions to repeat sentence patterns, and by placing significant terms in an emphatic position. The beginning and end of any unit of composition—sentence, paragraph, theme, chapter—are the most emphatic positions, whereas the middle of the unit is the proper place to tuck away less important items. It is especially important to "end with words that deserve distinction."

Evidence for Proof   If this text has a single aim, it is to teach the student constantly to use evidence for proof, to support every generalization with specific, concrete details. For example, should you say that a certain girl is overly sensitive, you must support this statement with evidence: she always thinks that other people are talking about her behind her back; she misinterprets casual remarks as insults; she wilts at the slightest critical comment—and these details could be further specified. Specific evidence convinces readers.

Example   See *Development*.

Fallacies   See pages 224–25.

Figurative Language   The use of figurative language is frequently an important means of communication. Through such language one does not convey literal meanings but imaginatively represents one thing in terms of another by means of figures of speech. Examples of figurative language would occupy a range from a simple comparison in which an unknown, or relatively unknown, thing is made clear by reference to something already known (as in this *simile:* The girl's movements were as delicate and graceful *as those of a doe*), to much more vivid and complex metaphorical assertions of likeness: for example, to praise the generosity of Mark Antony, Shakespeare's Cleopatra says,

> For his bounty,
> There was no winter in't: an autumn 'twas
> That grew the more by reaping. . . .

Generosity is not literally an autumn grain harvest; but if anyone's bounty is as great as the most bountiful autumn harvest, he can be most generous with constant gifts, as Mark Antony was consistently generous to his friends. The effect of this *metaphor* comes from the contrast of winter scarcity and a bountiful autumn harvest which is given even more force by the use of *hyperbole,* the figure of exaggeration, as Cleopatra asserts that Antony's autumn *grew the more by reaping.* This statement is very striking because it is a *paradox.* And there is more figurative complication here: the word *harvest* is not used, but *autumn* instead, an example of *metonymy,* a figure in which one word is substituted for another with which it has close association.

These figurative assertions of similarity do not of course insist that there is full identity between the things compared. In our first example—the simile *as those of a doe*—it is only in relation to her manner of moving that the girl is likened to a doe; and in Cleopatra's metaphor *bounty* is equated with autumn only insofar as autumn is a time of harvest.

Metaphors are the most vivid and powerful figures of speech. When two dissimilar ideas or things are brought together, just this once, in a comparison, they interact so as to raise, as it were, the voltage of communication. The bringing together of ideas or things with some newly discovered claim to likeness results in greater vividness, freshness, or broader implication of meaning that cannot be obtained in any other way. (Consider Ellington White's "the hot jangle of neon bursting red.") With its distillation of complexity by such economical means, metaphor creates breadth of enlightenment with a sense of immediacy and intensity. Metaphor is a verbal short-cut to understanding.

Metaphor can be expressed in different grammatical patterns. But metaphors seem to have special strength when they are expressed through verbs. Thus, however hard it may be to explain, we can all recognize the extraordinary effect of *sleep* in William Blake's

> I will not cease from mental fight,
> Nor shall my sword sleep in my hand. . . .

Likewise, when Steinbeck (page 9) describes Juan Chicoy's left hand ("the flesh was slightly mushroomed where the finger had been amputated"), what vividness comes from *mushroomed!*

Simile—a comparison with *like* or *as*—is often considered less forceful than metaphor, being more diluted, less economical; but this is a relative matter. This simile, however, written by a freshman, enlightens us: "To the city dweller, trying to fit into small town living is like dancing to a record on too slow a speed; he can hear the music but can't slow down enough to pick up the rhythm."

Only when figurative language is fresh and has some novelty can it be effective. Trite, over-used figures—of which there are many, like *as white as snow, eyes like stars*—must be eliminated from writing; they create dull reading and exasperated readers. Mixed metaphors—like

> All members of the staff should play ball by putting their shoulders to the wheel and pulling together—

though they may be amusing, are a sure indication of muddle-headedness.

An analogy is sometimes described as an extended metaphor, a rather detailed comparison of two different things with alleged similarities, such as an analogy of human life and the course of a river: a small stream at first (childhood), water dashing against boulders and forcing its way past them (overcoming life's difficulties), sunny pools in pleasant meadows (carefree recreation), a broad estuary merging with the sea (life ending with death). Analogies are used in exposition and argument to explain, exemplify, and try to persuade that similar situations demand similar treatment. Such carefully thought out and deliberate comparisons function differently from most metaphors, which are used to create an image.

Another kind of extended metaphor is allegory, in which *personification* is used; that is, abstractions are given life and considered as human. Thus in John Bunyan's allegory *The Pilgrim's Progress,* Christian, the hero, is imprisoned by Giant Despair. With the figure of *apostrophe* abstractions or absent persons are addressed as though human and present.

General–Specific General terms are useful for summarizing, as in "Crime rates are higher in this country, and processes of justice are slower, than in other nations." But such general statements lack the interest and the power to persuade that specific statements have. If we said: "Last year 8,463 robberies occurred, 3,541 more than in the year before, but only one-third of the robbers were captured, and, of these, 1,922 are young drug addicts not yet brought to trial by the district attorney," we would be providing a much clearer understanding of the crime situation. See *Abstract–Concrete* and *Definition*, page 181.

Idiom An idiom is a "cast-iron" expression, a set way of stating something that has been established by usage, that is peculiar to a language, and that often cannot be logically explained. Some examples are: *by and large, a home truth, strike a bargain.* Many idioms involve prepositions and adverbs, such as *on hand, on time, off his hands, hands off!, speak up, shut up, slip up, put up with, be hard up.* Idiomatic usage generally comes naturally to native speakers of a language, but students who have read little may have more than ordinary difficulty in writing idiomatically. Wide reading and consulting a dictionary will help them. Dictionaries usually provide guidance to correct idiomatic expression.

Illustration See *Development.*

Imagery Images are physical representations of people or things; therefore, imagery is the body of concrete details, literal or figurative, in writing, which suggests sensuous experience; or that element in writing which brings sensuous details into a reader's imagination. Writing that is rich in imagery produces strong sense-impressions of color, shape, size, movement, touch, hearing, taste, and texture. It makes a reader feel experience more intensely and intimately than does writing that lacks imagery.

Interpretation–Overinterpretation A writer should make clear to readers the significance or relevance of facts and illustrations that he uses, but overinterpretation of material is boring. Frequently it is effective to keep comment to a minimum and let facts speak for themselves. In the following paragraph Kipling does not interpret his feelings or those of his characters, but he makes clear how the characters feel, and he also gives his description a specific tone and creates a definite mood.

Then Mowgli picked out a shady place, and lay down and slept while the buffaloes grazed round him. Herding in India is one of the laziest things in the world. The cattle move and crunch, and lie down, and move on again, and they do not even low. They only grunt, and the buffaloes very seldom say anything, but get down into the muddy pools one after another, and work their way into the mud till only their noses and staring china-blue eyes show above the surface, and there they lie like logs. The sun makes the rocks dance in the heat, and the herd-children hear one kite (never any more) whistling almost out of sight overhead, and they know that if they died, or a cow died, that kite would sweep down, and the next kite miles away would see him drop and would follow, and the next, and the next, and almost before they were dead there would be a score of hungry kites come out of nowhere. Then they sleep and wake and sleep again, and weave little baskets of dried grass and put grasshoppers in them; or catch two praying-mantises and make them fight; or string a necklace of red and black jungle-nuts; or watch a lizard basking on a rock, or a snake hunting a frog near the wallows. Then they sing long, long songs with odd native quavers at the end of them, and the day seems longer than most people's whole lives, and perhaps they make a mud castle with mud figures of men and horses and buffaloes, and put reeds into the men's hands, and pretend that they are kings and the figures are their armies, or that they are gods to be worshipped. Then evening comes, and the children call, and the buffaloes lumber up out of the sticky mud with noises like gunshots going off one after the other, and they all string across the gray plain back to the twinkling village lights.

—Rudyard Kipling, "Tiger, Tiger!" in *The Jungle Book* (1894).

Other authors represented in this book who do not indulge in overinterpretation are Kinglake (page 3), Brown, Amory, and Dillard.

Interrupters   An interrupter is parenthetical material, frequently a phrasal or clausal modifier, an appositive, or sometimes a sentence, that interrupts the basic grammatical pattern of a sentence, often coming between subject and verb or between verb and complement. The skillful handling of interrupters is a real test of a writer's ability to manage long sentences. Interrupters, according to the degree of their separation from the main body of the sentence, are set off by commas, dashes, or parentheses. The italicized parts of the following sentence are interrupters. "Although she was certainly not pretty—*her long face usually looked sad or bitter, and when she was gay, wildly and almost desperately gay*—she radiated, *as if it were warmth from her body,* a passionate and angry vividness."—Alfred Kazin

Introductions   Although a writer should not assume that every essay requires a *formal* introduction (some writers need a caution against being stiffly and excessively mechanical), it is often good to begin by stating the main point of the paper with a thesis sentence. Another means of introduction is to present an illustration (perhaps through an anecdote) in order to catch the reader's interest. One can also lead into a subject by giving some background on it or its history or by discussion or comparison of a number of items in a class and then focusing on the one item that is to be the main topic. Occasionally writers open a discussion with a question—which is intended to arouse curiosity.

Logic   See pages 218–21.

Metaphor   See *Figurative Language.*

Objective–Subjective   Objective writing is that from which personal feelings and judgments are excluded. The product of pure objectivity is a scientific report. A narrative which limits itself to telling only what happened, without comment or interpretation, is said to be written from an objective viewpoint. Subjective writing is the opposite; it is personal, "comes from the heart," and includes the writer's own feelings, opinions, and interpretations.

Organization Common modes of organization are spatial, chronological, and logical. When we present material in a spatial order, we proceed from left to right, from higher to lower, and so on. The chronological order requires us to proceed from earlier events to later events. Logical order means going from least important to most important (order of climax) or *vice versa*, or using some similarly clear and reasonable method of organization. Much used methods are development from the general to the specific, the deductive type of organization, in which we start with a general proposition and then demonstrate it with examples or other details; and development from the specific to the general, the inductive type of organization, in which we first present details and then from them draw a general conclusion.

Outlines Preparing an outline before writing a paper helps many students because with the outline they have a plan of organization. The main requirements for an outline are logicality, clearness, and consistency.

To construct an outline, one should begin by formulating the central idea of the paper. The next step is to set down the main topics to be included. Then one indicates the supporting ideas, which will appear as subtopics. In a formal outline the main ideas (those of the first level) are indicated by Roman numerals, those of the second level (first subtopics) by capital letters, those of the third level by Arabic numerals, and those of the fourth level by small letters. One must remember that nothing can be divided into fewer than two parts; therefore there will never be a single subheading: where there is an A, there must be a B; where a 1, a 2. The most practical outline is a two-level outline, for setting down details of the third and fourth levels often stiffens up the imagination; consequently, students write duller papers because they adhere too closely to their wording of details on the third and fourth levels.

Types of outlines most used are the topic outline and the sentence outline. A topic outline does not have any complete sentences; each heading is a noun, which may have appropriate modifiers. The wording of the headings on each level should be as nearly parallel as possible. A sentence outline is clearer and more informative than a topic outline, for all the headings are complete statements. By writing sentences, one is forced to clarify his ideas.

The following brief sentence outline illustrates the principles just discussed.
Central Idea: I have increased my knowledge and appreciation of music by listening to the broadcasts from the Metropolitan Opera.
I. The broadcast gives a complete picture of the opera.
   A. An entire opera is broadcast every Satuday.
   B. Explanatory discussions are presented between the acts.
      1. They explain the plot.
      2. They tell about the composer and his career.
      3. They give information about the performers.
II. By listening to the broadcasts, I have developed my appreciation of music.
   A. I now read books and articles about music and musicians.
   B. I am making a collection of operatic records.

C. I have learned to distinguish between good and less good music.

D. I can understand and take part in discussions of operatic music.

Paragraph A paragraph is usually a group of sentences on a single topic which the sentences develop by various means, often by supporting evidence, that is, details to convince a reader that the central idea of the paragraph is true. Paragraphs vary in length from, say, 40 to 500 words, but today the typical paragraph in expository writing is likely to run from 100 to about 250 words. Shorter paragraphs, of one or two sentences, may be used for introduction, emphasis, transition, or summary.

Parallel Structure According to the principle of parallel structure, ideas of equal importance (coordinate ideas) should be expressed in identical grammatical structures. In a parallel series a noun will be followed by a noun, a verb by a verb, a phrase by a phrase, a clause by a clause, and so on. Thus Julius Caesar's "I came, I saw, I conquered" has three independent clauses with identical subjects; Pope's "To err is human, to forgive, divine" brings out a contrast with parallel infinitives as subjects; and Shakespeare's Brutus, saying of Caesar "As he was valiant, I honor him; but, as he was ambitious, I slew him," uses an identical pattern of grammar in his contrasting clauses. Very often appearing in balanced sentences, parallel structure is the easiest means to show balance of ideas and is thus a valuable aid to clearness. Repeating the same structure in successive sentences is also a device to secure emphasis.

Point of View Point of view is used in several ways. It can refer to an attitude, as in "President Hoover represented the Republican point of view." It can refer to ways in which a story is narrated: 1) first-person point of view, with "I," the teller, relating only what he saw or knew; 2) third-person omniscient, in which the teller knows all that happened, even the thoughts of all the characters; 3) selective omniscient, limited to the mind of only one character, generally the protagonist; 4) objective, which is a report without interpretation. Point of view can also indicate a moving or stationary position from which something is observed and described, or the age of the observer: a report from a child's point of view will not be the same as that from an adult's point of view. It is important for a writer to remember that he must maintain a consistent point of view and not switch from one observer or from one tense to another.

Process Analysis See page 79.

Repetition Careless repetition of unimportant words can be annoying, but to try to avoid all repetition by constant efforts to find synonyms (especially impressive terms from a thesaurus) is artificial. In fact, deliberate repetition of important words is a good device for achieving emphasis and driving ideas home in the reader's mind. Often the repetition of ideas in almost identical language is also effective. For examples of emphatic repetition see the selections by Steinbeck, Highet, Young, Boorstin, Adler, and Russell.

Restatement Restatement is expressing an idea again, frequently using different words and perhaps including some additional thought or approaching the thesis from a slightly different direction. It is not the same as summary, which merely pulls together the main ideas expressed before, but is a rhetorical device mainly for emphasis.

Sentences　In terms of grammatical make-up and complexity, sentences are classified as simple, compound, complex, and compound-complex. A simple sentence has only one independent clause. The fore-going definition is an example of a simple sentence: *sentence* is the subject; *has* is the verb; *clause* is the direct object of *has*. The statement consists of one independent clause. A compound sentence has two or more independent clauses: "I came, I saw, I conquered." A complex sentence has one independent and at least one dependent clause, as in "When better automobiles are built, Buick will build them"; whereas a compound-complex sentence has at least two independent clauses and at least one dependent clause. An example is: "While we were walking up the street, we saw black clouds, and we felt a few drops of rain."

In terms of rhetorical patterns, sentences are called loose, balanced, and periodic. A loose sentence generally has normal subject-verb-complement order; it makes a complete statement early, and dependent material comes after the sense is complete. An example is: "George was a thoroughly honest man because he had been carefully trained by his parents and other people who lived in his community always to tell the truth and to take pride in his reputation for upholding the principles of integrity and honor." If the fore-going sentence were reversed so that it began with *because,* it would become a periodic sentence—one in which the complete sense of the statement is held back until the end. Thus, *thoroughly honest man,* coming at the end, would receive very strong emphasis. A balanced sentence is typically a compound sentence, with clauses of equal importance: for example, "Training is intended primarily for the service of society; education is primarily for the individual."

Sentence Structure　Although we may find effective examples of writing in which the same type of sentence is used repeatedly (Steinbeck begins nearly all of his sentences in "Juan Chicoy" with the subject), people usually prefer to read material with varied sentence constructions. In order to avoid monotony and to promote interest, the apprentice writer frequently needs to strive for sentence variety, avoiding especially the overuse of the independent clause. The repetition of one independent clause after another in a Dick-and-Jane primer style makes for monotony and dullness. To secure variety, students will do well to consider both sentence length and sentence pattern. (See *Interrupters.*) Furthermore, they will make their writing more effective if they vary the beginnings of their sentences by starting some with the subject and others with dependent elements (introductory clauses or phrases) or transitional expressions (such as *in the meantime, moreover, nevertheless, on the other hand*) and by subordinating the less important ideas in each sentence. Possible subordinate constructions are dependent clauses (noun, adjective, adverb), phrases (prepositional, infinitive, participial, gerund), appositives, and nominative absolutes. We may use the following simple sentences as a basis for sentence improvement:——It was my first day at school. I was trying to find my classroom. I met a large man. He was somewhere in his middle sixties.

He waddled down the crowded hall. He had a broad smile on his face. With only a little thought we can combine these six dull short statements into one economical sentence, far more interesting and pleasingly rhythmical:——On my first day of school while trying to find my classroom, I met a large man somewhere in his middle sixties waddling down the hall with a broad smile on his face. Our essential operation here has been to reduce predication.

Another element in sentence structure we may call *pace*. In addition to creating special effects pace within the sentences can also produce variety. The beginning sentences of paragraph 2 of Amory's "Mrs. Jack Gardner" are short, choppy sentences which contrast with the rather lengthy and flowing sentences of paragraph 1. Amory's shift of pace is good; it stirs our attention with its staccato manner. Furthermore, the lack of a conjunction or conjunctive adverb between the clauses of the first sentence emphasizes the contrast.

The pace of the paragraph by Kipling (pages 296–97) makes one feel that "herding in India is one of the *l-a-z-i-e-s-t* things in the world." How does Kipling gain the effect of slowness? By using a great many *and*'s to slow the action, to say nothing of other coordinators. Yet none of the actions that Kipling describes are blurred or lost: his verbs and verbals are specific, exact, and numerous.

Simile   See *Figurative Language.*

Slang   See *Standard English.*

Specific–General   See *General–Specific.*

Standard English   Standard English, formal and informal, is established through the usage of educated people as acceptable throughout the English-speaking world. English on the formal level is used for dignified discourse, as in serious books and articles, speeches, and sermons. English on the informal or colloquial level is used by cultivated people in conversation and in writing where formality is not required. (*Colloquial* means conversational; it has nothing to do with location or region.) Nonstandard English consists of vernacular English and most slang. Vernacular English is characteristic of people with little education who confuse words such as *lie-lay, rise-raise,* and *sit-set* and who use ungrammatical constructions and illiteracies such as "I ain't goin' to lay down nohow, irregardless." Slang consists of novel terms originated and mostly used by persons who wish to challenge respectability or show that they are aware of the latest thing. Many slang terms are vivid and many are temporarily fashionable, but few slang terms become a part of standard English. Most dictionaries label words classified as colloquial or slang.

Subjective   See *Objective–Subjective.*

Suspense   Suspense is a feeling of tense and excited anticipation that we experience when reading a narrative or reading or watching a play. It comes from uncertainty, either concerning what will take place——what new turn the plot will take or how it will end——or concerning the manner and time in which an end that we foresee as inevitable will occur. When our uncertainty is over, our tension created by the anticipation, heightened emotion, and perhaps fear, disappears. Suspense is a strong means of creating interest.

Thesis Sentence   A thesis sentence is a statement of the main point of a theme, article, or book. Before writing a theme, you will find it helpful to formulate a thesis so that you can get clearly in mind the problem of communication ahead of you. Once you have such a controlling idea, you can make decisions efficiently about organization, vocabulary, tone, use of illustrations, and so forth. The best way to formulate a thesis is to narrow your topic and then decide what specific point you wish to make about it. You could not write a successful theme on such a broad subject, for example, as architecture or art. But you would be off to a good start if you narrowed it down and used a thesis like one of the following: I think the new Union Building is ugly; some of the handsomest buildings in Mexico were constructed from such ordinary material as concrete; I have come to admire the romantic glamour of Rembrandt's paintings. For examples of thesis sentences see selections by McCullers, H.N. Smith, Shahn, and Kipling (pages 296–97).

Time Sequence   In narratives, in accounts of processes, and in cause-effect analyses things happen, or actions are performed, over a period of time. It is very important for a writer to inform the reader clearly when events occur and in what order. For these purposes transitional devices are used—words such as *then, now, before, after, at the same time, simultaneously, as soon as, next.*

Tone   Tone refers to the dominant impression, mood, or emotional atmosphere that we feel when we read some pieces of writing. It is created especially through connotation and is frequently apparent in description. We recognize strongly contrasting tones in Poe's *The Raven*, Mark Twain's *Adventures of Huckleberry Finn*, the first scene of Shakespeare's *Hamlet*, and, in this text, the selections by Brown, Baldwin, E. White, Dick-Read, Didion, and O'Connor.

Topic Sentence   A topic sentence states the main idea of a paragraph. Often it is the first sentence in the paragraph though it does not have to be; it can come in the middle or elsewhere. If it comes early in the paragraph, it invites the reader to find out what the writer will say to back it up. With that sentence the writer enters a kind of contract to develop the idea he has stated; he must go on to convince the reader that the statement is true. A topic sentence may come at the end of a paragraph, where it is a conclusion to, or a summary or restatement of, what has been said in the paragraph. In some paragraphs the writer implies what the topic is rather than stating it.

Transition   Transition, which literally means "going across," is the linking of sentences and paragraphs by using logical order; by setting up statements in parallel structure; by repeating significant words; by using pronouns to refer to words in preceding sentences and at times even paragraphs; and by including special transitional devices, such as *therefore, next, in the second place, finally,* and many others. (But it is bad to overuse conjunctive adverbs like *moreover* and *therefore;* they are heavy and burdensome.) In long articles whole paragraphs are sometimes written just to provide transition. (See the selection by Young.) Clear transitional signals are essential to good writing.

Triteness Trite expressions—also called hackneyed expressions or clichés—are worn-out combinations of words that annoy readers because they are stale, dull, and ineffective. No single word is trite. Triteness always consists in some combination of terms, frequently an over-used simile or metaphor such as eyes like stars, teeth like pearls, hair like spun gold, straight as an arrow, diamond in the rough, making a shambles of the place; or acid test, the bottom line, depths of despair, sigh of relief, reign supreme, fast and furious. . . . Ready-made phrases like these reveal a writer's mental laziness or poverty of imagination. By using concrete terms and by being on their guard, students can usually avoid such rubber-stamp expressions.

Unity Unity is necessary to all effective writing. It is based on the idea that any literary work and indeed every element in composition should be related to some organizing principle that gives it oneness or wholeness. Practically, unity requires a writer to know clearly what his topic is and to stick to it, keeping out ideas that do not pertain to it and clearly indicating what relation illustrations, analogies, and so on have to the central idea that he is developing.

INDEX OF AUTHORS